The MIS Manager's Guide to Performance Appraisal

The MIS Manager's Guide to Performance Appraisal

Practical Guidelines
and Forms for
Evaluating and Appraising
Your MIS Staff

Lockwood Lyon

Fred A. Gluckson

McGraw-Hill, Inc.

New York St. Louis San Francisco Auckland Bogotá
Caracas Lisbon London Madrid Mexico Milan
Montreal New Delhi Paris San Juan São Paulo
Singapore Sydney Tokyo Toronto

Library of Congress Cataloging-in-Publication Data

Lyon, Lockwood.
    MIS manager's appraisal guide : practical guidelines and forms for
evaluating and appraising your MIS staff / Lockwood Lyon and Fred A.
Gluckson.
        p.   cm.
    Includes index.
    ISBN 0-07-039272-2
    1. Electronic data processing personnel—United States—Rating of.
I. Gluckson. Fred A.   II. Title.
HD8039.D372U64   1994
004'.068'3—dc20   93-41057
                                                                        CIP

1 2 3 4 5 6 7 8 9 0   DOC/DOC   9 9 8 7 6 5 4

ISBN 0-07-039272-2

*The sponsoring editors for this book were Jeanne Glasser and Marjorie
Spencer and the production supervisor was Donald F. Schmidt. It was
set in Century Schoolbook by North Market Street Graphics.*

Printed and bound by R. R. Donnelley & Sons Company.

*To order or receive additional information on these or any
other McGraw-Hill titles, in the United States please call
1-800-822-8158. In other countries, contact your local
McGraw-Hill representative.*   BC14BCZ

For Gary, Chris, Michele, and Ariel—
for their respect and inspiration

Contents

Part 2   The Performance Appraisal Process

Part 3   Optimizing Performance Appraisal

Preface

Why

Some of my most confusing experiences in data processing revolved around my performance and its appraisal. I always thought that I knew how well I was doing—after all, who would know better than I? These feelings seemed to be dashed regularly every year at appraisal time. My manager would explain how things that I did or didn't do nine months ago now assumed major significance, and my salary would be adjusted (or not adjusted) accordingly. I used to think that when I was a manager I would do a better job, giving feedback at the proper time, documenting employee progress, and so forth.

That actually came about. Becoming a manager, that is. I eagerly anticipated attending a training course in appraisal procedures, knowing that this would be a major help for me and my subordinates. Boy, was I disappointed. No course, no standard procedures, nothing concrete. Just a set of forms to fill out, some brief interview procedures ("establish rapport," "praise the employee," that sort of thing), and a "do it as best you can" from upper management.

I determined to study the subject, perhaps with an eye toward improving things. What I discovered was frustrating and disillusioning: except in academia, nowhere did there exist complete, correct, verifiable procedures for constructing and implementing an appraisal system for data processing professionals. Companies that had such systems had either copied them from forms and procedures used for other salaried or hourly workers, or had "adapted" them from other businesses. In most cases management claimed that their procedures were valid, useful, objective, and effective. Curiously, most employees felt that the systems were subjective, discriminatory, useless, unfair, and biased.

Company after company asserted their commitment to objective appraisals. Employee after employee complained about nebulous rating scales, bias, untrained managers, poor documentation, and prejudicial treatment. I resolved that managers and employees deserved better than this. Hence, this book.

How

I began, as many authors do, in bookstores and libraries, searching for what information exists on the subject of performance appraisal. Bookstores were interesting. Half of the books remotely alluding to appraisal were mostly about interviewing tactics. This seemed backward to me. How do you know what to talk about if you don't gather, interpret, and analyze the data first? And once this is done, doesn't the interview boil down to a simple summary of the data? How could so many interviewers be doing this so poorly that they buy books on interviewing?

Another favorite book topic was survival skills, with titles like "How to Survive the DP Jungle," "The Guerrilla Guide to Being Interviewed," and "Power-Packed Résumés." These are cases of cart-before-the-horse mentality, ways to obscure the real issues, and methods of faking it.

Libraries turned up little of value. Many managers seem to have written about performance appraisal, or at least they have tried. Most seem to rely on a how-to approach that emphasizes tactics like special forms, special procedures with interesting names like "hands-on" or "management by walking around," and, of course, how to conduct appraisal interviews. Few concentrated on what I needed to know—the questions starting with the word why?

Few books (actually, one) attempted to cover data processing people as a separate issue. While it was interesting and informative, it was somewhat out of date (1980). A lot has happened in DP since then! Or has it? Certainly technology has advanced, but have people changed that much? This gave me the first clue to the puzzle—my answer would probably be found in the realms of psychology and sociology.

To make a long story short, this book is the result of some research the authors have done, both in the "school of hard knocks" and in academia. We believe that we have addressed most of the "why" questions we originally had about effective performance appraisal of DP professionals. In addition, you will find lots of "how" information in this book, including recommendations for using different appraisal systems for maximum benefit, guidelines for supplementing forms, and some general advice on employee communications.

After twenty years in data processing as a programmer, systems analyst, database administrator, project leader, manager, and consultant, I have finally found and developed what I needed: a set of reasons for why we evaluate DP people, and a strategy for developing procedures for getting it done. I hope that the information contained herein helps you as much as it has helped me.

Who

I would like to thank Barbara, who inspired this book. In addition, my heartfelt thanks to the staff at McGraw-Hill for their tact, patience, tolerance, and persistence.

The authors appreciate comments from readers. We can be contacted on CompuServe at [71600,2673] or in care of the publisher.

Lockwood Lyon

Introduction

Employee performance appraisal is rarely done well—and it isn't the fault of the manager.

Typical managers will have time to concern themselves with it once every year when the evaluation interview must be scheduled. Without formal training in procedures such as fact-gathering, they accumulate such facts as they can remember about the preceding year, sometimes with special emphasis on negative items. They then spend a few minutes filling in an evaluation form as best they can, followed by several hours preparing for the interview with the employee where they feel they must justify their actions. Such interviews often begin with the manager handing the employee the "report card," or evaluation form. This form grades the employee in several poorly defined categories such as "communications," with nebulous ratings such as "3" or "satisfactory." These interviews are rarely constructive, and sometimes end up with the employee asking (or begging) for higher ratings.

These problems are worsened and aggravated in the field of data processing. As we shall discuss, data processing people are markedly different from those in other professions. Such differences must be taken into account when evaluating their work. Since many DP managers come from the programming ranks, the problems they had when being appraised are carried over to their new subordinates. A list of some of these problems follows.

Lack of available training in:

- appraisal forms and procedures
- interviewing techniques
- employee problem solving
- legal considerations (discrimination, objectivity, at-will employment, and so on)

Lack of commitment to:

- company and employee goal-setting
- employee career planning
- fair and objective performance standards
- fair compensation ("pay for performance")

An inability for an enterprise to:

- identify and rate employee potential
- identify training needs
- make quality business decisions

We feel that DP managers and employees deserve a better fate than this. While many companies and enterprises offer some training in policies and procedures, few explain what is going on underneath. Why do we appraise employees the way we do? Is it done objectively? Is it fair? How and why is data processing any different? Explaining these things is the purpose of this book.

A Brief Overview of the Book

What exactly is performance appraisal?

Webster's New World Dictionary defines *appraise* "to judge the quality or worth of (something)." Although this definition conveys some of the substance of performance appraisal, it tends to steer managers and employees in the wrong direction. *True performance appraisal* consists of two distinct procedures: *measurement,* followed by *judgment.* From this extended definition we derive the following principles.

The first step in proper performance appraisal is *gathering and recording facts.* Examples might include lists of employee results achieved, behaviors observed, important events that occur, and so on. From this we derive three basic rules: (1) some decision procedure must exist to determine which facts to gather; (2) some mechanisms or procedures must exist to gather facts at the earliest possible moment (i.e., as events occur); and (3) some medium must exist to record the facts for later use.

Few performance appraisal systems recognize these three basics— fewer still implement valid procedures for implementing them.

The next step in proper performance appraisal is *interpreting the facts.* Most performance appraisal systems fail miserably at this point. Interpreting a fact calls for a standard against which it will be measured. Many measurements are invalid or subject to misinterpretation unless the standard of measurement is given.

Consider the question, "How far is it to the airport?" An answer of "five miles" has several possible meanings. If you are traveling by car, then five miles may mean either "five miles as the crow flies" or "five more miles on the odometer." If you are traveling by airplane, then five miles means five *nautical* miles. (Note that the mileages given for automobile travel were in *statute* miles, something not stated, but assumed.) Another illustration involves directions. The term *north* may mean either "true north," "magnetic north," or "magnetic north corrected for local deviation." The correct interpretation of the facts depends upon assumptions and standards.

While these examples may not directly relate to data processing or employee behaviors, one thing should be clear: without a standard against which to measure it, a fact cannot be used as a sound basis for estimation, opinion, or judgment.

The next step is *analyzing the interpretations.* (Note that here we are still within the realm of measurement.) This step recognizes that several interpretations may exist for the same fact. How is this possible? This problem usually comes about either through miscommunication or misinterpretation of facts, standards, or definitions of terms. Consider the programmer who is told on Monday morning to "complete the coding on program A in six days." The following Monday the manager asks the programmer, "Is the coding done?" The programmer answers, "No." The manager then records the fact that the original goal of six calendar days was not met. The programmer records the fact that six days have not yet elapsed; after all, they have only spent five work days on the coding. This miscommunication of the definition of the term "six days" led to different interpretations of the facts, and consequently to a different judgment as to the programmer's performance.

Next comes *judgment.* It is here that subjectivity can play a large role. The supervisor forms an opinion as to how the facts will play a role in making decisions (the next step). Some of the areas where such judgment comes into play are:

- Making employment decisions (hire, fire, terminate, transfer)
- Performance improvement planning
- Compensation administration
- Identifying training needs

In each of these (and other) areas the manager and employee must either separately or jointly consider and determine how the facts should be used.

The last step is the *decision* step. Here the manager (and perhaps the employee) make decisions based on the results of the previous steps.

How appraisals are misused

Companies use appraisals (more properly, appraisal forms) as input to procedures such as these:

- Making termination decisions
- Improving employee performance
- Assigning employee work duties
- Identifying potential for promotion
- Salary administration
- Identifying training needs
- Employee career planning

As we shall see when we discuss forms and procedures, no one form can provide the information required to make all of the business decisions in each of these areas. Further, the procedures required are markedly different. For example, proper salary administration requires that the appraisal settle on a single, overall rating. This rating is then used to determine raises and bonuses. On the other hand, this overall rating and the procedures for determining it have little or no bearing on career planning.

The most common reasons for performance appraisal system failure include the following:

- Lack of objectives
- No definition of development
- Forms not related to system objectives
- No definition of performance
- Poor appraisal interviews

As we shall see, each of these problems can occur by itself or in combination with others. In this book we will examine each of these areas and offer specific recommendations.

Judgment—and misjudgment

Surprises during the appraisal meeting can range from being merely annoying to provoking embarrassment, humiliation, or rage. Managers and employees seem to forget that judgment is, by nature, subjective. *Webster's New World Dictionary* defines *judgment* as "an opinion or estimate." Curiously, supervisors and subordinates sometimes have differing opinions as to the subordinate's worth to the organization. Such lack of understanding as to when judgment should take place is covered in Part 3 of this book.

According to a report done in the early 1990s, in 1992 improving the IS (Information Systems) human resource ranked fifth among the top issues facing senior IS executives. This was up from a ranking of 13th the year before, and 11th in 1990. If senior management is only now confronting the realities of productivity enhancement, technical training, overcoming job stress, and a host of other ills, then the way that performance appraisal was done in the past will be inadequate.

People—The Forgotten Detail

Where do I stand?

In our competitive society, people demand to know where they stand. One former city mayor had a trademark expression when he visited his public: when he met the press, marched in parades, or appeared on talk shows, his familiar greeting was, "How'm I doin'?"

Like most of us, he wanted to be liked, he wanted to be respected, he wanted to hear that he was *doing a good job*. At four-year intervals, this mayor and others who hold office hear resoundingly and publicly how they are judged—either they are reelected, or they go down to defeat. For others, the message is not so clear.

Children understand performance appraisal better than their parents do. Without benefit of a formalized process, they know immediately "how they're doing." Children are in the business of constantly testing the limits of acceptable behavior. A child has to learn how much noise can be tolerated, when the playroom is too messy, and what forms of expression are acceptable. Even a young child knows instinctively the difference between a parent's approving smile and a threatening frown. Some parents think that for a sensitive child a raised eyebrow might be enough control. Other parents believe that the best form of encouragement is a pat on the back—especially if awarded "often enough, hard enough, and low enough."

Evaluation as a social issue

Society does not do a good job of evaluation. Unfortunately, materialism is often the basis for judging how well a colleague is doing. Too often the mayor's familiar refrain is answered by measuring the trappings of wealth. According to the bumper-sticker cliché, "He who dies with the most toys wins." For many people, however, accumulating wealth is not a measure of performance. Those driven only by money and power may lose sight of human values. Books, movies, even jails are full of people for whom money was an end rather than a by-product of quality performance. In fact, many people are driven by the joy of achieving, regardless of any reward. Olympic athletes strive to set a new record, no other goal in sight.

Others want to leave a mark on society that will live on after they are gone. The story is told of three stonemasons who were asked what they were doing. The first replied, "I am earning my wages." The second's response was, "I am cutting the finest stones that I can." And the third said, "I am building a cathedral." And their results were no doubt consistent with their aspirations.

Even those who seek the appearance of success through acquisition may be deeply in debt and living on overextended credit. Bank consumer lending officers tell of customers who buy big homes but allow them to remain empty because they cannot afford to furnish them. In 1990 the average balance owing on the major bank cards was $1230, while the average annual usage was nearly $2000. Thus, the average user owed six months' worth of charges. These figures include 200 million credit cards—a total indebtedness of a quarter trillion dollars! (*New York Times,* 2/7/90)

Indeed, with economic and competitive pressures increasing, the true test may be to achieve *balance* in life—gaining the proper trade-off between the needs of self, family, and job—for economic well-being; and for some investment in social issues, religion, or whatever institutions may be held dear.

How employment decisions are made

Motivation and performance. In his watershed work on motivation, Frederich Herzberg sampled 1685 employees, identifying events that caused job satisfaction and dissatisfaction. Factors related to salary were well toward the bottom in the list of influencers. Those salary events were equally balanced between satisfiers and dissatisfiers. Topping the chart of events leading to job satisfaction were the following:

- Achievement
- Recognition
- The work itself
- Responsibility
- Advancement
- Growth

The most frequently cited dissatisfiers were:

- Company policy and administration
- Supervision
- Work conditions

These results seem to put the lie to money as a motivator. Further, and of greater importance, effective performance appraisal can enhance many of the satisfiers cited by Herzberg and minimize some of the dissatisfiers. Although performance appraisal is not explicitly mentioned, it offers management and staff an important tool for enhancing satisfaction in the workplace.

Performance appraisal in business. So the business community had to step in where society had left a vacuum. Business requires a means of evaluating performance. Many functions critical to business require performance ratings. The wide scope of uses for performance appraisal data is shown in Figure I.1.

Some of the more important reasons are discussed in detail here:

Salary administration. Salary increases are often tied to performance appraisals. The free enterprise economy assumes that competition will arise where there is the opportunity for profit. Competition assures that the most efficient companies will prevail. Thus business must reward its best performers, discouraging them from quitting to join the competition.

Fostering improvements in work performance
- Review at completion of a probationary period
- Warning about unacceptable performance
- Recognition and rewards for past performance

Assigning work more effectively

Meeting employees' needs for growth

Assisting employees in setting career goals
- Career development on an individual basis

Recognizing potential for development to managerial positions
- Promotion based on merit
- Demotion or reduction in grade
- Lateral reassignment

Keeping employees advised of what is expected of them

Improving job placement

Layoff or termination based on merit
- Providing appraisal pursuant to laws or regulations

Identifying training needs
- Training needs on an individual basis

Validating employee selection procedures

Figure I.1   Business uses for performance appraisals.

However, salary administration should not be conducted at the same time as performance appraisal. The optimum timing is for the annual salary review to be conducted six months later than the performance review. They are related issues but should be separated in time. The performance appraisal is a time for discussion of job effectiveness, not financial reward.

Proper salary administration usually involves budgeting salary increases annually in advance. For example, the overall budget for annual merit raises might be 6 percent of the MIS (Management Information Systems) department's aggregate salary. This might be apportioned to each staff member, based on performance, in the range of 3 to 9 percent.

But it is important for good performance to be recognized at salary review time on an objective basis. Some systems professionals, particularly those with greater experience, may be jaded on the subject of performance appraisal. They may have seen performance appraisal used as a tool to gain the supervisor's ends, rather than an unbiased process. The appraisal results may be "rigged" to support the large (or small) raise preplanned by the supervisor. The employee will soon learn to mistrust the appraisal system. "Beware of the tool, lest it use *you*," Confucius may have said.

Subjective raises based on management whim or on favoritism are destructive to an enterprise.

Manpower planning.   Performance appraisal is an important tool in developing the overall MIS manpower plan. The manpower plan will include:

- Project staffing needs
- Anticipated turnover
- Promotion plans
- Hiring requirements

The performance appraisal interview, along with supplementary career path planning, will determine who may be a candidate for a promotion. Of course, an actual promotion will require that an opening be available and that a candidate be qualified.

Performance improvement.   Management requires that employees perform at some minimal level. Appraisals are used as the primary method for documenting poor performance. The review form then becomes a guide, setting the standards and goals for correcting any performance deficiencies.

Training requirements.   Poor or insufficient performance in one or more areas may point out the need for employee training. In addition, promotions may require augmenting an employee's skill sets. Training should be considered in the context of employee career planning.

The management of data processing people

Are data processing people different? That is, are there special techniques or circumstances that apply only to them? While these questions are covered in detail in Chap. 1, this section will deal with some of the situations unique to data processing personnel.

Controlling turnover. There are several categories of loss of systems staff. Consider these four:

1. People leave for health or family reasons. These losses are inevitable and uncontrollable, but fortunately few.

2. Sometimes resignations are suggested or encouraged by management. It is unfortunate that this should be necessary, but it is better for the organization in the long run that management step up to this difficult responsibility.

3. A third broad category is resignations that are not totally unexpected but not encouraged either. These are people that do not seem to be making the kind of progress in the organization that they would like. It may be that the incumbent felt qualified for a promotion but after careful consideration management decided to promote someone else—or worse, hired from the outside to fill the senior vacancy. There is room for disagreement among reasonable people on the qualifications of an individual for promotion. The manager must take a calculated risk—the kind they are paid for—on such a decision. But the disappointment to the unsuccessful staff member can be softened considerably through a counseling session, particularly if the employee can be told there are prospects for them in the future, given more experience, better personal communications skills, or upon successful completion of their current challenging project.

4. The fourth kind of resignation, and the most traumatic to the organization, is the unexpected loss of a highly valued contributor despite what seemed to be their rapid salary and career progress within the department. This kind of resignation sends shock waves through the staff and causes many to reexamine their own motives in staying. It is to prevent the fourth kind of separation, and to some extent the third, that we examine the next topic—that of staff retention.

Building loyalty. What are the motivators that keep good people with you or, if absent, drive them away? Certainly a key motivator is recognition. Computer professionals, being members of the human race, need their share of warm fuzzies. Recognition takes many forms. Certainly promotions, salary increases, and written performance appraisals are all forms of recognition. Others are less structured but more effective. For example:

- A note from a user department manager to an analyst's boss complimenting him or her on a clean and timely system modification.
- An opportunity for a systems programmer to teach a debugging technique to his/her peers.
- Invitation to a project leader to represent his or her company at a vendor presentation, or to join a professional society.
- Encouragement of a manager to give a speech or write a paper.

Sometimes simply the inclusion of a programmer in a status meeting with the customer will serve the double purpose of making them feel a valued member of the project team as well as giving them a first-hand view of the importance and urgency the user places on this project.

In summary

Hardware advances, new software, and new development environments have conspired in the last few years to transform the data processing environment. It is no longer enough for a programmer to write a program that is merely "correct." Indeed, the very idea of a *program* has changed.

These factors lead to the following obvious conclusion: *established methods of appraising the performance of data processing professionals are no longer valid in today's environment.* So what is needed? New forms? New procedures? Education and training?

The Purpose of This Book

This book focuses on the needs of the IS manager in the constantly changing world of data processing. Such managers must be informed as to current practices and future directions. This book will review current forms and methodologies and how they may be brought up-to-date. In addition, it will provide a road map for the future.

Part 1 concentrates on the career path of the data processing professional. Chapter 1 addresses DP personality types, and explores those things that satisfy, dissatisfy, and motivate DP-ers. Chapter 2 deals with data processing jobs, job descriptions, and productivity. Here, we will examine ways to measure productivity and professionalism.

Part 2 centers on the performance appraisal process. Although managers are familiar with their present company's evaluation process, many are unaware of the many alternative forms and procedures available. Chapter 3 considers many common misunderstandings about appraisals, and gives recommendations for managers and employees alike. Chapter 4 discusses the business use of appraisals. Here, we learn how a single form and procedure is used for many different purposes, sometimes with disastrous results. Chapter 5 reviews common (and uncommon) evaluation forms, and discusses their advantages and disadvantages. Should a manager find that one or more of these forms are being used in their company, recommendations are given for improving the forms and their corresponding procedures.

Lastly, Part 3 provides advice on the correct use of review forms and procedures. Chapter 6 concentrates on when and how performance appraisal systems fail, and how managers may adapt to this. It also contains several recommendations on how to make the employee evaluation process a success. Chapter 7 describes several common problems that occur during the appraisal process. Each problem is described in detail, with sample procedures, forms, alternatives, and recommendations. Chapter 8 analyzes each of the types of appraisal forms, their strengths and weaknesses. In addition, this chapter contains several suggestions for improving such forms. Chapter 9 examines techniques and procedures, and how appraisals can improve themselves and their methods. Finally, Chapter 10 contains several sample appraisal forms of different types. Each type is critiqued from the perspective of a manager appraising data processing personnel.

The Data Processing Career

1

DP Personalities:
Understanding and Coping

First, we need to understand what data processing is like, what DP people do, and how things will be different in the future. Each subsection ends with a *thought question* designed to stimulate discussion. (Experienced DP managers may choose to skim through this section, but should stop and ponder the thought questions.)

Data Processing in the 1990s

The latest technology

The word that best describes the current state of data processing is *change*—change in technology, change in software and systems, change in analysis and design methods, change in development environments, and finally change in the people themselves. Although rapid technological change does not always lead to a reordering or restyling of the human organization, recent advances have permanently altered the way that people interface with computers. *These changes will affect the way your organization deals with people.*

This section discusses some recent advances in information systems. These will serve as the background to the later discussion of people in data processing: how they interact with computers, how those people are managed, and how to determine the level of performance of data processing professionals.

Distributed processing. Distributed processing refers to a configuration of several computers where each of them is available to process data. (See Fig. 1.1.) Processing power is thus *distributed* among them.

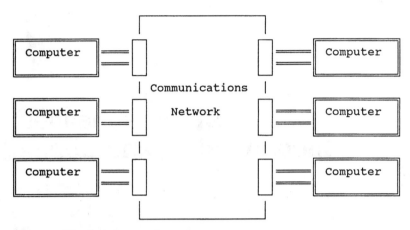

Figure 1.1 Distributed processing.

The great advantage of such a configuration is that the temporary outage of one or more processors still allows work to be done.

Users are usually not aware that processing power is distributed. They access the configuration through one of the computers. That computer then schedules the user's application to run on one (or more) of the processors. This gives users the freedom to run applications without needing to know where the processing is being done. In addition, application programmers can now write systems that take advantage of the particular hardware configuration.

With the advent of distributed processing, systems designers must deal with an additional level of complexity. As applications are designed, the designers must take into account the set of possible processors on which the programs may run. This may involve hardware internals, network configuration analysis, and special dataset management. In addition, programmers may be writing programs that must be able to interrogate the network to determine the availability of multiple processors. *This is a fundamental change in the body of knowledge that we as IS professionals mastered in previous years.* Such a radical change may make managers unsuitable, unwilling, or unable to appraise a programmer's or analyst's performance fairly. Indeed, it may be that their work seems completely foreign to us!

Question: How can you appraise employee performance when you don't understand what it is they do?

Question: Is it fair to appraise data processing professionals the same way now as in the previous ten years?

Networks. Closely related to the idea of distributed processing is that of computer networks. There are many methods of interconnecting computers. These methods are called *topologies,* referring to the physical configuration of the cabling connecting the computers. The names and arrangements of the various topologies is not important to us here, although several are shown in Fig. 1.2. It is enough to know that there are several ways to connect two or more processors, each with its own advantages and disadvantages.

Except for stand-alone microcomputers, it is very common for a computer to be connected to one or more others. Apart from distributed processing mentioned previously, such a connection allows computers to access data at other locations. This is called *distributed data.* Having access to distributed data frees users, allowing them to go beyond their own computer.

The convenience of having remote data available to local applications is not without cost. Specialists must be found to manage the network hardware and software. System designers must take into account special ways of updating remote data. For example, a bank may have assigned its checking account and savings account files to two different remote locations. A customer wishes to transfer $100 from checking to savings. A program on the network begins the transaction by updating the checking account file to reflect a withdrawal of $100. However, the program then abnormally terminates. What happens to the $100?

Situations like this one make the designers' and analysts' jobs more complex. Local and remote copies of data must be integrated, and processes that access them organized.

Question: How do we manage this staff? How do we measure their productivity? And how do we appraise their performance?

Computer speeds and parallel processing. Basic computer processor speeds are usually measured in terms of the number of computer instructions that are executed per second. Current mainframe speeds range from approximately 1 to 25 million instructions per second (MIPS) (see Fig. 1.3). These instructions are those internal to the central processor, and do not correspond one-to-one to the verbs programmers use in most programming languages. (There are some programming languages that allow for such coding; here, we are referring to the more common *high-level languages* such as COBOL, PL/I, and FORTRAN.)

Still, speeds in the tens of millions of instructions per second are awfully fast, and computers are getting faster. One way to speed up processing is for two or more computers to work on parts of the same problem at the same time. For example, two processors could work on

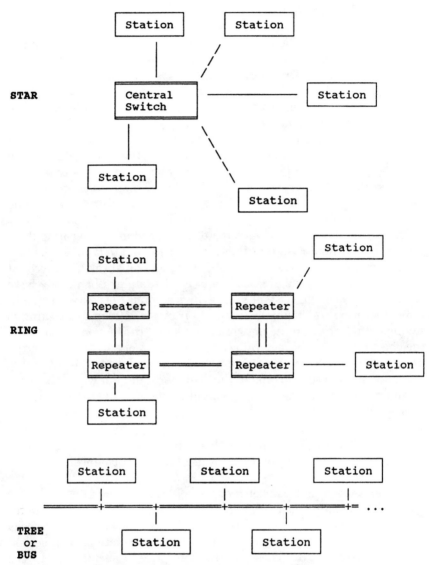

Figure 1.2 Some network topologies.

adding a list of 1000 numbers by having each of them add 500. The two would then combine their totals for the final answer. In this way, the problem can be solved in almost half the time.

Such *parallel processing* can be taken much further. Some computers on the market now contain several hundred internal processors. Assuming that programs can be written to take advantage of this power, 100 relatively slow (or cheap) processors can be configured in a

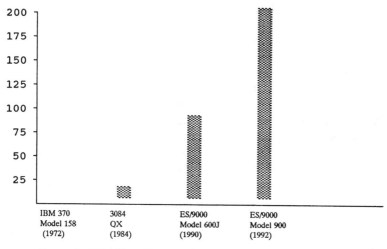

Processor Speeds in Millions of Instructions per Second (MIPs)

Figure 1.3   Computer processor speeds.

processor array that acts as if it is up to 100 times as fast as a single processor.

The advent of parallel processing makes the programmer's job more complex. Taking advantage of available parallel processing capability requires special programming languages, which may require extensive training to use efficiently. This additional complexity is difficult to measure and difficult to manage.

Question.   How will managers reward employees for excellent (or satisfactory) work in such an environment? Based upon final program efficiency? If so, how will that be measured?

Storage capacity.   Just as processor speed has increased, so has our ability to store information. The typical measure of data storage is the *byte*. Most computer systems can store one character of information, such as a letter or a digit, in a single byte. The number of bytes of storage is then roughly equivalent to the number of characters that may be stored. (Note that in many cases it is possible to *compress* character information so that it may be stored in a smaller space. Multiple blank spaces can be removed, for example.)

Perhaps the most recognizable form of data storage is the *diskette;* more properly, the 5¼-inch floppy disk, so called because of its flexibility. Now available in most retail stores in boxes of 10, current technology allows us to store approximately two million bytes of information on such a diskette. (This is roughly equivalent to the size of a large novel.) A more recent medium, the 3½-inch diskette, permits us to store about three million bytes. Lately, *optical media* (compact or optical disks) have greatly expanded this to hundreds of millions of bytes per diskette.

Going beyond the portable media, *hard disks* (those installed internally in microcomputers) can store up to one billion bytes, or the equivalent of 1000 novels. These hard disks typically measure about $3 \times 5 \times 2$ inches, or about the size of a paperback book. Imagine 1000 novels packed into the space of a paperback—continue by imagining a few hundred paperbacks (ten thousand novels) in a small box. It is now feasible to interconnect several hundred hard disks into something called a *disk array*. Such an array can be used by several thousand users to store information, and takes up less room than comparable mainframe direct access storage.

These advances in data storage will allow programmers and analysts to process large amounts of data *locally,* on microcomputers. This ability, once restricted to the realm of the mainframe, permits local processing of databases. Such processing may then easily be spread across multiple machines using multiple databases.

Question: How will managers appraise such employee skills? Are microcomputer programmers as valuable as their mainframe cousins? How can one measure such performance? Are such jobs comparable?

The latest software

Software is the programming, the instructions that are executed on the hardware. Usually equated with the statements of a programming language, software has become more than just a program listing. This has changed the way that we manage software developers. Let us briefly review some of the latest happenings in the software world.

Database management systems.   It was spreadsheet applications that "made" the microcomputer, and database applications were in a close second place. The reason for this is simple, if it is not obvious. Traditionally, programmers sat down at the computer and wrote programs in which they developed files. Those files were relatively simple—we call them *flat files*—and generally were able to supply all the immediate needs for the programs. Then, if another report was needed, another program was developed, and often another file. The user was totally dependent upon the programmer to develop both the files of data and the programs which manipulate that data. As the number of sizes of flat files proliferated, we began to call the aggregation of data a *database.*

The face of data processing had been changing for some years when the microcomputer appeared. People now learned that the duplication of data in multiple flat files had been both absurdly redundant and outrageously expensive. The proliferation of programs necessary to capture and access this data had itself increased at an alarming rate. Projects were delayed, costs escalated, and user frustration mounted. However, we learned that extensive collections of data could be developed (and therefore duplicate and redundant data could be eliminated) and alternative methods of accessing this information could be found. What remained was a useful and easy-to-use method to extract from that data useful reports. And then along came the microcomputer.

The microcomputer brought with it both data and operational independence. It put the power of the larger computer into the hands of the microcomputer user. And though it brought with it a higher degree of complexity than any prior item of office equipment, it brought a phenomenal amount of power. A major part of that power lies in the database application.

Question: Is knowledge of a database management system a useful skill? How do we measure design, analysis, or programming skills where a database is utilized? Would employees with such knowledge be paid more than other employees? What if the work they did was inferior?

Shareware. A recent phenomenon usually restricted to the microcomputer environment is *shareware.* Shareware is software, usually a program along with accompanying data, that is presented to the public at a very low initial cost (sometimes no cost at all). Shareware purchasers are then allowed to make copies of the shareware and furnish it to other potential users. These new users are then expected to pay a minimal fee to the original developer for this privilege.

The net result of this has been an explosion in the availability of new types of software. Calculators, word processors, spreadsheets, electronic mail, on-line databases, and many other services are now available to the microcomputer user. Such services were once the sole province of the mainframe computer, provided to users by request only, requiring programming by the mainframe development staff. These functions are now available at very low cost to users who are becoming less dependent on the mainframe programming staff.

Programmers are now being "migrated" to a different climate, one where the tasks they perform are more complex.

Question. How can you judge the worth of programmers if they use shareware in their work? Alternatively, should one reward a programmer for "reusing" working code?

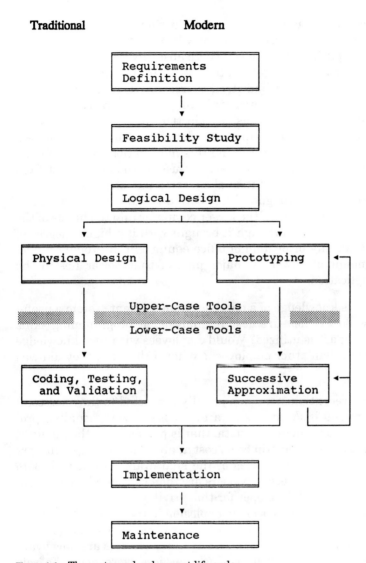

Figure 1.4   The systems development life cycle.

New development environments

Most programming is done as a standard part of the systems development life cycle (SDLC) (see Fig. 1.4). In this section we will take a close look at the environment programmers work in.

Development on mainframes.   This is the traditional environment for systems development. As data processing matured in the late 1970s, most large systems were designed and developed by analysts and programmers using *terminals* that connected to the mainframe computer. These terminals were initially very simple, consisting of little more than a keyboard and a cathode ray tube (CRT) screen. By the mid-1980s, microcomputers were taking the place of terminals as the basic programmer's workstation.

Using microcomputers to develop systems. By about 1987 the microcomputer revolution was in full swing, with millions of "micros" being installed in homes and businesses. It now became feasible to create business applications that were intended to execute solely on the microcomputer. Some enterprises took advantage of the concepts of networks and distributed processing, and created large distributed networks of microcomputers for their users. Data and programs were distributed across the networks, allowing users access to data and programs at remote *nodes*.

The next logical step was to develop mainframe systems using the microcomputer network as the development environment. Programmers wrote and tested programs using microcomputer tools. These tested programs were then transferred to the mainframe computer for final execution. There are several advantages of doing systems development in this environment:

- *Better usage of resources.* Programmers use microcomputer and network computer power and data storage during application development, rather than competing with production applications for CPU, magnetic tape, and disk storage.

- *Insulation from production environment.* Program abnormal terminations on the network do not affect the production environment.

- *Data sharing.* Test data and program modules are available to programmers, either across the network or through portable media such as diskettes. This allows testers rapid access to test data and results.

The microcomputer development environment is different and new. Programmers may now communicate electronically to obtain program specifications and test data. Microcomputer development tools make the job of writing a working program much easier.

Question: Are there two kinds of DP staff—those that develop on the mainframe itself, and those that develop mainframe applications using a microcomputer? Which are more valuable? Will there be two pay scales for programmers in your company?

Summary

Before the advent of disk arrays, parallel processing, networks, distributed processing, databases, shareware, and application development on the microcomputer, the programmer's major obstacles included writing "correct" or "efficient" programs; that is, coding programs so that CPU usage and storage resources were optimized. Programmers were graded on efficiency—special meetings called *walkthrus* were used to review program code for efficiency. Many enterprises with important applications required that programs run quickly and use minimal storage.

With the revolutions in storage capacity, processor speed, and hardware configurations, this emphasis on efficiency *will no longer be as important*. Instead, programmers will be made to concentrate on program correctness and maintainability. *This will require managers to measure employee performance in nontraditional ways.*

This book will serve as a guide for IS managers in measuring and appraising data processing employee performance.

Are Data Processing People Really Different?

Computer personnel are very much like noncomputer personnel in many of the traditional ways. But they arc also very different in many ways, and this section will concentrate upon the differences. Some in-depth research has been done in this area.*

The expanding backlog of work

The backlog of applications waiting to be developed is a serious problem, caused by five major factors:

1. *The increasing complexity of systems.*   New techniques have not increased productivity. The DP budget is rising significantly and personnel costs are rising within that budget (30 to 50 percent) between 1970 and 1980. Today data processing applications are far more complex and more effort is required. Labor costs are affected by inflation.

2. *Increasing quantity of systems.*   Knowledgeable users have multiplied their requests for service and, as has been stated before, have turned to the microcomputer. In short, DP personnel have done a pretty good job of acquainting user departments with what is possible—and have awakened a sleeping giant.

---

* *Motivating and Managing Computer Personnel,* by J. Daniel Couger & Robert A. Zawacki (John Wiley & Sons, Inc., 1980).

3. *Turnover.*   Surveys by Datamation show that turnover in data processing departments usually lies between 28 and 34 percent. This means a new employee learning curve—it also means that a large number of people simply aren't very happy.

4. *Increasing maintenance cost.*   More than 50 percent of some IS department budgets is spent on keeping applications afloat—sometimes called maintenance. This figure can vary, upward to 75 percent in some enterprises.

5. *A shortage of qualified personnel.*   Universities and colleges are not producing enough people with enough training, and this situation is a drain on time and budget resources.

Loyalty to the profession

Many people in data processing do not feel it necessary to follow their company's objectives and career paths. Rather, they tend to select another company in the industry and model their behavior after this enterprise. This behavior is magnified by a shortage of qualified technicians that permits programmers, analysts, managers, and other technicians to fulfill goals and receive rewards by changing organizations.

Key considerations

One measurement instrument used to gauge data processing employees is called the Job Diagnostic Survey (JDS), developed by J. Hackman (University of Illinois) and Greg Oldham (Yale). It describes five characteristics of a job (called core job dimensions): *skill variety, task identity, task significance, autonomy,* and *feedback.* Systems analysts and programmers rate very high on these scales compared to other professionals. The developers of the JDS note that this may be explained by three psychological states: *experienced meaningfulness, experienced responsibility,* and *knowledge of results.* These three terms bear definition:

Experienced meaningfulness: Individuals must perceive their work as worthwhile or important by some system of values they accept.

Experienced responsibility: They must believe that they personally are accountable for the outcomes of their efforts.

Knowledge of results: They must be able to determine, on some regular basis, whether the outcome of their work is satisfactory.

The outcomes of the JDS model compute a single summary index of the "motivating potential" of a job. The index is called the *motivating potential score* (MPS), and the formula for that is shown in Fig. 1.5.

Motivating Potential Score (MPS) =

$$
\left[\frac{\text{skill variety} + \text{task identity} + \text{task significance}}{3}\right] * \left[\text{autonomy}\right] * \left[\text{feedback from the job}\right]
$$

Figure 1.5   MPS formula.

Growth need strength

In a survey done by Couger and Zawacki, one of the things they tested was the *need for growth* of data processing professionals. In this area they could determine if a person who had a high *growth need strength* (GNS) absolutely required a position with the potential to satisfy that need. A person with a high GNS could not perform well in a job which did not require it. When compared to the MPS, there was a direct correspondence. The highest GNS corresponded to the highest MPS. In other words, *data processing people having high growth needs demand a job that motivates them.*

Social need strength

The question has often arisen as to whether or not a DP professional is a *loner* because he or she is a DP professional, or whether in fact loners are drawn to this field. Couger and Zawacki answer this by saying that they were very surprised that DP professionals were consistently and substantially *lower than all other professionals in the need to interact with people.* Programmers, it would seem, got along well with other programmers (to a degree) but with few others. A major cause for this is that the job itself was a key indicator of performance—the programmers knew just how well they were doing on the basis of interaction with the computer. Systems people, on the other hand, perform interpersonal relations as a part of their jobs—and yet their SNS was equally low—until it is realized that in both colleges and businesses the supply of people to the systems ranks comes largely from the programmer ranks. *Programmers, and systems people that were originally programmers, have generally lower social needs.*

Recognizing that people with inclinations to music have always fared well in data processing, some parallels may be drawn. The cello player (for one) is instantly aware of his or her position in the orchestra—yet the cello player is playing only to the cello player. The instrument (computer) is in direct communication with the player (programmer), and there is instant feedback.

The only significant difference seems to be that the music director is instantly aware of an audible boner—but the head cello player may not be. In short, DP people are critical of and unsatisfied by their supervision—and the reason may be that of the three types who make up the bulk of the department (programmer, systems, and operations), only programmers have the immediate feedback about their performance.

This may not be a problem for some data processing professionals at the moment, but consider: what happens when these people are promoted to supervisory or managerial positions? Such "people" jobs may not provide adequate feedback or motivation. And what about their employees?

The data processing profession and its supporting academic institutions have put an enormous amount of effort into improving design and programming techniques, but very little into improving the motivation for using the techniques. Some have said that what is happening to the DP professional world right now is what was happening to the automobile production world 40 years ago—that we have specialized the DP field too much. Job enlargement, wherein the scope of jobs is expanded to include several areas of responsibility and expertise, may be the only answer.

Motivating people in computer operations

The motivation situation is most acute in computer operations where employees may be only two-thirds as motivated as other DP professionals. According to the survey the MPS of these jobs is lower than any of the other 500 jobs in the Hackman/Oldham database—the computer operator is the least motivated of all employees anywhere. (Operators in this sense include data entry, data control, and computer operators.) Such people feel that their job is just as important, but feel that the organization does not agree and gives more support to the programming and systems people than to those in operations.

Growth and social need strengths
of operations personnel

The survey pointed out that there is a very high GNS for operations personnel, essentially because they do not feel challenged by the work they must do. It is much closer to those of programmers and analysts than to other employees, but only about two-thirds of those in the systems department.

Social need strength for this group is, interestingly, much higher than that of programmers and analysts. They interact with more people. There is also generally a high feeling of satisfaction (except for pay) among these people, for growth is available in DP operations, in terms of a general growth of the department. There is also enough pay satisfaction (it may not be high enough to suit, but is substantially higher than other persons in the organization) to offset the lack of challenge.

Despite this, there was evidence that these people recognized that the future would be bright in the DP career field and they were willing to pay their dues.

Feedback

Humans desire feedback. Because a programming manager is frequently an ex-programmer, his or her SNS doesn't measurably increase simply because the individual's position has escalated and the need for an increased SNS is evident. The survey suggests the following:

1. Data processing professionals have high growth needs, and must be provided with challenging jobs.
2. Departments where feedback is not produced naturally—because of low SNS of personnel—need more formalized feedback procedures. Training in effective feedback approaches can improve application of the procedure.

Summary of survey findings

1. While their general satisfaction is higher than that of other professionals, DP professionals are less satisfied with their supervision.
2. Growth need strength is high for DP professionals compared to other professionals and other job categories.
3. Social need strength is substantially lower for DP professionals compared to other professionals in other fields.
4. DP job specialization could be improved by reversing the trend toward specialization, and concentrating as much upon the fulfillment of the employee as upon the techniques they are called upon to employ.

What Motivates DP People?

A Columbia University study sponsored by *Business Week* magazine in the mid-1980s describes the factors that data processing professionals rate most highly about their jobs. Columbia investigators surveyed 117 managers and 624 computer specialists. A summary of their findings appears in Fig. 1.6. As can be seen in the table, specialists considered learning new skills their highest priority in choosing a job. In comparison, managers selected responsibility as their highest priority. And while managers considered autonomy and job title as important, specialists considered these least important.

In general, computer people deem growth, skills, and personal fulfillment as the most important aspects of their jobs. This indicates that

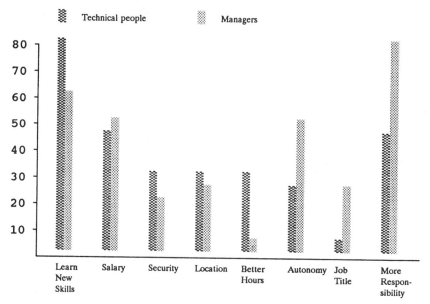

Figure 1.6   Factors DP professionals rate highly about their jobs.

managers of data processing professionals need to use different skills in managing their people than do traditional managers. Rewards for achievement in traditional organizations include money (higher salaries, bonuses, and stock options), additional responsibility, and advancement. In a data processing environment, these are not strong motivators. Instead, managers should use those things that influence their people, such as education and training, and free them from cramping management styles.

The U.S. Government's Office of Personnel Management did a five-year study* of the job structure of its computer professionals. This study involved thousands of DP professionals in government service. It found that programmers responded to training and education, while systems analysts responded to interpersonal contact.

Satisfaction

A recent survey† of job satisfaction in the DP industry indicates that many practitioners are less satisfied than in the past. They feel more

---

* Occupational Data Report, Computer Specialist Series, GS-334, 1981.

† Computerworld's Sixth Annual Job Satisfaction Survey, September 1992.

stress due to increased workloads and increased demands from business. By far, most respondents indicated that job satisfaction was their top concern. Further, the most common reason chosen for leaving a position was for "career advancement."

Growth

"Growth is so important because in the data processing industry skills are outdated every three years," says J. Daniel Couger, professor of computer science at the University of Colorado. "Data processing people tend to be individualists [who] look for working environments where they have a career path that allows for growth."

The idea that skills can become outdated so quickly in data processing is reinforced by the explosion in hardware and software described in the Introduction. In the area of microcomputers alone, the last five years have seen the introduction of:

- A new operating system, OS/2, for the IBM PS/2 personal computer

- Relational database management systems

- Packages that simulate the IBM mainframe environment, including CICS, IMS, and DB2

Companies using microcomputers to do mainframe application design are well aware of the extraordinary learning curve required to master this new technology. To offset it, they are devising comprehensive training and education programs that will assist their employees in mastering these new areas of data processing. Being able to positively motivate these employees will become one of the management challenges of the 1990s.

Data processing personalities

Many data processing people consider themselves to be somehow *different* from other professionals in other industries. Why is this? What makes a data processing person different (if at all) from others? In this section we will describe one theory of personality description that may point us in the right direction.

The Myers Briggs Type Indicator. The Myers Briggs Type Indicator (MBTI) has grown out of the work of Carl Jung, who postulated that people are different in fundamental ways. In the early 1920s many psychologists disagreed as to how people could be classified into personality or psychological types. Each had their own names for the types. Some of these were:

- Choleric, phlegmatic, melancholic, sanguine (Hippocrates)
- Dogmatic, agnostic, traditional, innovative (Adickes)
- Hyperesthetic, anesthetic, melancholic, hypomanic (Kretschmer)
- Religious, theoretic, economic, artistic (Spranger)

In the 1950s Isabel Myers and Katheryn Briggs revived Jung's personality types and devised a test that measured a person's propensity to act in certain ways. There are four categories of behavior, or *temperaments;* this leads to sixteen different personality *types,* depending upon one's leanings in each of the temperaments. Note that each category is not absolute. A person only tends to act a certain way to a certain degree, and is not said to actually *be* one of the types.

Every temperament has a range from one extreme to the other. Each of these extremes is identified with a one-word description and a single letter. These are:

- Extroversion (E) and Introversion (I)
- Intuition (N) and Sensation (S)
- Thinking (T) and Feeling (F)
- Judging (J) and Perceiving (P)

Extroversion and introversion.   This category refers to the way that a person interacts and relates to other people. A person who chooses people as a source of energy probably prefers extroversion, while the person who prefers solitude to recover energy may tend toward introversion. The extrovert prefers talking to people, and experiences loneliness when not in contact with people. On the other hand, the introvert desires peace and privacy. Introverts may enjoy interacting with people, but it drains their energy. About 75 percent of the population tends toward extroversion.

Intuition and sensation.   Those preferring sensation probably describe themselves as practical, while those having a natural preference for intuition probably choose to describe themselves as innovative. Sensation-preferring or *sensible* people want facts, trust experience, and want to deal with the actual as opposed to the theoretical. The intuitive, however, looks to the future, to daydreams, to imagination, and to inspiration. About 75 percent of the population tends toward sensation.

Thinking and feeling.   This is sometimes seen as the difference between being personal and impersonal. Thinking types tend to be logical, impersonal, and objective. Feeling types tend to be emotional or personal, may be somewhat subjective, and are inclined toward persuasion. These types occur in about equal proportions in the general population.

Judging and perceiving. Judging types prefer closure, and are likely to feel uncomfortable until a decision has been made. They are apt to establish deadlines and take them seriously. Perceiving types prefer open options, and wish to gather more information. They sometimes look upon deadlines as mere alarm clocks that signal time for action. These types occur in about equal proportions in the general population.

Comparison of categories. Each of the category ranges can be illustrated most clearly using the phrases shown in Table 1.1.

Using the letters that signify each end of the range of the types, we end up with sixteen distinct personalities. Each of the personalities is described with a word deemed most descriptive of that type. These types are listed in Table 1.2.

Typical data processing personalities

Many recent studies of data processing personalities predicted that the most common DP personality would be ESTJ—that is, extroverted, sensing, thinking, judging. In fact, the most common personalities actually found were ISTJ and INTJ. ISTJ personalities, occurring in only 6 percent of the general population, were found to occur in almost 25 percent of the data processing professionals tested. The INTJ type, occurring in less than 1 percent of the general population, occurred in 16 percent of those tested. Although these were the most common personality types found, it was decided that the extroversion/introversion category was far less significant than the three others. The general conclusion was that TJ personalities predominate in data processing.

These results are significant in that they point to a large number of data processing people being described by a few personality types. Referring back to Fig. 1.3, we find that DP people can be described predominantly as objective, impersonal, and analytical; as tending toward making decisions, being well-planned, and getting things done. Managers in data processing can now use these results as guidelines in predicting what kinds of things will motivate their employees, and in how best to appraise performance.

As a large portion of DP people are analytical and tend toward laws, rules, and standards, managers should try to ensure that the appraisal process is well-defined. Forms should be self-explanatory, and procedures should be in writing. Performance appraisal meetings should follow a standard format, and all employee performance data should be documented. Further, regular status meetings should con-

TABLE 1.1   Personality Category Ranges

Extrovert	Introvert
Sociability	Territoriality
Interaction	Concentration
External	Internal
Extensive	Intensive
Multiplicity of relationships	Limited relationships
Expenditure of energies	Conservation of energies
Interest in external events	Interest in internal reaction
Sensation	*Intuition*
Experience	Hunches
Past	Future
Realistic	Speculative
Actual	Possible
Down-to-earth	Head-in-clouds
Utility	Fantasy
Fact	Fiction
Practicality	Ingenuity
Sensible	Imaginative
Thinking	*Feeling*
Objective	Subjective
Principles	Values
Policy	Social values
Laws	Extenuating circumstances
Firmness	Persuasion
Impersonal	Personal
Justice	Humane
Analysis	Sympathy
Judging	*Perceiving*
Settled	Pending
Decided	Gather more data
Fixed	Flexible
Plan ahead	Adapt as you go
Closure	Open options
Planned	Open-ended
Completed	Emergent
Decisive	Tentative
Urgency	There is plenty of time

TABLE 1.2   The Sixteen Personality Types

INTP	Architect	ESFJ	Seller
ENTP	Inventor	ISFJ	Conservator
INTJ	Scientist	ESFP	Entertainer
ENTJ	Field marshal	ISFP	Artist
INFP	Questor	ESTJ	Administrator
ENFP	Journalist	ISTJ	Trustee
INFJ	Author	ESTP	Promoter
ENFJ	Pedagogue	ISTP	Artisan

centrate on the facts and their interpretation, rather than on extenuating circumstances.

These guidelines should be taken as advice only, as they may not apply to all data processing people. Indeed, the manager should make an attempt to determine how an employee fits into the various personality categories. This should be done on an informal basis.

Dealing with computer egos

The worst problem a manager can have is an employee who feels mentally superior to others. This type of employee requires careful handling by management, so that any impending employee revolts can be dealt with before they occur.

According to Don Berardo, a management counselor at The Meld Group, West Hartford, CT, every organization should consider implementing a screening method to eliminate possible problem employees during the hiring process. He suggests establishing a hiring model within the corporate structure to do this. Once a vain or arrogant person slips through the hiring process or develops such a personality trait on the job, the manager must adjust and conform tactics to the new situation.

"Managers must continue to act as facilitators and avoid taking mental power personally," says Berardo. "You must gain the personal respect of the *prima donna* so that the power boundaries remain clear to both parties. It's important to make everyone feel wanted and equal within the DP department."

The manager should use problem-solving techniques with such employees, listing the behaviors that they feel are inappropriate, and explaining how they are deemed unacceptable. They should make it the employee's responsibility to monitor and change their own behavior. These points should be documented in status reports, as they will affect the outcome of the performance appraisal. This point is one that most employees will understand.

Motivational factors: satisfiers and dissatisfiers

In his watershed work on motivation, Frederic Herzberg sampled 1685 employees, identifying events that caused job satisfaction and dissatisfaction. Factors related to salary were well down the list of influencers. Those salary events were equally balanced between satisfiers and dissatisfiers. Topping the chart of events leading to job satisfaction were achievement, recognition, the work itself, responsibility, advancement, and growth. The most frequently cited dissatisfiers were company policy and administration, supervision, and working conditions. These results clearly put the lie to money as a motivator.

Frederic Herzberg's work on job satisfaction predates the era of the computing professional. What, then, *does* motivate computer professionals? Experience, discussion, and literature surveys suggest the factors mentioned in the following section. Further, and of greater importance, effective performance appraisal can enhance many of the satisfiers cited by Herzberg and minimize some of the dissatisfiers. Although performance appraisal is not explicitly mentioned in that work, it offers management and supervisors an important tool for enhancing satisfaction in the workplace.

Adequate working conditions.   Most workers need a comfortable environment in order to be productive. But it is even more important to the intense, intellectually challenging work of programming. On the other hand, programmers do not need, or even want, opulent surroundings. Thus, paintings on the walls and fountains in the lobby might better serve in the Marketing Department.

1. *Floor space.*   An eight-by-ten-foot workstation is about right. Programmers with this much space seem to perform best in the Coding War Games. Tom DeMarco and Timothy Lister set up these productivity studies over several years and discussed the results in *Peopleware* (Dorset House, 1987). Programmers who performed in the first quartile reported 78 sq. ft. of dedicated work space, while those in the fourth quartile had 46 sq. ft. Of course, other variables were operating as well.

2. *Furniture.*   There should be a comfortable, height-adjustable, posture-correct chair so that long hours at a terminal do not become drudgery. The work surface should accommodate two 11" by 14" listings open side by side to compare reports. Six feet of overhead cabinets will hold textbooks and manuals. Auxiliary lighting is usually provided under the cabinets. Plenty of personal bulletin board space is needed. Some stations may require both a terminal and a PC, with its CPU on the floor to save desk space. A guest chair for impromptu discussions is a luxury.

3. *Telephones.*   Phones are intrusive, but necessary. Nothing is more disturbing than to have to listen to someone else's phone calls. Fortunately, acoustic panels on workstations help mask voices. The phone's ringer level should be adjusted down. Most workers find that voice recording systems are a real improvement in the workplace. Failing that, a message center or receptionist should intercept incoming calls after the third ring, so everyone else can go back to

work. Although computers can be set to mask interrupts, most people cannot.

4. *Air.* We take good air for granted but that's not always the case. Many buildings are now smoke-free, but who has not seen a systems person having a secret smoke in the confines of the workstation? Report this to Big Brother. Air conditioning is great except for the unlucky worker whose neck is right under the vent. And some buildings shut down the ventilation system at 5 p.m. Friday, and start it up again at 6 a.m. Monday. But what about Weekend Warriors? Some shops will provide weekend air conditioning on request.

5. *Dress code.* More and more companies are subscribing to relaxed dress codes. In some cases it may be a casual day, say on Friday. In other installations, casual dress is acceptable at all times. Care must be taken to maintain a neat and businesslike workplace. It is difficult to do quality work in a sloppy environment. A written dress code that covers the subject without being offensive is difficult to achieve. Such efforts usually end with the statement "at the discretion of your manager."

6. *Other factors.* To round out excellent working conditions, complimentary coffee and tea are a nice touch. One large hotel company has a racquetball court and showers in its headquarters complex! Nice, but expensive. But how about a volleyball court outdoors for lunchtime use? Or a jogging and walking path? And park benches? Many of these facilities can be provided at modest cost but go a long way toward motivating systems staff.

Having use of up-to-date tools. Many used to feel that the issue was whether to work in a large DP installation or a small shop. In a small organization, the systems person could enjoy a broader job description. They could be development programmers, but also double as systems programmers and do SYSGENs. They could do capacity planning when the need arose, and write standards from time to time. Such were the diverse opportunities of small DP installations. Well, there are relatively few small shops anymore. Through mergers, centralization of remote data centers, and other systemic changes in the workplace, most of those in commercial data processing toil in large installations.

In such an environment the work is more narrowly focused. Even development and maintenance of the same application might be separated. But one overwhelming advantage of a large shop is in the resources available. Large companies have the budget and can find justification to stay abreast of new technology. And systems professionals, for the most part, want to have access to the latest tool set.

Development has traditionally been done on mainframe terminals under an on-line editor such as TSO or ROSCOE. But more and more,

PC-based tools are making an impact in the marketplace. Programmers and analysts will not be *truly* happy without one or more packages from these categories:

Word processing. Preparing documentation is the bane of the applications programmer. Access to one of the popular word processing PC packages (such as WordPerfect, Word, and Displaywrite) can make this chore more palatable.

Desktop publishing. These packages, such as Aldus Pagemaker, Ventura Publisher, and others, can make user manuals look truly first-class. Mastering them requires considerable experience, so usually they are operated by a publishing department rather than by systems professionals. But availability and use of publishing tools—even for meeting notices and training announcements—lends an aura of quality to the organization.

Programming aids. PC-based programming aids enable programs to be written and debugged on a stand-alone PC and then uploaded to the mainframe. No more waiting in TSO queues when these tools are available. MicroFocus COBOL can open an on-screen window in which selected variables can be observed to change in slow time as highlighted instructions execute in the background. Programmers are excited to come to work in a shop that offers such facilities.

CASE tools. Computer Aided Software Engineering tools are still evolving and seeking their place in the market. They offer assistance to the systems builder by representing and storing systems designs. There is usually a repository for data names, descriptions, and relationships. They may include mouse-based programs for drawing dataflow diagrams and structure charts. Career-minded systems designers will be happy if their organization is evaluating rather than ignoring CASE tools. It is noteworthy that the new federal job description for Programmer/Analyst includes an oblique reference to software engineering: "May use computer-aided software tools, such as flowchart design and code generation, in each stage of system development . . ."

Tools are not limited to hardware and software. *Procedural* tools are also important. As one example, the *structured walkthru* is recommended by most recent textbooks on systems development. But how many installations are actually using it? There is a short-term cost—the time and attention of qualified reviewers—while the benefits are long-term and less easily identified. Yet some authors say (*Bugs in the Program, Problems in Federal Government Computer Software Development and Regulation,* April 1990) that a defect identified in the design stage can cost a hundred times less to repair than one that has found its way into the finished software product. Systems professionals want to be part of a team that recognizes and follows such precepts.

Opportunity to learn from senior professionals.   Few people aspire to be the smartest in the work group. Computer people are motivated to hone their skills (or improve their resume, if you prefer). It is comforting to know that one can find help with a thorny issue among colleagues. Another, subtler, factor is at work: If this company can hold as well-qualified a system designer as Sally, it's good enough for me also.

The chance to teach junior staff.   In addition to the opportunity to learn, many systems professionals welcome a chance to participate in the career development of less senior people. Some companies have an entry-level training program and draw instructors from the ranks. The sequence might consist of a few days on each of the following topics:

- Introduction to Hardware and Software
- Systems Development Methodology
- COBOL Lecture and Workshop
- TSO (or other development tool)
- Fundamentals of JCL
- Program and System Testing
- Installation Standards

Peer recognition is enhanced for those willing and able to contribute. One has not thoroughly mastered a subject until he or she has prepared and taught it to others. A steady diet of teaching can be grueling, but the occasional stint in a classroom is a boost to self-esteem for many people. Incidentally, trainees are also motivated by their experience. Empirical studies have shown that junior staff who have come up through the ranks are more loyal than those hired with experience.

Technical and professional growth.   The systems people most in demand are those interested in their own career development. Such staff members will be motivated in an organization that fosters such growth. Often there is short-term pain to achieve long-term gain. For example, cross-training involves taking people off applications they know well in order to prepare them for another assignment. The penalty could be slippage of a project, but the alternative is to risk the resignation of valued staff members—or to have them "retire on the job."

Another practice that motivates by encouraging professional growth is that of *job posting*. Vacancies are posted on bulletin boards with job description, requirements, and salary range. Interested and qualified people are encouraged to apply. Thus promotional opportunities are made available to current staff instead of hiring from the outside. There could be some bruised egos among those who are not offered the position but, on the whole, morale is increased in such an open organization.

Certainly an active training program is important in an organization that seeks to motivate its systems professionals. The half-life of computer knowledge is about five years. Those who mastered Assembler Language find it of little value today. And how many remember Visicalc, the precursor of Lotus 1-2-3? It is the responsibility of the company to offer its people the knowledge they need in today's and tomorrow's workplace. The wise company budgets 2 percent of staff salary and 4 percent of staff time to be invested in training.

Technical library. Providing a library for the systems and data processing staff is an important contribution to the professional environment. There should be subscriptions to mainframe and PC magazines—perhaps a dozen in all. Staff members who belong to professional societies might be encouraged to bring in their monthly journals. Vendor reference manuals can become a part of this library. Flip-top racks are an orderly, inexpensive way to display magazines.

Books should be purchased out of the annual budget for that purpose. Staff members may request and substantiate the importance of new books. It is no good to lock them up. There is no sense in buying books, then making them inaccessible. A card sign-out system must be set up so absent books can be traced. If the library grows too big—a good sign—a secretary or part-time librarian may be needed. Yes, books are expensive. But systems professionals will be very responsive to this investment, and job applicants as well as clients will invariably notice the library and carry away the impression of a top-notch organization.

Professional societies. At a certain level in the organization, such as Senior Analyst, membership in a professional society should be sponsored by the company. Attendance at monthly meetings and annual conferences, and browsing the several journals available, can enrich the thinking of one who has long been in the same company. Incidentally, when they see how things are done elsewhere they often realize that "my company isn't so bad after all."

Professional societies span a broad range of interests.* The ACM (Association for Computing Machinery) and IEEE (Institute for Electronic and Electrical Engineering) emphasize hardware and software. ASM (Association for Systems Management) and DPMA (Data Process-

---

* For a list of some representative societies and associations, see App. A.

ing Management Association) are more process-oriented. And there are more theory-oriented organizations such as TIMS (The Institute for Management Science) and newer groups that study the systems life cycle and the use of CASE tools. There is a society for almost every systems interest, and that interest must be encouraged by a forward-thinking company. A famous Japanese company has the motto: Material resources are limited, but human resources know no bounds.

Educational library.   An adjunct to the technical library is a repository of educational resources. This might include college catalogs, vendor class schedules, certification study materials, adult education courses, and so forth.

College catalogs.   Most installations encourage staff members to continue their education, usually in evening courses. Rare companies may grant an educational leave of absence to a key senior professional or manager. (IBM has sponsored sabbaticals for people to teach at the university level.)

Such encouragement might include tuition reimbursement, especially if good grades are earned. The educational library should house current catalogs of nearby universities, colleges, and community colleges. Often courses in data processing that are most closely applicable to the workplace are found at two-year colleges (where working professionals are instructing) rather than at universities.

Vendor class schedules.   The in-house education program recommends certain courses conducted by training and software vendors. The technical library is the place to keep all such course descriptions and schedules. Here they can be accessed by interested management and staff.

Certification study materials.   Staff members who are interested in earning the Certificate in Data Processing will need introductory materials, application blanks, sample test questions, and any information that might be available on refresher courses.

Adult education courses.   These are usually introductory-level courses thus may not be reimbursable by the company. Still, they are of value and should be encouraged. Provide current course listings and the names of some staff members who have further information about the courses.

Caring management.   Management's job, loosely defined, is to provide a productive opportunity for work and then to stand back. In a systems development effort this opportunity includes fixed targets with reasonable dates. Ideally, the systems team should participate in setting the delivery dates. But in the real world the team may not yet be in place when planning is undertaken. In fact, preliminary estimates must be made in order to seek funding approval—before little is known about the actual design of the system. Caring management will realize that these estimates are subject to change as the design becomes more specific. Indeed, time estimates are subject to *stepwise refinement*. When locked in to unreasonable schedules, systems professionals will become frustrated and motivation will suffer. Ultimately they may vote with their feet.

On the other hand, another obligation of systems management is to attempt to hold the boundaries of the project fixed. Projects have a tendency to grow like Topsy as the client begins to request new functionality that was not in the original estimate. This is a credit to the users' involvement in the project—they have begun to envision "what might be." The process is known as *scope creep*. Adding more features in the same development time can be demoralizing to the project team. In *The Terrors of Ice and Darkness* by Christoph Ransmayr, we are told that the secret of good sledging is to excite the dogs with a goal and make them believe they are heading straight for it all the time.

Kerzner (*Project Management—A Systems Approach to Planning, Scheduling, and Controlling,* Van Nostrand Reinhold, 1989) provides a useful summary of the needs for which management must provide in order for systems team members to realize their true potential:

- Interesting and challenging work
- A professionally stimulating environment
- Technical expertise within the team
- Management assistance in problem solving
- Clearly defined objectives
- Good interpersonal relations
- Proper planning
- Clear role definition
- Open communications
- A minimum of changes

Being part of a winning team.   Our society adulates a winner. "Winning is not the *main* thing—it's the *only* thing!" exhorted Vince Lombardi, legendary coach of the Green Bay Packers. A systems project, like the Packers, is a true team effort. Walter Mitty need not apply. In fact, the wise Project Manager will quietly spirit away the supercoder, since he or she is disruptive to the team effort.

But programmers are highly motivated to be recognized by their peers as valued members of a successful team. The word *synergy* does apply: the whole is greater than the sum of its parts. A smooth project team has been likened to a practiced surgical team. Every doctor, nurse, and assistant has a specific role to play—and each has learned to rely on the others, under the direction of the Chief Surgeon. The concept of the Chief Programmer Team had its 15 minutes of fame. It will work once—or a few times. But egos tend to get in the way.

Some Project Managers go as far as providing "Winning Team" hats or t-shirts, emblazoned with the company logo, at the team pizza party. Others believe their professionals would find this a little corny. There's room for reasonable managers to disagree on this.

Making a difference. Thoughtful people are motivated by the idea that their work matters. That is why some folks join the Peace Corps instead of Wall Street investment firms. Many systems workers find a home in maintenance programming because they are willing to work all night to get a recalcitrant system back on the air—the roar of the greasepaint, the smell of the crowd. They say, "Development programming? Are you kidding? They can work for months or years before enjoying the fruits of their labors!" One friend who worked his way through college by doing construction work during the summer points with pride to a particular beam in a highway bridge: "I remember helping to lay that beam." People need to be proud of their contribution.

The wise Project Manager will respond to that need by instilling in the project team the importance to the company—nay, to mankind!—of this endeavor. And the systems professionals will give their all, then tell their grandchildren (if they are computer literate).

In the classic book *Motivation and Personality* by Abraham Maslow (Harper and Brothers, 1954), we learn of the hierarchy of human needs. Some systems professionals are among the fortunate few who have fulfilled the lower and middle levels of need. They are seeking *self-actualization* through:

- Constant self-development
- Full realization of one's potential
- The desire to be truly creative

On the other hand, what factors don't matter very much?

Working hours. For the most part computer people are young, ambitious, and task-oriented. They may not observe regular working hours. It may make sense to come in early and/or stay late to have access to CPU cycles. Night and weekend work goes with the territory. Project Managers should encourage this kind of commitment and allow casual time off as compensation. And many will prefer to work at home. In recognition of time saved and ecology benefits of home work, many companies are lending terminals, PCs, and documentation to qualified people. There must be an understanding, oral or written, that certain days are office time for everyone so meetings can be scheduled.

Company bowling league. Systems staff are not motivated by traditional company functions like bowling, bingo, or being interviewed for the in-house newspaper. On the other hand, many are fitness buffs and will turn out for the company 10K run or bicycle trip. They will help clean up trash from a stream or paint houses in the inner city. And they will be responsive to the organization that sponsors such valued events.

Retirement program. Programmers and analysts are not excited by the company's pension benefits. They are many years from retirement and are likely to make several job changes before that distant event. They are more interested in the here and now.

Endless meetings. Meetings are generally construed as a waste of precious time. Management fulfills its mission by calling meetings and enjoying face time with the project team—but the latter find them demotivating. Necessary meetings should be kept short, on track, and to the point. Providing healthy snack food may make these meetings more palatable.

2

Data Processing Jobs and Standards

Job Descriptions

Purpose and content

Most every employee is familiar with the general term *job description,* even though they may not have seen their own in writing. In this section we will concentrate on why job descriptions are important, how they are created, and how they tie in to the performance appraisal process.

The purpose of job descriptions. A company needs job descriptions of its employees for several reasons.

Informing employees of job responsibilities. The best way to familiarize new employees with their job responsibilities is to provide a job description. Such a description may describe either expected results, correct behaviors, or tasks to be performed. Without this information, the only good alternative is on-the-job training (OJT). Many companies use OJT, and for good reasons. Reading about the assembly line is one thing—actually doing the job is another. Understanding the job description for (say) a "cyclist" may be interesting, but it will not be of much use to someone learning to ride a bicycle.

Personnel planning. As a company grows, it must expand its product line or its services, its market areas, and its employee base. To grow an employee base by planning how many jobs of what type and expertise level will be required is called *personnel planning*. Such a plan may become a critical factor in the organization's future success.

The plan can be used as a guide to staff growth (or downsizing). It requires facing up to the anticipated resignations in each job category, along with planned promotions. The outcome is the number of newly hired employees required in each job so planned recruiting can begin early and proceed on a level basis throughout the year.

In many industries, employee compensation and new employee recruiting account for over half of total expenses. Acquiring new employees that have the correct skill sets and training current employees represent a major investment. Complete and accurate job descriptions are a must.

For example, assume a systems development department has about 100 professionals. Assume also that approved projects and projected staffing needs will grow by 2 percent in the first year and 7 percent in the second year.

First, count the noses already on board and consider the current budgeted vacancies. Consult personnel reports to guess what the turnover rate might be in each job. If records are not in good order, consider the state of the local economy and apply an educated guess. Convert these percentages to full-time equivalents.

Next, lay in the growth positions mandated by project plans. Based on performance evaluations and human resource department guidelines, estimate the number of people expected to be promoted to and from all job titles in the coming year. Addition and subtraction will reveal the hiring requirements for the year (see Fig. 2.1).

Use of a model such as this one can be a valuable part of the personnel planning process. With it, staff deficits are less likely to occur unexpectedly or to creep up slowly until they reach crisis proportions. Finally, performance appraisal is an integral part of such staff planning. A good employee evaluation process is a good predictor of promotions—or terminations.

Apprising employees of job openings. Career path planning for employees is always difficult. Employees are generally not well-informed about all available career opportunities, and managers are seldom qualified to act as career counselors. The best that can be done is that managers solicit personal goals from employees and assist them in matching those goals with those of the company. To assist in this endeavor, managers are responsible for informing employees about job opportunities in other departments.

Another related subject is that of *promotion from within*. This involves giving current employees priority when assigning people to jobs. This is an excellent policy for several reasons. First, employees do not feel threatened that outsiders will be brought in and made

1993 Personnel Plan	Pgmr. Trainees	Prog. & Sr. Prog.	Anal. & Sr. Anal.	Sys. Pgmr. Sr. S.P.
1. Presently on board	3	37	29	12
2. Current vacancies	1	6	6	4
3. Estimated turnover (%)	0	20	10	15
4. Est. turnover (1 * 3)	0	8	3	2
5. Budgeted additions	0	0	2	0
6. Promotions (from)	3	2	1	0
7. Promotions (to)	0	3	1	1
8. Needed hires (2 + 4 + 5 + 6 − 7)	4	13	11	5
9. Final staff (1 − 4 − 6 + 7 + 8)	4	43	37	16
1994 Personnel Plan				
1. Presently on board	4	43	37	16
2. Current vacancies	0	0	0	0
3. Estimated turnover (%)	30	25	15	20
4. Est. turnover (1 * 3)	1	11	6	3
5. Budgeted additions	1	2	3	2
6. Promotions (from)	4	3	2	1
7. Promotions (to)	0	4	2	2
8. Needed hires (2 + 4 + 5 + 6 − 7)	6	12	9	4
9. Final staff (1 − 4 − 6 + 7 + 8)	5	45	40	18

Figure 2.1   A personnel planning model.

their managers. Thus, management tends to consist of employees who have been with the company for some time and are familiar with policies, procedures, and culture. Second, competent employees are assured that they will be considered for promotional opportunities. Third, knowing that future leaders will be brought up through the organization makes upper management confident that promotees understand the company from the ground up.

Newly created jobs. Jobs that are brand-new seldom remain the same after a period of time. Still, management should only create jobs to complete tasks that they wish to be performed. Finding an employee (or potential employee) to fill such a job is difficult to do fairly, and requires care. Management must be sensitive to possible discrimination and other hiring biases. The best way to minimize hiring or promotion mistakes is with a clear and concise job description. A list of responsibilities, tasks, and requirements eases this process, especially if it has been developed and validated through job analysis.

Creating performance appraisal documentation and procedures. This last reason for job descriptions is the one companies seem to think of last. Apparently, it is sometimes more important to grow the business in the short term than to plan for measuring and evaluating the employee's performance in the future. Most companies understand this and grapple with creating some kind of job description that will lead to a performance appraisal system. What they end up with is either a system "borrowed" from a similar enterprise or one that is designed to meet too many business demands. (These problems will be discussed in Chap. 6.)

How job descriptions are created.   Usually a fledgling business develops job descriptions during its expansion. Sometimes this is accomplished by borrowing or copying standard job descriptions from other similar companies. Common sources of job descriptions include trade associations, university research projects, and the federal government.

For example, Fig. 2.2 contains a short list of job titles taken from the Department of Labor. These job titles are for computer-related occupations in the federal government.

Let's look briefly at one of these job titles, and see how it has evolved over several years. Figure 2.3 is drawn from the Department of Labor 1977 *Dictionary of Occupational Titles*. It presents the job description for a Programmer Analyst.

Figure 2.4 shows the latest version of this job description, drawn from the most recent publication.

By far the most logical way to create job descriptions is to systematically develop them by analyzing the business's current employee base (and perhaps the employees of similar business concerns). This last method is called *job analysis.*

Conducting a job analysis.   There are many ways to effect a job analysis for a company. Some of the more relevant are listed here.

1. *Critical incidents.*   Using this method, a task force of employees and managers gathers information from several employees and supervisors in all job capacities. In all cases the task force concentrates on gathering data about specific instances of job behavior. These examples of job behaviors are called *critical incidents.* Sets of incidents (or behaviors) for a particular job category (say, programmer) are grouped into categories; these categories and the incidents within them then make up the job description for that type of employee.

   This technique is an excellent one for developing performance appraisal forms and procedures; however, it sometimes fails in several respects. First, the information gained about job behaviors is typically not evaluated as to its applicability for a particular job. An atypical employee behavior may be inadvertently included in a job description simply because an employee was doing it, and not because that behavior was appropriate or correct. One example of such a behavior would be a programmer who spent most of the day

---

Computer-Related Occupations

030.062-010	Software Engineer
030.162-010	Computer Programmer
030.162-014	Programmer-Analyst
030.162-018	Programmer, Engineering and Scientific
030.162-022	Systems Programmer
030.167-010	Chief, Computer Programmer
030.167-014	Systems Analyst
031.132-010	Supervisor, Network Control Operators
031.262-010	Data Communications Analyst
031.262-014	Network Control Operator
032.132-010	User Support Analyst Supervisor
032.262-010	User Support Analyst
033.162-010	Computer Security Coordinator
033.162-014	Data Recovery Planner
033.162-018	Technical Support Specialist
033.167-010	Computer Systems Hardware Analyst
033.262-010	Quality Assurance Analyst
033.362-010	Computer Security Specialist
039.162-010	Data Base Administrator
039.162-014	Data Base Design Analyst
039.264-010	Microcomputer Support Specialist
160.162-030	Auditor, Data Processing
169.167-030	Manager, Data Processing
169.167-082	Manager, Computer Operations
203.582-054	Data Entry Clerk
206.367-018	Tape Librarian
213.132-010	Supervisor, Computer Operations
213.362-010	Computer Operator
213.382-010	Computer Peripheral Equipment Operator
221.362-030	Computer Processing Scheduler
823.261-030	Data Communications Technician

Figure 2.2   Computer-related job titles in the federal government.

answering telephone calls. Although answering calls and dealing with questions and concerns of callers might be that programmer's responsibility, the behavior should not be included in the general "programmer" job description.

A second problem with the critical incident technique is that it gives managers little or no information about the distribution of skills within the company's work force. While a job description of this type shows how employees in a particular category behave, it does not show whether they are behaving correctly, how many are

Analyzes business procedures and problems to refine data and convert it to programmable form for electronic data processing; confers with personnel in organizational units involved to ascertain specific output requirements, such as types of breakouts, degree of data summarization, and format for management reports; studies existing data handling systems to evaluate effectiveness and develops new systems to improve production or work flow as required; specifies in detail logic and/or mathematical operations to be performed by various equipment units and/or comprehensive computer programs and operations to be performed by personnel in system. A programmer analyst also conducts special studies and investigations pertaining to development of new information systems to meet current and projected needs; plans and prepares technical reports, memoranda, and instructional manuals relative to the establishment and functioning of complete operational systems; may prepare programs for computer use.

Figure 2.3   1977 Federal government job description for Programmer Analyst.

030.162-014 PROGRAMMER-ANALYST (profess. & kin.).
Alternate title: Applications Analyst-Programmer.

Plans, develops, tests, and documents computer programs, applying knowledge of programming techniques and computer systems. Evaluates user request for new or modified program, such as for financial or human resource management systems, clinical research trial results, statistical study of traffic patterns, or analyzing and developing specifications for bridge design, to determine feasibility, cost and time required, compatibility with current system, and computer capabilities. Consults with user to identify current operation procedures and clarify program objectives. Reads manuals, periodicals, and technical reports to learn ways to develop programs that meet user requirements. Formulates plan outlining steps required to develop program, using structured analysis and design. Submits plans to user for approval. Prepares flow charts and diagrams to illustrate sequence of steps program must follow and to describe logical operations involved. Designs computer terminal screen displays to accomplish goals of user request. Converts project specifications, using flow charts and diagrams, into sequence of detailed instructions and logical steps for coding into language processable by computer, applying knowledge of computer programming techniques and computer languages. Enters program code into computer system. Enters commands into computer to run and test program. Reads computer printouts or observes display screen to detect syntax or logic errors during program test, or uses diagnostic software to detect errors. Replaces, deletes, or modifies codes to correct errors. Analyzes, reviews, and alters program to increase operating efficiency or adapt to new requirements. Writes documentation to describe program development, logic, coding, and corrections. Writes manual for users to describe installation and operation procedures. Assists users to solve operating problems. Recreates steps taken by user to locate source of problem and rewrites program to correct errors. May use computer-aided software tools, such as flow chart design and code generation, in each stage of system development. May train users to use program. May oversee installation of hardware and software. May provide technical assistance to program users. May install and test program at user site. May monitor performance of program after implementation. May specialize in developing programs for business or technical applications.

Figure 2.4   1991 Federal government job description for Programmer Analyst.

behaving in that manner, or which employees with what skills can be transferred, trained, or promoted.

To avoid these problems, the job analysis team must be objective and fair in its observations. In addition, the team must record and track job information using tools that permit a detailed analysis of the data.

2. *Functional job analysis.* Using this technique, a professional *task analyst* gathers information about what *tasks* people perform, what *data* is needed, and what *things* are used. Included are any requirements for task instructions, reasoning skills, mathematics, or language. This information is collected from managers and their employees. The task analyst prepares a preliminary draft of job standards. This is then reviewed by a *subject matter expert*—someone with an in-depth knowledge of the tasks, data, and things observed. The subject matter expert and the task analyst together refine the task descriptions. When completed, they submit the descriptions to a task force of subject matter experts, who produce the final documents. These will be job descriptions, each consisting of the tasks performed by that job, the requirements for successful task completion, the required minimal employee skill sets, and the standard way each task is to be accomplished.

Although this method is excellent for developing objective performance appraisal documents and appraisals, it is seldom perceived as such. Employees and managers are rarely willing to accept a procedure developed by outside experts based solely on task observation. A common complaint is the inability of this method to correctly value people-oriented behaviors such as oral communication skills, leadership skills, and charisma.

Another difficulty is that this technique usually generates a large number of task elements for each job, sometimes as many as 100. Appraising an employee on 100 different task elements is quite a lot of work. In many cases, the task force responsible for developing the final document eliminates many of the task elements. Though this makes appraisal forms manageable, it dilutes the applicability of the job descriptions.

One final issue raised by this system is that it ignores the problem of actually measuring the extent to which each job standard is attained. The best one can do is to note whether or not an employee has performed a task. How well it was performed and whether that employee should have performed the task are not addressed.

3. *Job elements.* This method is relatively common, and is used for jobs that are considered simple or easy to analyze. Here, the personnel department or outside consultants gather information from subject matter experts. They then analyze the knowledge, skills,

abilities, and other personal characteristics required for each job. From this they develop job descriptions, performance appraisal forms, and procedures.

This technique is usually used for unskilled jobs or those where workers perform a limited number of relatively simple tasks. Some examples of such jobs might include assembly-line worker, chauffeur, receptionist, and usher. Another time this technique is useful is when a job does not yet exist. For example, a company installing a database management system might need a job description for *database analyst*.

While common, this method is useful only for relatively simple jobs (or newly existing ones). It does, however, provide management with a practical procedure for screening job applicants, for personnel planning, and for informing employees about job responsibilities. Regretfully, it tends to alienate employees. They feel left out of the job analysis process and believe that they have been "pigeonholed."

4. *Position analysis.* This method is an improvement on the previous one. In this case, trained *job analysts* interview present employees and managers, collecting specific job behaviors. Like the job element method, this requires skilled professionals—but, in this case, employees and managers are included in the analysis process. The job analysts act as more than simple data gatherers as they collect behavior. These behaviors are verified with employees and management before being included in any final documents.

5. *Task analysis.* Using this technique, a task force of employees, managers, and experts from the personnel department identify general *job functions* and specific *roles* (leader, scribe, doer) within those functions, and *tasks* performed. Current employees are then interviewed to determine how important these functions, roles, and tasks are for their particular jobs. The task force rounds out these items by including any additional job requirements.

Once a list of functions, roles, and tasks is complete, the task force gives the documentation to managers. The managers are now responsible for reviewing each task and providing examples of both good and bad behaviors for each one. These examples are then ranked by the managers, and form the basis for judging whether an employee correctly completes a task. This method is an excellent one for developing performance appraisal forms and procedures, and is also good for informing employees of job responsibilities.

Job analysis problems. As described above, no one technique for job analysis is without its problems. Some overall problems that are common to most of these methods are the following.

The standardization myth.   Many companies say that their attempt to do job analysis results in job descriptions that are "standard" for their organization. What they sometimes forget is that the tasks comprising jobs with similar titles (e.g., programmer) actually involve separate job functions, or even totally different jobs altogether. The job title "programmer," for example, may involve entirely different tasks for programmers working in a mainframe environment coding in COBOL, compared with programmers developing systems for microcomputers coding in C.

The problem here is that job analysis does not differentiate across similar job titles. The "standard programmer" job title may lead to a standard performance appraisal package that is inequitable across all types of programmers. The net result is that such standardization treats each position as interchangeable with others having the same job title.

Suppression of individuality.   This problem is related to the previous one. Most job analysis ignores any characteristics that are unique to individual positions. These positions may be distributed across different hardware platforms (IBM, DEC, Unisys), across different business divisions (payroll, personnel, manufacturing, retail sales), and across functional lines (management, sales, administration). In each set of environments the job being analyzed may have taken on attributes unique to positions in that environment.

In this case, the problem can be avoided by assigning similar jobs different temporary titles (Programmer A, Programmer B) during job analysis. Jobs with similar behaviors can be combined later if the situation warrants it.

No allowance for abnormal demands.   Performance appraisal systems based upon formal job analysis tend to be all-encompassing—they assume that all of those positions across the company are doing similar work under similar conditions. This ignores cases where some divisions, projects, or employees are working under abnormally high demands. Examples of such demands include working overtime to meet tight schedules or deadlines, working in a group using new or complicated computer-assisted software engineering (CASE) tools or database management systems, and working under high-security conditions.

Since job descriptions (and the resulting performance appraisal system) regard all jobs with the same title as equal, those employees finding themselves in such circumstances are unfairly penalized, as they are expected to perform up to the same standards as other employees having an easier time. Similarly, employees that are not under the gun are unfairly rewarded and are able to meet objectives and complete tasks with relative ease.

Unable to compare similar jobs.   The other side of the coin is the problem of *not* standardizing. Many performance appraisal programs use *ranking* techniques to compare employees. If the job descriptions don't standardize what the employees do, then how can one compare similar jobs, or people in similar positions? Regrettably, some form of standardization may be required.

Dimension weighting.   A topic not addressed by many performance appraisal systems is the *weighting* of job dimensions. For example, entry-level programmers should be rated more heavily on their technical knowledge and skills, as they will need these for career advancement. Alternatively, expert programmers should be rated more heavily on their written and oral communication skills, as it is these skills they will be using when developing user requirements, writing program specifications, and compiling system documentation.

Few job analysis methods make a point of analyzing the importance of various job tasks and behaviors so that such weightings can be derived. This is usually left to the discretion of the manager in charge of the employee's appraisal. Regrettably, managers sometimes wait until the annual review meeting to inform the employee of the weightings they have chosen. In cases like this employees feel cheated—if they had known how their job behaviors would be weighted, maybe they would have performed differently for the last year!

The 1980s

It is interesting to compare the data processing job descriptions in the 1980s with those 10 years later. Hardware and software advances have changed the ways we look at these jobs: there are more programming languages, more hardware platforms, many new and different development environments, and a plethora of new job opportunities. These transformations have modified the way that information systems are designed, built, tested, and installed. Surely they have affected the way that DP people are managed and appraised.

Manager of Data Processing.   Reports to the VP for Administration. Manages the Supervisor of Systems Analysis, Supervisor of Programming, Supervisor of Machine Operations, Supervisor of Production Control.

Responsibilities include management specifics of DP activities. Technical duties include review and evaluation of computer systems, requests for additional services, new equipment or vendor's proposals, equipment and personnel utilization, education, and training.

Administrative duties include budgeting, personnel recruitment, evaluation, policy matters, departmental coordination, and planning.

Desirable qualifications should include a business-oriented degree, specialized training in the currently installed hardware system, if possible, and five to ten years of directly related experience.

Supervisor of Systems Analysis. Reports to the Manager of DP. Supervises two or more senior systems analysts. Responsibilities include providing technical and analytical assistance in the identification and solution of data systems problems; defining information requirements and prescribing procedures; organizing studies on system matters, including resource costs of time, personnel, and money; and evaluating the advantages of and alternative efforts to management.

Desirable qualifications should include a business-oriented degree, specialized training in systems and pertinent hardware capabilities, and four to seven years of direct experience.

Senior Systems Analyst. Reports to Supervisor of Systems Analysis. Supervises one or more Systems Analysts. Responsibilities include providing technical and analytical assistance in analysis and design of data processing systems; assistance in defining information repositories and dataflows; help in conducting studies on systems matters, including resource costs of time, personnel, and money; developing and presenting alternatives to management.

Desirable qualifications should include a business-oriented degree, specialized training in systems and pertinent hardware capabilities, and two to five years of direct experience.

Supervisor of Programming. Reports to the Manager of DP. Supervises two or more senior programmers. Responsibilities include providing technical and administrative assistance in the development of new programs and the maintenance of operational programs. Also schedules revisions to operational programs.

The candidate for this position must be knowledgeable in the details of the databases, programs, and products of all systems. Qualifications may specify a business degree as desirable (but not mandatory), specialized training in appropriate hardware systems and programming languages, and four to six years direct programming experiences.

Supervisor of Machine Operations. Reports to the Manager of DP. Supervises shift leaders, tape librarians, data entry and support equipment supervisors, software support activities (in some instances), database administration (in some instances), computer performance monitors, and distribution personnel. Responsibilities include supervision of the I/O control function; ensuring effective utilization of EDP equipment and personnel in accordance with schedules, operation run books, standards manuals, and equipment operation manuals; maintaining logs of operation, equipment utilization, downtime and maintenance, tape library controls, and input/output.

The candidate must be acquainted with file structures, procedures, and products of major applications systems. Qualifications should include some college courses, as desirable, and specialized training in the current hardware system, as well as four to seven years of directly related experience.

The 1990s

In these new job descriptions we see the effects of the new information systems environments mentioned previously.

Manager of Data Processing. In more and more progressive companies the Manager of Data Processing reports to a new position: the Chief Information Officer (CIO), who reports directly to the President of the company.

Many organizations have moved away from a totally centralized DP shop approach toward a more division-centered or user-centered one. This typically includes companies whose user communities are geographically spread out, as well as multinational corporations. This decentralization allows each division or department to develop specific expertise in developing systems, and relieves upper management of the burden of maintaining a single, massive DP organization.

As the users become decentralized, so does the DP organization and its supporting hardware. This sometimes leads to separate, distinct DP organizations, each servicing one particular user or set of users. Each organization may then consist of a manager, supporting supervisors, and other DP personnel.

Further, as we march into the networking and distributed processing world, the Manager of DP will probably manage the Supervisor of Network Control and the Supervisor of Distributed Data Base Services. These positions are somewhat self-explanatory; however, please note that both must be concerned with intercommunication among multiple hardware platforms, multiple DBMSs, and perhaps transborder dataflow.

In addition to the above, the Manager of DP will review and evaluate requests for outside services. This includes contract programming, consulting, outsourcing, and system integration. Also, as DP organizations have grown, it has become apparent that there is a need for ongoing training, both technical and business-related. These needs are sometimes handled by an internal training organization headed by a Manager of Technical Training. Occasionally this will include a provision for the acquisition of training from outside vendors.

Although the typical manager's duties have not changed much, the new DP Manager must take into account the personalities and egos of computer people. Much has been written on this subject recently, and managers are becoming increasingly aware of some of these new management techniques.

Managers are becoming less dependent upon specific hardware platforms and their attendant software and DBMSs. There will be many different hardware platforms in the DP shop of the future (mainframe, minicomputer, and micro). To combat the dependence upon a specific machine, IBM has proposed a set of standards, interfaces, and protocols called Systems Application Architecture (SAA). As we move through the 1990s, the DP Manager will need less specialized knowledge about hardware.

To counterbalance this, the DP Manager must have a broader business background. Initially, data processing systems supported only a very narrow spectrum of applications: at first, accounting; later, personnel and payroll. Today, DP applications span the gamut of business systems from the traditional (general ledger, payables, receivables, materials management, payroll) to the modern (point-of-sale, electronic data interchange, airline reservations, industrial process control, CAD/CAM) to the futuristic (multimedia imaging systems, Strategic Defense Initiative [SDI] battle management, voice-actuated data input). Such areas of business that a company enters will require the DP Manager to acquire a background of knowledge and expertise in order to better manage personnel and resources.

Supervisor of Systems Analysis.   As hinted previously, this Supervisor may not exist as a single individual; rather, systems analysis, design, and development will be bundled into a single group of people that is together responsible to a particular user community. Using matrix management techniques, this group may then be responsible to several supervisors. Figure 2.5 shows one kind of DP matrix organization in which programmers, analysts, and other IS employees report both to line managers and to project managers.

The job of Senior Systems Analyst (described below) has changed radically in the last decade. As analysts have taken a larger role in multisystem applications, networks, distributed database, and micro-mainframe usage, they may now report to several managers. Using matrix management techniques, supervisors of systems analysis now cross-report to each other and direct the work of many subgroups.

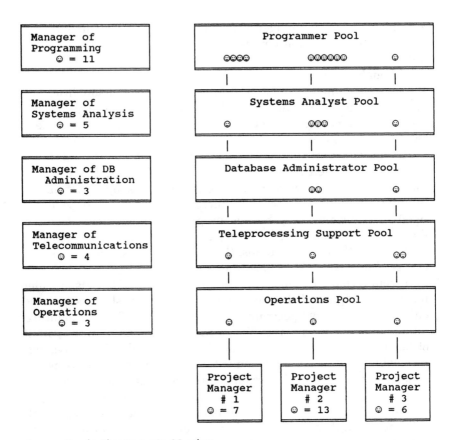

where ☺ indicates staff size.

Figure 2.5   A data processing matrix organization.

With the explosion of new data processing hardware and software of the past decade, the Supervisor of Systems Analysts now rarely provides specific technical assistance unless it is within his or her own area(s) of expertise. More and more this supervisor is responsible for budget analysis, analysis of vendor proposals, and management of external resources such as outsourced vendor personnel and system integration staff.

Again, this supervisor needs less specialized hardware or software training, and more knowledge and experience in managing people. In addition, a business-oriented degree helps when attempting to integrate a wide set of diverse applications into the specific company's environment.

Senior Systems Analyst.   As described above, new areas of expertise are forcing senior systems analysts to specialize in particular hardware platforms, application areas, and even specific software packages. This, and the concept of *matrix management,* dictates that analysts may report to several superiors. For example, a senior systems analyst with expertise in DASD capacity planning and financial systems may support data center operations and financial application development, thus encouraging reporting to both the Manager of Operations and a Supervisor of Systems Analysis for financial systems.

Little has changed in this area in the past decade. Many data processing development projects are managed with a standard hierarchy of line management and technical support. In a few cases, though, the concept of Joint Application Development (JAD) leads to a single Systems Analyst supervising a team of analysts, designers, database analysts, users, and managers. This relatively new methodology has received some attention in the trade press.

These responsibilities have been expanded to include attention to matters typically left to management, such as performance appraisal, proposal preparation and presentation, and evaluation of hardware and software tools.

The business-oriented degree is becoming more important, as companies acquire other companies and expand internationally. This forces middle management to become more aware of what the business is about, both in terms of integrating diverse applications and consolidating disparate or dissimilar business data models.

Supervisor of Programming.   This was the standard in many organizations where the data processing department was organized traditionally. In a more modern, decentralized organization, there may not be a single Manager of DP. Further, programmers and senior programmers may work for several teams on several projects simultaneously. Programmers will then typically report to one or more Project Leaders, who will manage their work.

The title "senior programmer" is an old one. In the modern data processing shop, programming itself has taken on a wide variety of meanings, covering a broad base of knowledge, skills, expertise, and experience. A supervisor of programmers has almost become a contradiction in terms.

These responsibilities have been shifted to several kinds of technical specialists, including network analysts, database analysts, system administrators, and quality assurance staff.

As this position has diffused into those of several other staff members, these qualifications are no longer relevant.

Supervisor of Machine Operations.   In traditional organizations this reporting structure is sound. In more modern DP shops (especially those that have decentralized or distributed DP operations) each hardware complex may require separate management. These supervisors may report both to a divisional data processing manager and to a central point (probably a Chief Information Officer).

This still holds true, with the addition of new hardware (such as magnetic tape cartridges, CD-ROM storage, terminal networks, and satellite communication networks) and new software (such as distributed database management systems, I/O subsystems, and third-party application packages).

This position's responsibilities also include management and evaluation of hardware alternatives, parallel-testing various hardware and software configurations, and monitoring network activity.

College courses are becoming less important for operations staff as the number and complexity of hardware platforms and software packages increase. Far more important is specialized training.

What jobs will be in demand?   According to Robert Half International Inc., the jobs least in demand in the 1990s will be:

- Mainframe system software programmers
- Batch programmers
- Nontechnical administrative managers
- Mainframe programmers
- PC generalists

Among the most sought-after will be:

- Network administrators
- PC support technicians that specialize in a particular area like hardware, databases, or e-mail
- Client/server development specialists
- IBM midrange programmers
- Information engineers

Recommendations for DP Job Analysis

Each of the following categories was mentioned as a possible problem or trouble spot that might arise during job analysis. In each category we have included a brief recapitulation of the problem and our recommendations.

The standardization myth

The problem. Many companies do a job analysis that results in job descriptions that are "standard" for their entire organization. The problem here is that their job analysis may not have differentiated across similar job titles. The "standard programmer" job title may lead to a standard performance appraisal package that is inequitable for some types of programmers. The net result is that such standardization treats each position as interchangeable with others having the same job title.

The solution. To help prevent this problem, the job analysis team should include representatives from each of the proposed job categories. These representatives are then made responsible for differentiating between similar jobs. For example, many IS departments are now experimenting with a *microcomputer development environment.* Here, programmers use microcomputers to create and test programs that will eventually be executed on mainframe computers. In this environment, programmers may use software tools and techniques that are completely foreign to their mainframe counterparts, even though both may have the job title "programmer." In this case, it would be the responsibility of the programming representative of the job analysis team to ensure that each variety of programmer be assigned a unique job description.

Suppression of individuality

The problem. Most job analyses ignore any characteristics that are unique to individual positions or people. A company with many one-of-a-kind positions may find itself doing a complete job analysis for every employee in the company. This will be a time-consuming, laborious process. Further, when the analysis is complete, any changes that have occurred in the specific job descriptions will need to be incorporated on a regular basis.

The solution. An analysis that indicates many one-of-a-kind jobs is probably examining jobs and job responsibilities to an excessive level of detail. While such thoroughness is laudable, the result may be worthless. In this case, the problem can be avoided by first assigning similar jobs different temporary titles (Programmer A, Programmer B, and so forth) during job analysis. At the end, each set of similar job titles should be analyzed as a group for common characteristics (codes programs, creates test data, and the like). It will be these common characteristics that are placed in the final job description.

One caution is in order: Job analysts should be wary of falling into the standardization myth described above. Similar jobs may still require separate job descriptions in order to analyze their performance fairly. One common method of deciding whether two similar jobs are, in fact, the same is to ask those who hold them for feedback.

No allowance for abnormal demands

The problem. Performance appraisal systems developed from a formal job analysis tend to end up trying to be all things to all people by assuming that all of those positions across the company are doing similar work under similar conditions. This ignores cases where some divisions, projects, or employees are working under abnormally high demands. Since job descriptions (and the resulting performance appraisal system) regard all jobs with the same title as equal, those employees finding themselves in such circumstances are unfairly penalized, as they are expected to perform up to the same standards as other employees having an easier time.

The solution. The simplest approach to the solution of this problem is for the job analyst to recognize the difference between *duties, behaviors,* and *tasks performed* in the context of specific jobs. After lists of job tasks are accumulated, the team must analyze the data to determine which behaviors were appropriate. At this point, the analysts should solicit feedback from job holders and their managers as to their superiors' expectations, the level of effort required on the current project, and the "normal" requirements of the job. This information must then be carefully examined. Analysts must avoid grouping dissimilar jobs under the same job description (e.g., programmer and senior programmer), and must also avoid differentiating between the same job performed by two employees with different expertise.

Dimension weighting

The problem. A topic not covered by many performance appraisal systems is the *weighting* of job dimensions. For example, entry-level programmers may be rated more heavily on their technical knowledge and skills, as they will need these for career advancement. Few job analysis methods make a point of analyzing the importance of various job tasks and behaviors so that such weightings can be derived. This is usually left to the discretion of the manager in charge of the employee's appraisal. Regrettably, managers sometimes wait until the annual review meeting to inform the employee of the weightings they have chosen.

The solution. This problem can be the cause for low morale and even employee unrest and rebellion. The fairest solution is to require that each job (say, programmer) be defined in terms of *levels*. Each level is then assigned a set of weightings for that job's task and behaviors. The entire set of levels and weightings is then included in any published performance appraisal forms. The supervisor and subordinate then meet at the beginning of the review period to discuss the level at which the employee is functioning and will be evaluated on for that period.

If such weightings are not produced as a part of job analysis, an alternative solution would be to require managers that will be doing their own weightings to discuss them with employees at the beginning of the review period. This communication and agreement at the beginning of the review period is vital, as it defines the manager's (and the company's) expectations, and will set the stage for the employee's appraisal.

Measuring Productivity

How do we measure data processing productivity? Since most data processing activities seem to center on programs, it is only natural that management has concentrated on trying to measure programmer productivity. In this section we review some of the more common programmer productivity measures, along with the problems associated with them.

Results-oriented approaches

Lines of code. With this method we measure the number of lines of source code produced by the programmer. This method has suffered over the years by the failure of DP departments to define exactly what is meant by "lines of code." Some of the possible interpretations are:

- Number of language verbs in source code
- Number of source program records (i.e., "lines in the listing")
- Number of source program statements (counting a statement that spans multiple lines as one program statement)
- Number of *debugged* source statements
- Number of source statements excluding *data definitions*
- Number of source statements *excluding* comments
- Number of source statements *including* comments

There are several other problems associated with this metric. One is the inherent boost given high-level languages. For example, 10 lines of

COBOL source code can be the equivalent of hundreds of lines of assembler code. Another problem is that the programming activity commonly includes other work not measured here, such as producing documentation, attending meetings, assisting with specifications, and so forth.

Function points. Briefly, a program can be measured by counting program inputs, outputs, files, interfaces, and transactions processed, and then weighting each of these for complexity. The result is then adjusted based on system characteristics (on-line versus batch, critical versus noncritical, and so forth). The derived total score is the number of function points contained in the program. More on function point analysis appears in App. C.

Cost per defect. This metric is usually measured by comparing the number and quality of defects in software with the cost required to fix the defects. This measure penalizes high-quality programs, in that there are always some fixed costs associated with programs, such as defect removal activities. As these fixed costs become a large percentage of the total cost of a program, the cost per defect goes up, even though there are relatively few defects.

The goal-oriented approach

This approach to productivity measures concentrates on the goals or standards set at the beginning of the process. Most programming projects, for example, are tracked using some kind of *project management system*. With these systems, project personnel such as analysts, designers, managers, project leaders, programmers, and technical writers are given *tasks*. Each task is assigned a *start date,* a *duration* (usually in hours), and a *deadline* (for an example document, see Fig. 2.6). The project management software collects all these tasks and, using additional input regarding the order in which tasks must be completed,

Task Assignment Worksheet

Task ID	Subtask ID	Description	Start Date	Duration	Deadline	Hours Worked this Period
2000	001	Code Program	03/01/92	32.0	03/29/92	.
2000	002	Test Program	03/01/92	8.0	03/29/92	.
2000	004	Create Test Data	03/01/92	4.0	03/05/92	.
6999	001	Report Status	03/01/92	1.0	03/01/92	.

Figure 2.6   Programmer task assignments.

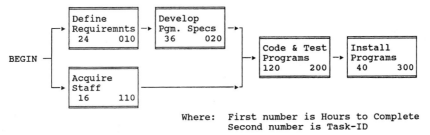

Where: First number is Hours to Complete
        Second number is Task-ID

Figure 2.7 A project network.

places the tasks into a *network* (see Fig. 2.7). This resultant network can then be analyzed to determine how long the project will take, how many staff members having each job description will be required, and sometimes even how much the project will cost.

With this kind of system, employees work on and complete *tasks.* As an employee completes a task, he or she enters that information into the project management system. The overall result is that employees are judged based upon the number and type of tasks that they complete. Goals set at the beginning of the review period are based on the number of tasks to be completed per unit of time (a week, a month). This simplifies performance appraisal for purposes of compensation and personnel planning, but drastically limits its use for training, career development, and performance improvement. In particular, knowing that an employee is not completing enough tasks on time provides little information about *what* the employee should be doing about it.

Process-oriented approaches

These techniques concentrate on the *way* that employees perform tasks, not on the tasks themselves. The theory is that managers can manage only employee behaviors, as it is these behaviors that they observe.

Development methodologies. In the past 20 years many well-known authors have concocted their own methodologies for designing, coding, testing, and implementing systems. These methodologies usually include some types of diagramming methods for portraying data and processing relationships, and some standards for proceeding. The diagrams took on the names of the authors of the methodologies in most cases (Yourdon charts, Warnier-Orr diagrams, Nassi-Schneiderman charts, Jackson diagrams, and so on), while the methodologies took on more generic names (Structured Programming and Design, Data Flow Design, Entity-Relationship Design, and so forth). See Fig. 2.8 for a list of some of these methodologies and diagramming standards.

Time Period	Methodologies	Diagramming Techniques
Early 1970s	Structured Coding Conventions Top-Down Programming Information Hiding (Parnas) Levels of Abstraction (Dijkstra) Stepwise Refinement (Wirth)	Flowcharts HIPO Diagrams
Mid 1970s	Structured Design (Yourdon-Constantine) Jackson Design Methodology Warnier-Orr Design Methodology	Jackson Diagrams Nassi-Schneiderman Diagrams Structure Charts Warnier-Orr Diagrams
Late 1970s	DeMarco Structured Analysis Gane and Sarson Structured Analysis SADT Requirements Design Language	Data Flow Diagrams Data Navigation Diagrams Dependency Diagrams Entity-Relationship Diagrams Pseudocode State Transition Diagrams Structured English
Early 1980s	HOS Axiomatic Verification Automated Data Modeling Intelligent Data Models Nonprocedural Languages Action Diagrams	Action Diagrams Higher-order Software (HOS) Diagrams CASE Tools with Graphic User Interfaces (GUIs)

Figure 2.8 Structured programming methodologies and diagramming standards.

Many companies then took these methodologies and inserted them into their own in-house procedures, resulting in a "customized" means of designing systems. Data processing departments then took these new procedures and incorporated them into their performance review process. Managers measured performance based upon the employee's conformance to the methodology.

While this technique of measuring productivity does give employees and managers an idea of how well everyone is complying with policies and procedures, it fails when the procedures are themselves inadequate. Many design and programming methodologies base themselves on business data that is structured hierarchically. This is adequate for many business problems, but not all. Business data that was not structured this way caused *network structures* and *relational databases* to come into being. In these cases, some of the old methodologies may prove to be detrimental to an enterprise.

One answer to this problem is to adopt a new methodology, one that is more in keeping with business data structures and current hardware, software, and database technology. There are several such methodologies available. Another alternative is to bring in CASE tools. These tools assist information systems staff in automating the systems design process.

Quality Assurance (Q/A). Another current trend in software design is the establishment of a software quality assurance program. Such programs usually aim to provide a higher-quality finished software product. There are several ways to accomplish this. One way is to institute procedures that severely test programs before they are installed. The emphasis here is on creating the necessary and sufficient test data, performing proper tests, integrating program tests into systems tests, and so on. Test data creation seems to be an art form—several books exist for this topic alone. Most books recommend one of two methods. The first is to do a complete analysis of the required output of a program. This will determine the number of different conditions and output results that are possible. These conditions then determine the test data. The second method is to analyze the program code, and then create test data that ensures that every program statement is executed at least once, and that every logic path of the program is tested for all possible conditions.

Another way to begin a Q/A program is to analyze current problems and address them one at a time. For example, suppose that a set of programs had a tendency to abnormally terminate due to invalid data. Management could then institute Q/A procedures that required every program to validate input data before processing it. Another example might involve measurements indicating that some applications are running more slowly then expected. After analysis of the problem, management may institute Q/A procedures that ensure that every database design be approved by a database task force for efficiency and conformance to the business data model. In addition, all programs assessing the databases must have their program logic reviewed and approved by a database analyst before installation.

There exist several quality metrics. Some of these are:

- *Number of failures.* This is usually defined as a deviation from the program specifications, regardless of the intent of the specs. It is usually shown as the number of failures per line of code, or number of failures during a certain time period.

- *Technical quality.* This is a consolidation of subjective and objective measures relating to the stability, amount of maintenance required, "structuredness" of design, and performance or efficiency of the program.

- *User-perceived quality.* This is another composite score, including user satisfaction, reliability, accuracy, processing speed, turnaround time, and meeting service-level agreements.

The watershed work on these types of metrics is *Programming Productivity* by Capers Jones (McGraw-Hill, 1986). In his book, Jones notes that measuring lines of code is "not mathematically consistent and there is zero correlation between the lines of code and productivity." He considers using lines of code a harmful mistake, ". . . [like] treating an illness with bleeding or operating without washing." He also recommends using function points as the primary programmer productivity measure.

Summary

Although there is currently no one measurement of programmer productivity agreed upon by data processing practitioners, the function point seems to have acquired a following in academic circles and in some companies as well. At the time of this writing (winter, 1993) there are over 25 software tools that measure productivity in the CASE environment. Such measures use the inputs to and outputs from the CASE tools as a basis for developing estimates of function points and other metrics. Companies that have made a commitment to developing applications in the CASE environment will have a tremendous advantage in developing productivity measures using these tools.

Professionalism

The term *professionalism* is usually used to denote a set of practitioners that perform tasks according to certain self-imposed standards, based upon a body of knowledge. This operative definition of a *profession* requires at least two things:

A common body of knowledge.   Computers as we know them today came into existence in the late 1940s. Data processing (using computers) didn't really exist in a commercial sense until the mid-1950s. Data processing, therefore, is a fairly new profession. Considering the latest hardware and software advances, any collection of a standardized DP body of knowledge would be out-of-date within months. At best, one can say that data processing knowledge is an ever-expanding moving target.

Some associations have attempted to codify a *data processing curriculum* at the university level. These efforts are aimed in the right direction, as many college and university graduates enter the job market in data processing positions. Regrettably, such curricula have not kept pace with recent hardware and software innovations.

A set of standards.   Standards include a Code of Ethics and a Code of Conduct, along with professional associations that will enforce them. Although several organizations have proposed and published such standards, there is no industrywide acceptance of any of them.

It is not yet clear whether data processing will eventually fit this description. Still, assuming that this will eventually come to pass, some groups are beginning to look forward to the next steps: certification and licensing.

Certification and licensing

There are more than 100 competency designations available in various fields of business, each awarded by a professional association to recognize individuals who have met certain requirements.

This is according to Mona Milbrath, author of *Credentials: A Guide to Business Designations* (Blue River Publishing Co., 1980).

Certification provides recognition of achievement. Success on a certification examination allows you to measure your competency against a standard; however, certification is not a legal requirement for the professional. Many certification examinations have a feedback feature, which allows evaluation of one's strengths and weaknesses. Analysis of areas requiring improvement provides information to you regarding possible programs for improvement.

Passing a certification exam demonstrates your expertise and provides recognition of your knowledge. It is also a positive achievement to show to a potential employer.

Licensing is a legal matter. Many states require that people practicing certain professions must be licensed. Such licenses are sometimes controlled by the state, sometimes by professional organizations.

Certification programs in data processing

The Institute for Certification of Computer Professionals. The Institute for Certification of Computer Professionals (ICCP) was formed in 1973 by several societies of professionals in data processing. This organization was a not-for-profit corporation established for the primary purpose of developing a computing profession. It began by acquiring the Registered Business Programmer examination from the Data Processing Management Association (DPMA), and converting it into a new exam, the Certified Data Processor (CDP) exam. This exam was one of the first attempts to measure the knowledge and skills of the data processing profession. To date, over 50,000 people have passed the exam.

Available certification programs. There are four certification programs available from the ICCP at the time of this writing. One is an entry-level program. The other three examinations are professional examinations to be taken by people working in the field.

An entry-level examination, the Associate Computer Professional (ACP) exam is designed to measure the competencies of people aspiring to enter the computer profession or who have worked in the field a short time. Generally, people just graduating from college will take this program.

The Certified Computer Programmer (CCP) examination is designed for the senior-level programmer or analyst who has been working in the computer field for several years. Candidates who lack extensive experience will find the exam difficult.

The Certified Data Processor (CDP) examination is aimed at managers of information processing areas. Candidates must have 60 months of full-time experience in computer information systems.

The Certified Systems Professional (CSP) examination is directed at senior-level personnel in systems analysis and design. It also has a 60-month full-time experience requirement.

The three professional examinations (CCP, CDP, and CSP) each require that the successful candidate recertify his or her professional skills every three years effective the first of January following the examination data. The recertification process may be accomplished through retesting or through involvement in approved continuing education.

A self-assessment feature of the examinations provides feedback to the candidate regarding the candidate's strengths and weaknesses on the examination. The purpose of this is to provide the candidate with insight regarding the self-improvement programs to be pursued.

Current certification programs

The Institute for Certification of Computer Professionals (ICCP) has made major changes in certification examination format and contents, beginning with the January 1993 exams. These changes represent a substantial departure from the previous exams. Potential candidates should understand these differences so they will be able to decide which certification program is most appropriate for them.

The Certified Computer Programmer (CCP), Certified Data Processor (CDP), and Certified Systems Professional (CSP) designations are still separate certifications programs, each with different objectives. Beginning in 1994, however, the examination requirements for the designations will be combined into a single program. Instead of separate exams for each of the designations, the ICCP has merged all three exams into a single, multipart exam and will award a single designation, Certified Computer Professional (CCP). This new exam consists of a Core examination and nine Specialty examinations of 110 questions. A passing score is 70% for each examination.

To satisfy the examination requirements for the CCP designation, a candidate must pass all of the following:

- The Core examination
- A required Specialty exam
- Any other Specialty exam

The list of Specialty examinations available in 1993 was:

- Procedural Programming
- Management
- Systems Development
- Business Information Systems
- Communications
- Office Information Systems
- Information Resource Management
- Software Engineering
- Systems Programming
- Systems Security

Those who already hold a CCP, CDP, or CSP may convert their certification to the current designator by notifying the ICCP.

Note that the experience and professional qualifications for the three designations are now identical. A candidate must have at least 48 months of full-time (or part-time equivalent) direct experience in computer-based information systems. The 48 months need not be consecutive or in a single position. Candidates having less than 48 months' work experience may substitute postsecondary academic work for up to 24 months of experience. Interested candidates should contact the ICCP (address given later in this chapter).

Current certificate holders keep their designations, depending upon their recertification status. Candidates that have passed portions of the CCP, CDP, or CSP exams may still complete their examination requirements under the "old" exam formats as they are phased out.

There is a movement afoot to have future examinations processed in real time. That is, the candidate would make an appointment at almost any time during the year for a time slot at an electronic testing center. The questions would be presented by a microcomputer and the applicant would answer on-line. At the end of the testing session a final grade (pass/fail) would be given almost immediately, along with an analysis of right and wrong answers by topic area. The ICCP would be notified automatically by the software to mail a certificate, assuming the candidate passed the appropriate exam(s).

Recertification requirements. The requirements for recertifying certificates remain in effect. You must accumulate 120 contact hours in a three-year period to maintain the currency of your certificate. Taking and passing additional Specialty exams qualifies for contact hours as well. The price structure for the 1993 examination(s) is shown in Fig. 2.9.

An alternative program. Candidates who feel they do not have enough experience for the CCP, CDP, or CSP should consider the Associated Computer Professional (ACP) program. The ACP designation is awarded to any candidate who passes the ACP exam. This exam consists of a general section and seven specialty sections. Each specialty section covers a particular programming language. Available languages include Ada, BASIC, C, COBOL, FORTRAN, Pascal, and RPG. Only one specialty exam need be taken.

The ACP program is aimed at data processing professionals with only a year or two of experience. No recertification is required. In addition, several colleges and universities give academic credit to those who have passed the ACP exam.

The advantages of certification

Certification provides recognition of achievement. Only a small percentage of candidates pass the exams every year. Success on a certification examination allows you to measure your competency against a standard. The exams also have a feedback feature that allows evaluation of one's strengths and weaknesses. Analysis of areas requiring

---

CCP, CDP, CSP Fees

Testing Fee (required):	$ 45
Core Examination:	75
Specialty Exam #1:	75
Specialty Exam #2:	75
	$270

ACP Fees

Testing Fee (required):	$ 25
Core Examination:	75
Language Section:	30
	$130

Figure 2.9 ICCP 1993 examination costs.

improvement provides information to you regarding possible programs for improvement.

For more information

Institute for Certification of Computer Professionals
2200 East Devon Street
Suite 268
Des Plaines, Illinois 60018
(708) 299-4227

The future

What will certification mean for the future of the DP manager and their staff?

While licensing of data processing personnel may be far in the future, certification is seen as a necessary first step. Many other professionals are liable under the law for the work they perform, and are measured against standards of excellence and performance. Data processing is, or should be, no different.

Professional certification will provide DP personnel with recognition among their peers. It will allow them to measure themselves against a standard. And it will serve as an achievement to show a prospective employer. In addition, they will be taking the first step toward professionalism.

It is in the interests of all DP managers and supervisors to encourage and support these efforts, for the following reasons:

- The general level of data processing expertise among the staff will increase.

- Support for certification efforts indicates to everyone that the company supports a standard of ethics.

- Certification enhances the reputation of the staff in the eyes of the public and the user community.

Career Path Planning

In this section, we approach the notion of the *career* from the employee's point of view. In this way, we hope to give the manager a different perspective on how people view a company's attempts to provide career paths, training, education, job enrichment, job enlargement, promotional opportunities, and, of course, performance appraisal. In particular, we will concentrate on the employee with little or no experience. This section is general, in that it is not specific to data processing. (Such considerations will be covered in the next section.)

Supervisors should approach this section with performance evaluation in mind, remembering that new employees have few preconceptions about appraisals or career opportunities. Their first few months on the job may be extremely important in determining how they will perform in the future.

The curse of entering the workforce

We have bad news.

There is a new disease that is becoming more and more widespread in our society. Its principal victims are young students who are now graduating from our finest institutions. It strikes everywhere, and there is no known cure.

Yes, we are referring to "Entrylevelitis."

Common symptoms

The most common symptom of Entrylevelitis is a feeling of inadequacy. This feeling comes about when a job-hunting graduate looks through the "Help Wanted" section of the newspaper, only to find the words "Two Years of Experience Required."

Another symptom, which appears in the later stages of the disease, is sometimes called Beginner's Syndrome, named for the label others attach to you. It arises when an interviewer says, "Have you ever been employed full-time?" or "Your experience (or education) doesn't seem to fit any of our qualifications."

Another symptom is a lack of education. It becomes evident when you begin competing with four-year college graduates for jobs.

There is no known cure for Entrylevelitis; however, symptomatic relief is available. If you suffer from this common malady, the following should be of some help.

Skill building

The feelings of inadequacy generated by lack of relevant experience can be overwhelming. It is important to realize, however, that people who do have such experience are not very different from yourself. The skills they've gained during their years of experience are the following:

- Skills involving interacting with people
- A track record of success and increasing responsibility

- The ability to communicate
- A history of being able to solve problems

While some of these skills and abilities may come naturally with job experience, they also can be "acquired." This means that you can control the way interviewers (and others) perceive you.

People interaction skills involve your abilities to relate to others. Do you make friends easily? How about enemies? Can you handle praise, criticism, apathy, sympathy, rejection, or anger?

It is important to realize that the way you interact with your fellow human beings may have a greater impact on an interviewer's perception of you than your experience (or lack of it). One of an employer's greatest concerns is that employees cooperate with one another and work as a team. To do this, they must interact without friction. Can you fit into their environment?

Acquiring these skills is not difficult, but it may take some time. Begin today by deliberately interacting more with people. Your goal is simple: make friends. One way to do this is to participate in outside activities where you must deal with others. These might include co-op, teaching, work-study, assisting coaches, camp counseling, working as a research assistant, ushering, waiting on tables, and many other things. The list is almost endless. In all cases, try to be helpful, courteous, and friendly. Treat each person you meet as a potential "best friend." Smile. Learn to take any rudeness or unwarranted criticism in stride—no one is perfect.

The track record

Another aspect of having experience is one's track record; that is, what have you done, and how did you do it? When you start a project, do you finish it? Do you accept responsibility? Do you take on challenges, and try to do your best?

It isn't necessary to be employed to be successful. You don't have to have a full-time job to acquire a good track record. Perform your duties in a professional manner and take on any added responsibilities as a challenge. A history of accepting challenges, meeting deadlines, and reaching goals is quite an accomplishment, something interviewers (and employers) like to see.

Another aspect of experience is the ability to communicate. This skill may be the most important because almost every aspect of our daily lives involves communicating. Asking questions, giving answers, discussing alternatives, giving orders, taking orders, teaching, learning, speaking, listening—these activities all involve communicating.

The word *communication* implies a sender and a receiver. This leads to the sometimes surprising conclusion that about half of your time spent communicating will be as the receiver; that is, listening.

Some experts say the typical adult forgets more than half of what they have heard within the first few seconds of hearing it. Since about half of your time spent communicating will be as a listener, listening is at least as important as speaking.

The most important point to be made about listening is that it takes practice to do it well. Listen to a news broadcast. Can you repeat the gist of each story immediately after hearing it?

While listening to someone speak, do you spend most of your time preparing your reply? Do you sometimes speak just for the enjoyment of hearing your own voice? If you think your listening skills could be improved, perhaps it's time you did something about it.

The last major aspect of experience is solving problems. People with experience seldom have a week go by without dealing with (and solving) problems. These include social, technical, and personal problems. To deal with problems, they must either: (1) have solved a problem like it before, or (2) have acquired skills which enable them to approach problem solving with confidence. Either way, there comes a time in everyone's life when they must deal with a certain type of problem for the very first time. How do they do it?

René Descartes, the 17th-century French mathematician and philosopher, attempted to generalize problem solving. He defined several principles of what he called *analysis*. One of these principles could be called the *divide-and-conquer* approach. It involves dividing a complicated problem into several smaller problems, which are easier to understand and solve. Another way is to redefine the problem so it is similar to one you have solved before. The solution to the previous problem then becomes a model for the present one. Solving these smaller problems and assembling the solutions provides the answer to the original problem. Descartes' analysis formed the basis for what we now know as the *scientific method.*

Further, principles such as these are the basic tools we use to deal with our environment. Several good books on learning to solve problems exist. In addition, a regular reading schedule helps. Almost anything having to do with people will do, either fiction or nonfiction. Keep in mind the conflicts you read about and how people deal with their problems. Television is also a good way to see how people can deal with conflict.

Apart from the facts learned about the body of knowledge one studies, a bachelor's degree or other four-year degree tells a prospective employer something about its holder. College graduates have learned problem-solving skills, and have had to memorize facts. They must have had to manage their time effectively and organize their work. Finally, and perhaps most importantly, they have *learned to learn.*

While it is beyond the scope of this book to give you a college education, you can acquire the equivalent of one. Several books on memorization, time management, and getting organized exist, and adult education, community education, and college extension services will be of help. Visit the library and check out books on these subjects. Study them, and practice the principles you learn.

Learning to learn is not a skill that can be acquired in a short time. While help does exist in this area in the form of books and classes, it can be most difficult. We recommend a wide variety of reading in as many areas or disciplines as possible. Don't limit yourself to those areas in which you are interested; a wide variety of subjects will introduce you to new ways of thinking about things.

Feeling of inadequacy

This symptom appears in the later stages of Entrylevelitis, and is the most difficult to treat. Sufferers may feel hopelessly primitive and immature, and may spend hours bemoaning their fate, staring into space.

All is not lost, however. The feeling of immaturity is natural; in fact, many people who have been employed for years share this feeling. It's composed of four separate attitudes about one's life and one's work:

- Commitment
- Ethics
- Image
- Reputation

Commitment means that you are dedicated to getting a job done to the best of your abilities. You spend your work hours finishing tasks and meeting deadlines, not socializing. While you realize that your relationships with your coworkers are important, you feel that your top priority is the completion of your work to your supervisor's satisfaction.

An *ethical* attitude doesn't deal solely with coming in to work on time or with theft. It means that you believe in Pay for Performance. You believe in doing an honest day's work, and receiving fair compensation for it. You believe that excellent or superior performance should result in higher pay and greater responsibilities. Do you feel that society owes you a good job and a decent life? If so, perhaps you should reevaluate your ethics.

Your *image* depends to a large extent upon the way you dress. Much has been said and written about dressing for success. A well-known manager once said, "You never get a second chance at a first impression." Considering that we typically cover most of our bodies with clothing, we conclude that clothing and the way it is worn constitutes a large portion of that first impression.

Think about the images you convey of yourself with your clothing. How do others see you? Are you clean, neat, unkempt, disheveled, or slovenly? Do you seem to care about your appearance? People can't help but get an impression about you from your appearance.

Reputation. Are you honest and trusted? Do you have the respect of your fellow workers and your friends? Do you treat others courteously? Are you well-mannered? A good reputation and good manners are almost a necessity for advancement.

Changing your attitude. Psychologists say that major behavioral changes take years to become automatic. You can get a good start, however, by working on your image. Acquire dress skills by reading or comparing notes with friends.

Finish any job that you start, and don't take on things you aren't willing to complete. Do the best work you can, and let people know. This enhances your reputation.

Find people whom you admire, and ask their advice. If you admire historical figures, read about their lives, how they dealt with problems, how they acted, and what they believed.

A prescription

It takes time to overcome Entrylevelitis. Sufferers sometimes take months (or years) to recover. Those who do recover have probably used the following four-part treatment. This prescription should be taken as often as necessary to relieve the symptoms of Entrylevelitis.

1. Buy and read books on dress skills, grooming, listening, problem solving, memorization, organizing, and time management. Study these books, and discuss what you learn with your friends. Promise yourself that you will use these tools to improve yourself, then keep that promise.

2. Take classes or get training in dealing with people, ethics, speed-reading and comprehension, and creating an image. Schedule time for this training or reading so that you can put what you learn to good use.

3. Deal with people. Ask them how they solved particular problems and what they learned from the experience. Practice listening skills by asking for advice and then carefully summarizing what they say.

4. Set yourself a schedule and stick to it. Choose a topic, a book, or a class, set a deadline for absorbing it, and meet that deadline. Manage your time so that you will have an unbroken string of successful accomplishments.

For the manager

The authors hope that the preceding section has given managers and supervisors a new outlook on the entry-level employee. While our recommendations are not specific to data processing personnel, they are relevant. With the changes we foresee coming to data processing in the near future (see the Introduction), even the meaning of the term "programmer" may evolve to the point where we won't recognize it. With our newest employees acquiring new skills in problem solving, organization, time management, listening, and the like, we must be prepared to challenge them enough so that they remain. The most important part of this process is providing feedback on their performance: *performance appraisal.*

Data Processing Career Alternatives

Career path choices in data processing have changed greatly in the past decade. In the 1970s, computer-related job opportunities were limited to programming, analysis, and management, because computers were rudimentary and business applications were relatively straightforward. The 1980s saw the appearance of many data processing hardware and software advances such as multiprogramming, multiprocessing, data communications, databases, and high-level languages. The 1990s will see distributed processing, distributed databases, advanced telecommunications, and applications expressly designed for microcomputers.

Under these circumstances, data processing job descriptions and career alternatives will be quite different from those of today. In the context of performance appraisal, how will managers measure and appraise the performance of these professionals? In this section, we address the job opportunities available at the lower, nonmanagement levels of data processing, with special attention to performance appraisal.

Analysis and design

In the past. The science of systems analysis existed long before computers came on the scene. Analysts were responsible for investigating problems, gathering data, evaluating alternatives, and recommending solutions. With the advent of computers and computer application systems, the *systems analyst* (or simply *analyst*) appeared. Systems analysts are now responsible for determining whether portions of systems, or entire systems, should be automated using computers.

The analyst usually began by interviewing potential users to determine their business requirements. On some occasions, users presented their needs to a *data processing steering committee,* which then prioritized the users' needs.

With requirements in hand, the analyst conducted a *feasibility study* to determine if a system that was both practical and useful could be developed. If so, the analyst listed the various possible alternative designs. These designs did not necessarily involve computers. The analyst then evaluated the alternatives in terms of their costs and benefits. This evaluation then became the basis for a decision as to whether or not to proceed with system design.

With the decision to proceed, the analyst then used the original user request and the *cost benefit analysis* to expand the system description into a *system requirements* document. This document was then further expanded to create report formats, file descriptions, and application program specifications. These specifications were then given to programmers for coding and testing.

Performance appraisal. As analysts' jobs were somewhat unstructured, their managers had a great deal of difficulty measuring their performance. Attempts to quantify the work that analysts did usually led to some kind of *trait-based* performance appraisal system, where analysts were rated on communications skills, attendance, punctuality, attitude, dependability, and sometimes even appearance.

While it is possible to measure such traits, they are a poor basis for meaningful performance appraisal. (For more on this subject, see Chap. 3.)

The present—the future. The systems analyst's job in the future will remain mostly as it is now. As their basic task is to improve and automate business systems, the changes in computer hardware platforms and software tools change only the way that computers can be applied as part of an overall systems solution. Still, analysts must keep abreast of the latest development, as these may become part of future alternative system designs and, therefore, future systems.

Performance appraisal. The job of the systems analyst will not change substantially in the near future; still, current performance appraisal procedures and techniques must be updated so that they are less subjective and trait-based.

Programming

In the past. Computer programmers are the people who tell computers what to do. Programmers, sometimes called coders, created directions to the computer called *programs*. The computer then interpreted and executed these programs to accomplish one or more tasks. These tasks were sometimes simple, such as printing a report of a file or database. They were sometimes much more difficult, such as controlling the robots in an automobile assembly line. Some of the more complex computer programs consisted of hundreds of thousands of lines of computer language code. These programs were typically written by teams of people and took several years to complete.

Programmers wrote these programs in many languages. These languages consisted of strings of characters that both the computer and the programmer could understand (perhaps with a little bit of translation). Before coding a program, however, the programmer required written specifications that stated what tasks the computer was to perform. The programmer used these specifications as a guide to writing the program. Sometimes the programmer extended or rewrote the specifications into one of several formats that were more suitable for translation into a program. Some of these formats included flow charts, hierarchical input-process-output (HIPO) diagrams, and structure charts.

Measuring the programmer's performance was relatively easy. Programmers were assigned only a small variety of tasks, and these were easily measurable. The majority of these tasks were as follows:

Analyze specifications. Programmers were required to analyze the specifications they were given, for several reasons. First, if there were any ambiguities or obvious errors in the specs, the programmer was expected to notice them and bring them to the analyst's attention. Second, in many cases programmers had several years of experience writing either similar applications or applications for a particular business unit. Their expertise in these areas made them particularly good at writing certain kinds of programs. Last, as the programmers finished coding the program, they were required to present their code to the analyst during a program walkthru. This kind of meeting was held to detect possible coding errors. To do this, the program was compared with the specifications to see how closely they were followed.

Create flow diagrams. There were (and still are) several methodologies and diagramming standards for creating process flow diagrams. Programmers created these diagrams by studying the logic flow of the specifications and the structures of the data. Occasionally, the programmer would also develop a dataflow diagram that described how input data was transformed at various points within the program.

Code the initial program.   The programmer, using either pencil and paper or an on-line data entry system, would devise program language statements from the program flow chart. Sometimes the programmer would use another program as a starting point, deleting the sections that did not apply to the current program, and adding any necessary code.

Test the program.   Programmers were sometimes responsible for writing a formal program test plan, in addition to creating test data and testing the program. This testing usually took quite a long time, as errors in the program would cause it to abnormally terminate.

Create required documentation.   Many data processing organizations had standards regarding the documentation that was required to accompany a program. This usually included a list of the program statements, the original specifications, a text description of the purpose of the program, the formal test plan, test results, sample reports, and program execution information. This last item was primarily for use by computer operators, as they would be responsible for executing the program.

Performance appraisal.   In the past, management graded programmers on how well they performed these few tasks; in general, the more work accomplished in a given period, the better the measured performance. This concept was sometimes revised and expanded to take into account that a program didn't work as expected. The fewer errors a program made, the better the programmer's performance.

The present—the future.   The programmer's role in the future is greatly expanded. Software is becoming more complex, and many new and interesting languages now exist. New business applications that did not exist in the past are becoming a reality. Some of these include industrial process control, network performance monitoring, storage capacity planning, and computer-aided graphic design.

With the changes mentioned at the beginning of this section, how will the programmer's job change? Some of the factors are listed here.

Specification writing and software tools.   Programmers will assist analysts and user representatives in writing program specifications. To assist them in this effort, many computer-aided software engineering (CASE) tools will be available. Programmers (by then probably called programmer analysts) will enter high-level system design information into a CASE tool. The tool will then analyze the design, produce the required diagrams (such as flow charts), and, for advanced CASE tools, even generate the program itself.

Another kind of CASE tool is the prototyping tool. Using this tool, the programmer analyst can quickly construct a working model of the final system. This model can then be shown to the users, and serves as a basis for discussion and refinement.

Logic diagramming.   With the tools mentioned above, the programmer will no longer need to diagram the logic flow of a program before beginning to code. In many cases, the CASE tool will create diagrams automatically. In others, tools are able to convert designs directly into executable programs, completely bypassing the diagramming steps.

Program coding.   In those situations where a tool is used to generate the program, the programmer will no longer be responsible for the initial programming. Instead, there will probably be enhancements, additions, or perhaps some customization required. There are no CASE tools available at the time of this writing that can produce complete, functioning programs from design input. There are several, however, that can create almost-complete programs that require only minor modifications on the part of a programmer.

Program testing.   This segment of the programmer's job will change greatly in the future. Rather than a laborious, time-consuming task involving many scores of tests with reams of data, program testing will involve many new and different software environments. The database environment will require expertise in the database management system, including displaying and modifying databases while testing. Telecommunications links will compel the programmer to master communication protocols. In many cases, the programmer must master several different disciplines to be able to determine if a program is working correctly.

Documentation.   Little documentation will be needed in the future. In addition to the current popular trend toward a paperless environment, many companies will depend upon CASE tools for their documentation. Should program errors appear, they may not be fixed by changing the program; instead, the programmer or the analyst will go directly to the design, make the appropriate changes, and recreate the corrected program in its entirety.

Execution information will not be required either, as data centers shift toward automated operations. Computer operators will not be needed to handle magnetic tapes, as new types of automatic tape-handling equipment appear. Further, program abnormal terminations can now be fixed on-line, rather than requiring a programmer to wade through an immense storage dump. Also, most data processing installations have now installed job scheduling systems that automatically schedule jobs for execution.

Microcomputer-based development. This recent advancement in application development strategy will change the way that programming is accomplished. Tools now exist that allow programmers to design, code, and test mainframe applications using a microcomputer. These tools simulate the mainframe environment on the microcomputer, almost entirely eliminating the programmer's need for specific microcomputer experience. As the programmer develops and tests programs, the resources used are those of the microcomputer, not the mainframe. Should a problem occur with program testing, such as an abnormal termination, this will not affect mainframe processing.

Performance appraisal. With these changes in the programmers' basic work assignments, how will management measure their performance? There will be little choice: management will be forced to shift from *process-oriented* measurements to *results-oriented* measurements.

For example, programmers cannot be appraised based on their coding habits because coding, as such, will no longer exist. Instead, managers must rely on quality measurements such as their ability to develop specifications, the number and complexity of programs they successfully complete, and their expertise in the use of CASE tools.

Project leader

In the past. Programmers and analysts rarely exist in a vacuum. Large business systems usually require teams of analysts and programmers working together. Sometimes large programs are divided into sections, with one or more programmers working on each section. During testing, programs that depend on others for input or output must be tested together, either in sequence or in parallel.

To handle these situations, project leaders were responsible for coordinating the efforts of several analysts and programmers. In addition to supervising work efforts, the project leader monitored project progress using a project management system.

Performance appraisal. As the project leader was held accountable for the success or failure of a project, performance appraisal was relatively straightforward. Typical measures of performance included project elapsed time, whether deadlines were met, total budget expended, and percentage and distribution of errors. However, the most important criterion of success was whether the delivered system met the objectives defined in the user's specifications.

The present—the future. Project leaders now have the advantage of software tools that assist them in project status monitoring and tracking. These tools include the ability to answer "What if?" questions such as the following:

What would be the effect on the project deadline if:

- additional new programmers were assigned?
- some tasks were reassigned among the staff?
- the order of some tasks was rearranged?

What would be the effect on the project budget if:

- several entry-level staff were replaced by one or two highly skilled staff?
- time spent programming was decreased by 20 percent, and time spent testing increased by 20 percent?
- the project deadline were extended, allowing fewer staff to be used, but for a longer period of time?

These questions are important ones for the project leader—answers to them may form the basis for management decisions that will affect staff assignments, deadline dates, budgets, and delivery of application systems that are critical to an enterprise's business.

Another interesting evolution in project operations is that of microcomputer-based application development. (This was described in an earlier section.) Using these techniques, team members can function almost independently during the coding and testing phases of a project. This relieves the project leaders of some of the stress inherent in managing people. In addition, it permits the project leader to automate project progress tracking, since all of the programs and test data can be made available on a network.

Performance appraisal. Microcomputer-based application development and project management systems have made the project leader's job a more organized and controllable one; hence, performance measures will be even easier to come by. Management may even be able to automate the performance appraisal process, as all of the measures of project success may be available as reporting elements of the project tracking system.

The only component missing is the *human factor*. Things such as morale, team spirit, and employee development must be included as additional duties. As their ability to manage larger and larger projects increases, project leaders will be given more and more such responsibilities—at some point, the project leader may become a manager, responsible for the performance appraisal of project team members. Appraising the appraiser then becomes an issue.

Systems programming

In the past. The systems programmer is a special kind of programmer who specializes in computer system programs. Examples of such programs include the operating system, compilers, interpreters, input/output systems, telecommunications systems, database managers, and utilities. These programs are usually provided with the hardware by the computer vendor, although sometimes data processing installations will write their own.

The systems programmer is responsible for monitoring and maintaining system programs. This requires knowledge of the internal design of the computer hardware, special system programming languages, performance measurement tools, and sometimes advanced topics such as database management and telecommunications.

Performance appraisal. It has always been difficult to measure the performance of systems programmers, as what they do and how they do it is usually not understood by management. Sometimes the only measurement available is that the computer is currently working (or not working). Appraisal systems for systems programmers usually concentrated on *potential*—that is, their current level of knowledge and skills relating to the hardware and software they maintained.

The present—the future. Even though new data processing developments are changing the way that business systems are being built, the only change in the systems programmers' job is the set of specific hardware and software skills they must possess.

The only thing that may change is the way the systems programmer must interact with others. As computers become more and more interconnected, systems software and information will begin to reside in several places. This distributed processing and distributed data environment means that the systems programmer must now consider multiple sites when evaluating a system or diagnosing a problem.

Performance appraisal. Performance appraisal for the systems programmer will probably remain in approximately its current state, although behavior-oriented appraisal procedures will become more applicable. (See Chap. 4 for more information.)

Computer operations

In the past. In the 1960s and 1970s, the computer operator was responsible for directing hardware operations. This usually consisted of deciding what program or job was to execute next, and preparing the computer and its peripheral devices (such as magnetic tape drives, disk drives, card readers, printers, and so forth) for job execution. The programmer's instructions usually specified what data files the program required and how the operator was to find them. Tape reels, for example, were usually identified by a six-character serial number and stored on a rack in serial sequence.

The operator performed many manual tasks. These included finding the required tapes and cards for a job, preparing the printers with the correct paper, starting the job, and monitoring its execution. After successful execution the operator sometimes collected the printed reports, separated them into (perhaps) multiple copies, and distributed them. If a program failed to run correctly, the operator was sometimes responsible for diagnosing and correcting the problem. At the very least, the operator documented the problem so that the programmer could fix it at an appropriate time.

Performance appraisal. Because the operators did so much manual labor, it was relatively easy to gauge how well they performed. Errors such as getting the wrong input tape or directing reports to the incorrect destination were easily measurable.

The present—the future. The data processing operations center of the future will be almost completely automated. Even now, many data centers are functioning in *lights out,* or unattended mode. Magnetic tapes are retrieved from vaults, mounted on tape drives, and restored to the vault by automatic equipment. Computer jobs are scheduled automatically by job-scheduling software tools. The only jobs that may be left for computer operators are the following:

Peripheral operator. Some computer input and output devices, called peripherals, require almost constant attention. For example, reports must be removed from printers and delivered to their destinations, and blank paper must be inserted into printers. Files shared between data centers may be created as magnetic tapes, requiring an operator to remove a tape and dispatch it to the other center.

Console operations. The computer console is the nerve center of the computer. On it, an operator is in complete command of everything happening. Should a system problem occur, the operator is usually notified immediately for corrective action.

As the number and complexity of hardware and software solutions become reality, computer operators must be prepared to deal with a wide variety of intricate and sophisticated systems.

Network operations.   Even now, many computers and data centers are electronically connected using networks. These networks usually require an operator to monitor them and to handle problems.

Performance appraisal.   As the job of computer operator steadily shifts from manual labor to skilled systems and network operations, performance measurement becomes more difficult. Operators, through training and education, will be acquiring technical skills they need for complex operations. This transformation will radically change the operator's job description, and the performance appraisal system must change to match.

Database administrator

In the past.   Up until the mid-1970s, databases didn't exist in large numbers on mainframe computers. Those professionals who were the forerunners of the database administrator were sometimes called *data administrators*. They were responsible for arranging, managing, and maintaining a company's business data in an organized fashion. They interfaced with security specialists who were responsible for protecting company data from improper access.

The present—the future.   With the appearance of database management systems, there came a need for people who would organize and manage database access by business systems. Database administrators (DBAs) were put in charge of database definition, creation, backup, recovery, performance monitoring, and tuning. Application developers then came to depend on the DBAs to design their database structures, create test database data, and assist them with program design.

In the future, as companies begin to disperse data and computer power across multiple sites, database administrators will become responsible for distributed databases. Such a database may exist either in several parts with one or more parts at separate sites, or as a single entity with multiple copies coexisting at two or more sites. DBAs will require tools to help them manage this data. In addition, application developers will need help designing programs to access such databases.

Performance appraisal.   The database administrator's job in the future will become extremely technically sophisticated. DBAs will need specialized training in database management systems, system internals, distributed processing, and networks. Measuring their performance will be difficult, as poor performance will be hard to detect. Many of the newer relational database management systems do not yet perform well in transaction processing environments—slow-running systems may be caused by system problems, rather than a poorly designed database.

The bottom line when measuring DBA performance is to concentrate on the way that the DBA supports the application development process. Since the database administrator is an integral part of the project team, management should use project deliverables as the basis for generating DBA goals and objectives. For example, if a project requires that a database be fully designed prior to writing program specifications, the design task should be included in the project plan with the DBA responsible assigned to it. The DBA must now finish the design on time per the project plan. This performance objective may now be included in the DBA's performance appraisal.

Data processing education

In the past. When computers first appeared in quantity executing business applications, there was no organized data processing training function. At best, training consisted of manuals and books made available to programmers as references.

In the 1970s, data processing systems became widespread. Colleges and universities began offering degrees in data processing and computer science. Educational companies began to appear that specialized in data processing training. As the number and types of different hardware platforms and software environments multiplied, companies became concerned that their staffs would not be able to keep current on the latest developments. Many companies instituted internal training departments. These departments were staffed with a faculty that specialized in DP curricula. DP instructors had to be somewhat technically oriented, as well as being good communicators and teachers. Typical classes included programming languages, debugging skills, written communications, specific hardware internals, and project management.

Performance appraisal. The most common error made in measuring instructor performance was to confuse *teaching* with *learning*. It was relatively simple to judge whether teaching had taken place—after all, classes were scheduled and students appeared. The mistake made was to regard this as sufficient evidence to warrant a good appraisal.

In reality, what should have been measured was whether learning took place. As data processing departments matured in the mid-1980s, most companies began to use one or more of the following methods for measuring learning.

Pre-tests and post-tests. Two tests with similar content are created for each class subject. Class attendees take the first (the pre-test), and the results are reviewed. At the end of the class, attendees take the post-test, and compare their scores with their results from the pre-test. The difference in their scores is a rough measurement of the amount of learning that has taken place.

Although this method provides a general gauge of the students' progress, pre-tests and post-tests are difficult to develop. They must accurately reflect the course content, be technically accurate, and be kept up-to-date as technology advances. In addition, it is impossible to compare results across different classes. For example, consider the following data from classes given on two different subjects.

- Class A: Pre-test mean = 10; Post-test mean = 75.
- Class B: Pre-test mean = 70; Post-test mean = 95.

Superficially one might infer that more learning took place in Class A, since that class had the highest mean absolute difference between pre-test and post-test results. This would be a false conclusion. This result may have been because the material in Class A covered material that was relatively new to the students (hence, the low pre-test mean). It could also mean that such material was easier to learn. Note that the students in Class B achieved a higher post-test mean score. Perhaps they are ready to practice what they have learned, while the students in Class A only know 75 percent of the material.

Despite these drawbacks, many companies consider such testing to be the only accurate assessment of student learning. Since the purpose of data processing training is to impart knowledge and skills to the students, such an assessment should have a direct impact on the instructor's performance appraisal.

Class evaluations. Using this method, students evaluate the various attributes of the class on a form constructed for that purpose. Common questions ask the students to rate the following on a scale from low to high:

- Relevance of the class topic to their work
- Enthusiasm of the instructor
- Quality of the class materials
- Usefulness of the workshops

These elements are rather subjective. Students may not be able to correctly assess the usefulness of the class until long after they have put what they have learned into practice. Also, this method suffers the same problems of other rating scales—scale measurements mean different things to different people. Still, many shops use these evaluations as measurements for instructor performance appraisal.

Direct instructor measurement. This technique involves placing an instructor in a situation where he or she must perform as a practitioner. COBOL programming instructors are asked to write COBOL programs; database instructors are required to assist a user in creating, populating, and accessing a database. A variant of this system is to interview instructors using experienced technical practitioners.

While these methods may be useful for determining the level of an instructor's knowledge, they fail to ascertain how well the instructor teaches—that is, how much do their students learn.

The present—the future. While hardware and software technology march steadily onward and upward, the instructor's job remains almost the same. There are more things to teach, and new things to learn. Still, their basic task is to impart knowledge and teach skills.

The late 1980s have added a number of additional media alternatives to the instructor's arsenal. Computer-based training (CBT) is a system of computer software that directs the students training program. The software displays information for the student to read, and then tests the student's comprehension. This method allows students to proceed at their own pace, and usually provides a record of their progress. Projection television and electroluminescent displays allow the instructor to demonstrate a live terminal session as if seen on an overhead projector. Many students can then follow a live demonstration comfortably from their seats, rather than crowding around a single terminal screen.

Performance appraisal. Advances in performance appraisal methods and procedures now provide instructors with more objective measurements of their performance. Following are some of the newer techniques being used in progressive data processing organizations.

Work-relevant workshops. Using this method, class workshops consist of actual elements from the student's work environment. For example, a COBOL programming class would contain workshops requiring students to write and test programs that are part the student's actual work assignments. This had two purposes: it provides workshops that are relevant to the students' particular environment, making the training more meaningful; and it allows students to complete job tasks while in class.

In terms of the instructor's performance, this technique permits management to directly measure the results of training by evaluating the work completed by the students. In effect, the student's performance measures are incorporated directly into that of the instructor.

Interactive training. Here, the instructor is at the center of a network consisting of student workstations. Each workstation is a microcomputer containing specially designed computer-based training software that allows the instructor to control each student's station, either as a group or on an individual basis. Typically, the instructor will demonstrate one or more class topics, which will be mirrored on the student's workstations. After this the students proceed to the workshops, where the instructor may monitor their progress. Should students require assistance, the instructor can aid them interactively.

Using this method requires a sophisticated software and hardware system, as well as an experienced instructor. Performance appraisal is based on student achievement, and can be monitored automatically by the software.

Computer consultant

In the past. While some of the larger accounting and consulting firms have had data processing consulting departments since the 1960s, computer consultants didn't appear in large numbers until the mid-1970s. This was primarily due to the introduction of third-generation programming languages, which for the first time enabled programmers to code programs without having an extensive hardware background. As coding became easier, some experienced programmers promoted themselves to consultants and formed their own companies. The industry sometimes referred to these professionals as *contract programmers,* and treated them as temporary workers in the general category of *contractors.* Groups of contractors sometimes formed companies to sell their services in teams or projects. Such companies were sometimes called *service firms.*

Contractors were usually used to supplement the data processing staff, and were given work space in the data processing installation. They performed tasks assigned by lead analysts or project managers.

The advantages of such a contract staff are many. A company with a large backlog of unfinished systems could hire contract programmers to complete the work. When the project finishes, these people can be let go. This is much better than hiring employees that must then either be reassigned or laid off. Another advantage is that a company can bring in a contract staff with the exact skills required for development. In this way, they do not need to provide for staff training, job reassignment, or a possibly long and expensive recruiting drive.

There are disadvantages to this approach. When a contractor leaves the project, his or her experience leaves with that person. Knowledge gained and skills acquired are lost, perhaps to be used on a project for a competitor. Last, as the contractor is not a company employee, loyalties may be unclear.

Performance appraisal. From the manager's perspective, performance appraisal of contract programmers was not an issue, as they were not company employees. Contractors (or consultants) did no formal appraisals of themselves, as they had no managers. In these cases, the contracting company would appraise its employees (the individual contract programmers); however, this appraisal was usually subjective and trait-based.

The present—the future. As data processing systems become more complex, data processing installations may be forced more and more to rely on outside experts to augment their own staff during application development. Such outsourcing can be a positive strategic business maneuver, as it permits a company to install automated and computerized systems quickly. This can sometimes mean the difference between success and failure in business, as competitors may be trying to do the same thing.

In the future, consultants must specialize more. It will not be enough for a consultant to know one programming language (such as COBOL) or be limited to one hardware platform (such as IBM). With distributed data, distributed processing, microcomputer-based application development, data communication networks, relational database management systems, and new high-level languages, the successful computer consultant must be an expert in several areas to be perceived as useful.

Performance appraisal. Appraisal of consultants will depend on their usefulness to their clients. Clients will compare consultants based on price and perceived value; that is, the amount of work they produce in a period of time, and their billing rate. Expensive consultants that produce little work will be replaced by cheaper workers that *do* work.

From the consultant's point of view, performance may be measured in several different ways. Some of these are:

Marketability. In other words, how many potential clients could a consultant service. A broad experience base and an excellent track record with past clients guarantee the consultant a job.

Revenues earned. Here, the company measures the total amount of money the consultant commands in a review period, regardless of the number of clients serviced or the level of billing rates.

Client satisfaction. Many enterprising consulting firms use this method, where they rely on customer feedback as to the worth of their consultants. The theory is that only the client can properly measure a consultant's performance, and that good performance should be rewarded.

In general, this is the best method of objectively appraising consultant performance. It addresses the most important problem—namely, that the consultant works for one company but gets paid by another.

Tools for career development

Several software packages exist that can help you structure your career plan. Only two are mentioned here; for more information, consult the current trade press.

Career design. This package is an interactive self-help package that puts you through a series of exercises such as determining your basic, specific, and personality skills. It helps identify your likes and dislikes involving work conditions and type of personalities you interact with best. The program gives constant feedback to the users about their answers, even leading to extended discussions on some topics.

After the information-gathering step, the program then organizes your approach: how to set goals, gather data on possible employers, and generate contacts.

Career Design Software
P.O. Box 95624
Atlanta, GA 30347
(800) 346-8007
(404) 321-6100

Peterson's career options. This program begins with a set of assessment exercises designed to measure your interest in career categories such as social service, data processing, or engineering. It then continues with a host of specific questions to determine which areas you prefer, and to narrow the list of potential careers. After generating a pool of possibilities the program attempts to reduce the number to manageable size by analyzing your preferences and skill levels.

Regrettably, by unrealistically restricting your preferences you will reduce your choice of possible careers to none. You must then go back and reanswer some questions or redo certain of the assessments.

The package also allows exploring specific careers by area and topic, including description and education/training required. Unfortunately, it does not include salary range and projections for future jobs. Still, as a place to start, the package has possibilities.

Peterson's
P.O. Box 2123
Princeton, NJ 08543-2123
(800) 338-3282

Bibliography

The following list of books is a sample of what is available on some of the subjects mentioned earlier in this chapter.

Communication skills

McCormack, Mark H., *What They Don't Teach You at Harvard Business School,* Bantam, 1984.
Steil, Lyman, Barker, L., and Watson, K., *Effective Listening: Key to Your Success,* Addison-Wesley, 1983.

Problem solving

Bonoma, Thomas, and Slevin, D., *Executive Survival Manual: A Program for Managerial Effectiveness,* Wadsworth, 1978.
Ritti, R. Richard and G. Ray Funkhouser, *The Ropes To Skip & The Ropes To Know,* John Wiley & Sons, 1987.

Memorization

Lorayne, Harry, *How to Develop a Super-Power Memory,* New America Library, 1957.

Organizing

Albrecht, Karl, *Executive Tune-Up: Personal Effectiveness Skills for Business and Professional People,* Prentice-Hall, 1981.
Winston, Stephanie, *Getting Organized: The Easy Way to Put Your Life in Order,* W. W. Norton, 1978.
Winston, Stephanie, *The Organized Executive: New Ways to Manage Time, Paper, and People,* W. W. Norton, 1983.

Time management

Lebov, Myrna, *Practical Tools and Techniques for Managing Time,* Executive Enterprises, 1980.
Mackenzie, R. Alec, *The Time Trap: How to Get More Done in Less Time,* McGraw-Hill, 1975.

Dress and grooming

Bixler, Susan, *The Professional Image,* G. P. Putnam's Sons, 1984.
Molloy, John T., *John T. Molloy's New Dress For Success,* Warner Books, 1988.
Molloy, John T., *Molloy's Live For Success,* Perigord Bantam Books, 1981.

Dealing with people

de Bono, Edward, *Tactics: The Art and Science of Success,* Little, Brown, 1984.
Karp, H. B., *Personal Power: An Unorthodox Guide To Success,* AMACOM, 1985.
Keirsey, David, and Bates, Marilyn, *Please Understand Me: Character and Temperament Types,* Gnosology Books, 1984.
Lareau, William, *Conduct Expected: The Unwritten Rules for a Successful Business Career,* New Century, 1985.

The Performance Appraisal Process

3

Common Misunderstandings about Appraisal

Doing performance appraisals of MIS professionals competently and fairly can be downright impossible. The lack of good job descriptions, a highly technical environment, and a widely skewed salary structure make it difficult for managers to do employees justice. Small wonder that employees don't look forward to appraisals, and managers don't like doing them.

Performance appraisals (or performance reviews) must satisfy several of the company's needs. They help determine employee compensation, assist in monitoring performance improvement, guide career development, and provide documentation for hire/fire decisions. With all this riding on a single document, appraisals must be impartial, unbiased, and equitable. Here's how to make employees look forward to their yearly reviews, along with some advice on how to prepare for them yourself.

Webster's New World Dictionary defines *appraise* as ". . . to judge the quality or worth of (something)." An appraisal, therefore, is a judgment of the quality or worth of your employee's results. To appraise your employees, you must first review the events during the appraisal period. Then, you must summarize the goals set and results achieved. After gathering the facts, you judge the employee's performance.

Many new employees are unaware of these attributes of performance reviews. This lack of knowledge may make it difficult for them to understand the review process, and may cause anxiety.

Briefly, a performance review is a set of measurements made during a specified period, including a judgment of these measurements. This judgment is then used as a basis for further action. Here's how each of these attributes relate to their particular situation.

Measurement versus Judgment

The appraisal process consists of two separate and distinct procedures: *measurement* and *judgment*. Measurement involves gathering facts, while judgment involves making decisions based on the facts. It is the blurring together of these two procedures that causes many performance reviews to go wrong.

The process of measurement

The major portion of any performance review should concentrate on the observed facts during the review period. This is the measurement process. It starts at the beginning of the employee's review period, and continues to either the end of the review period or the appraisal review meeting. Just as companies and governments have a fiscal year, so should employees in terms of their appraisals. (We will cover the review period itself in detail in the next section.)

It is only after all the measurements have taken place that the judging process may then begin. This means that the entire review period should be history; further, employee behaviors, critical incidents, and status reports must be complete, recorded, documented, and filed before the act of appraisal.

It is important to separate the act of measuring from that of appraising, or judging. This prevents judgments of some behaviors or results from clouding other judgments. It also provides an organized agenda for the review meetings between the employee and the manager.

Judgment day

Now that all measurements are complete, true appraisal can begin. Since the beginning of the review period, the employee and manager have both observed and documented incidents and behaviors. This documentation usually takes the form of status reports or "mini" appraisals. During the review period it is the responsibility of each party to interpret such reports in the context of the appraisal process, thus providing feedback on appropriateness of the employee's behavior and the effects of performance on promotional opportunities and compensation. In some cases, this ongoing analysis may prompt the manager to develop a *work improvement plan* for the employee.

Another responsibility of the two parties during the review period is that they both note how the various incidents which occur will be viewed by the eventual appraisal process. This preappraisal review requires that the performance appraisal forms and procedures explicitly state how various incidents will be rated or valued. Not only will this prevent any unforeseen or embarrassing "surprises" during the appraisal interview, it permits the manager and the employee to *tune* the employee's behavior during the review period. This tuning will result in a better employee, and will make the judgment process one of agreement rather than contention.

The Review Period

An entire period

In basic terms, work efforts extend over time. Results occur at points in time and change over time. A performance review, therefore, is a review of a period of results, not just a status report of results to date. It should cover the entire review period and contain examples of results achieved throughout that period.

This means that an employee's review is more than a simple "where they are now." It relates where they came from to how they got there. In addition, it tells whether or not they are learning and improving their skills and knowledge.

Failure to consider an employee's performance as occurring over a period of time leads to several errors. Some of these are described below.

What have you done recently? This is the tendency of raters to weigh recent events more highly than those at the beginning of the review period. Recent poor results or unacceptable behavior on the part of the employee may overshadow excellent earlier performance, thus leading to a review that is unfairly low. Conversely, a recent success can influence a manager to rate an employee too highly.

The status report. By not concentrating on the entire review period, the performance appraisal begins to take the form of a status report. This report then describes an employee's knowledge, skills, and expertise at the end of the review period. This is useful information, at least as far as personnel planning and promotability is concerned. What is missing is an index of the employee's *growth,* or *improvement.*

The report card. Here, the review takes the form of a scorecard that reports a list of goals and whether or not they were achieved. Sometimes this is expanded to include the extent to which unfinished goals were realized, and whether some goals were met beyond expectations.

The disadvantage is that the scoring itself tells the employee and the organization nothing about how the goals were met—whether or not they were challenging, too simple, or too difficult. Further, there is no information to help the employee improve his or her performance. For example, what would it mean if an employee achieved 95 percent of his or her goals? Is this good? Is it bad? How can the employee improve?

The "blurry" review period.   This common problem is too often unnoticed. It deals with the tendency of managers to look at an appraisal period in terms of their contact with the employee, or the employee's task assignments. Here are a few examples.

- An employee transfers into a new department in March. During the employee's review in December, the manager considers the review period to be March through December, even though the review period is actually January through December. The tendency here is to consider January and February outside the review period. Some progressive managers will address this issue by requiring the employee's previous manager to provide input to the review process for those months.

- An employee starts a new project in November that is expected to last for 18 months. During the employee's review in December, the manager ignores November and December, as nothing has happened (yet) on that project. The tendency here is to consider November and December as part of the *next* review period. Unfortunately, the manager sometimes forgets this a year later.

- An employee is promoted to a new position in June. During the employee's review in December, the manager considers the review period to be June through December. Here, the manager considers data from January through June as irrelevant, as it applied to the employee's previous position. The employee feels cheated, as six months of excellent work goes unrewarded. (Sometimes the opposite is true, as six months of goofing off goes unpunished!)

To avoid these problems, the appraisal system must take into account that appraisals measure behaviors and activities during the entire review period. The easiest way to make sure that events early in the period are reflected fairly in the final review is to document them.

Status reporting.   Status reporting takes many forms, probably as many as there are managers. Some of these types of status reports are described below:

The weekly status report.   This report is usually used by managers to report progress to their superiors. Typical sections in the weekly status report are:

- Things accomplished this week
- Plans for next week
- Problems or obstacles foreseen
- Comments

A sample weekly status report appears in Fig. 3.1.

Weekly Status Report

Name: Paul Programmer   **Date:** 03/01/92

Accomplishments for the Week

    1.   Completed coding of Module PR2001
    2.   Created test data for module
    3.   Began flowchart for Module PR2002
    4.   Chaired subsystem status meeting

Plans for Next Week

    1.   Begin testing Module PR2001
    2.   Begin coding module PR2002
    3.   Prepare agenda for monthly status meeting

Problems or Obstacles

    1.   User vacations have delayed acceptance testing of
         Module PR2000

Comments

    1.   Chairing the subsystem status meeting was a new
         experience for me. I got valuable pointers from
         attendees, and learned a lot.

Figure 3.1   A weekly status report.

The project task report.   This report has a list of the employee's tasks to be completed. For each task, the employee fills in the number of hours they worked, how many hours to completion, and any tasks completed that week. This information is then input to the project management system that the manager uses to track the progress of the project. A sample project task report appears in Fig. 3.2.

The monthly status report.   This report is similar to the weekly status report, but contains additional information such as:

- Classes completed
- Career planning session results
- A summary of goals completed
- Work in progress

Name: Paul Programmer   **Project Task Report**   **Date:** 03/05/92

Task	Subtask	Description	Hrs. Worked	Hrs. to Complete	Comp?
PR2000	001	Catalog Inquiry Pgm	32.0	8.0	
PR2000	002	Ctlg Inq Test Data	6.0	0.0	Y
PR2001	001	Part DB Print Pgm	0.0	48.0	
ST6001	001	Status Reporting	2.0	38.0	
Total Hours Worked This Period			40.0		

Figure 3.2 A project task report.

This information is used by both the manager and the employee. In particular, it is used as a vehicle for discussion in meetings regarding career planning, goal setting, and personnel planning. A sample monthly status report appears in Fig. 3.3.

These status reports have one thing in common: they contain information about the employee's *behaviors* and *results achieved* during the review period. As such, a combination of such reports should serve the employee and manager alike as documentation for the upcoming performance appraisal.

The review period begins. At the beginning of the review period, the manager and the employee should meet to discuss the review period and the next appraisal meeting. They should agree on the following:

- What will be the employer's goals for the review period?
- How will the goals be measured?
- What condition(s) determine whether goals will be added, changed, or discarded?
- What will be the form and content of the weekly and monthly status reports?

The status reports should contain all of the information (the *measurements*) that the manager will require at the end of the review period. This will allow the manager to rate (*judge*) the employee fairly, as there will be sufficient documentation available. This has several advantages:

- Problems associated with the definition of the review period, the form or amount of data gathered, or the weight of recent or past

---

Monthly Status Report

Name: Paul Programmer   **Date:** 03/31/92

Accomplishments for the Month

1. Completed coding and testing of two major subsystem modules.
2. Chaired two subsystem status meetings, one monthly status meeting.
3. Attended and completed Structured Design class.
4. Began attending weekly CDP Review Class.

Work in Progress

1. Continuing as lead programmer for Catalog subsystem.
2. The Parts Maintenance subsystem development team has asked for my assistance in debugging some of their programs.
3. Continuing to work towards attaining a CDP in May.

Career Planning Session

1. Discussed classes and training required for promotion to Senior Programmer with Martha Manager. She suggested that I concentrate on speaking skills. **Action Plan:** I will continue to chair status meetings, and will ask about teaching night classes.

2. Discussed upcoming (June) performance appraisal with Sam Supervisor. She reviewed forms and their contents with me, and I agreed to evaluate them for suitability to my job position. **Action Plan:** I will check company procedures manuals and the Employee Performance Review Handbook for relevant materials. I will assess the forms and write down my opinions for discussion at the next monthly meeting.

Comments

1. None this period.

Figure 3.3   A monthly status report.

events is minimized or eliminated. The status reports hold all relevant information, were written at regular intervals, and are dated.

■ Any "surprises" are eliminated from the appraisal meeting. The employee and the manager already know what will be discussed, and what events have occurred. Each should have complete documentation of all events.

- The appraisal review meeting will not be delayed because the manager is "not ready." The manager has had 12 months to prepare for the meeting—in effect, each monthly status report constitutes a mini-appraisal.

Succeeding periods. As each week or month passes, the employee is responsible for filling out the required status report. The manager then reviews it. As this report is the primary documentation of the employee's performance, the manager and the employee must agree on the accuracy of its contents. If they do not, the status reporting system fails as a measurement of the employee's behaviors, results, and performance for the period.

The first few reports will probably be a trial-and-error process for manager and employee. Both should keep in mind that the purpose of the status report is not to *judge* the employee's worth, but to *document* what happened during the period. It may become necessary to refine the report format or contents, either as to scope or degree of detail. Sometimes, however, there will be disagreements.

Should there be disagreements regarding *facts,* they should write down their understandings of the facts as they perceive them and submit these writings to an unbiased third party. This may be someone in the personnel department, an employee ombudsman, or another manager whom both parties feel will treat the matter seriously and objectively.

Disagreements about *opinions,* while they may exist, have no place in the status report. Opinions are beliefs or feelings; that is, *judgments.* Such things do not belong in status reports. Personal opinions may be documented by either party for a separate discussion at a later date.

Setting goals. Disagreements about goals should be resolved as soon as possible. Goals, and the standards for meeting them, usually form the basis for most performance appraisal systems. There are several possible obstacles that may arise regarding goals. These are described below, along with some examples.

- *Behavioral.* Goal statements should emphasize the activities that lead to goals, not the end results.

  Poor: Conduct COBOL programming classes for all staff.

  Better: Assure that 20 programmers attain competency in COBOL programming.

- *Flexible.* Rather than specify a goal as a single objective to be achieved at the end of the review period, split it into several subgoals that can be monitored. This allows the manager and the employee to reprioritize or reschedule goal attainment, if required.

Poor: Install a complete personnel system by the end of the review period.

Better: (1) Complete specifications for the personnel system by May 31; (2) Complete programming of personnel modules by August 31; (3) Complete unit testing by October 31; (4) Have users accept system by December 1.

- *Measurable.* As goals are intended to be used to measure an employee's performance, they should be measurable.

Poor: Ensure that all programs have high quality.

Better: Ensure that all programs pass quality standards as described in quality assurance procedures.

- *Precise.* Goals should be defined accurately and specifically. When possible, use numbers, preferably those that are easily measured automatically.

Poor: Significantly decrease coding errors.

Better: Decrease coding errors per 1000 lines of code by 25 percent.

- *Reasonable.* An employee should have goals that are challenging, yet attainable.

Poor: Totally eliminate all errors in code moved to Production.

Better: Reduce errors in code moved to Production to a level consistent with other programmers with the same skill level.

- *Unambiguous:* Goals should be expressed in terms that both parties can understand.

Poor: Ensure that programs installed in Production have the fastest response time consistent with our costs and our intended level of customer satisfaction.

Better: Develop cost and performance measurements for programs, and provide to users and management a set of cost/performance alternatives.

Follow-up. As the review period progresses, the manager should review goals and status report information with the employee on a regular basis. This review meeting is the manager's best opportunity to provide the employee with feedback regarding his or her performance to date. This meeting should also be used to document any disagreements regarding goals or status. This document then forms the basis for a dialogue between the manager and the employee.

The manager's feedback should be specific, and concentrate on the employee's behaviors during the past status period. The effect of such documentation, meetings, and feedback is to divide the entire performance review period into many smaller periods, each having a minireview. At the end of the review period the set of minireviews is consolidated into a single document. This then becomes the core of the employee's performance appraisal, at least as far as measurement is concerned. Feedback from the minireviews becomes, in part, the judgment of the employee's behaviors, along with a summary statement of goal status and attainment.

Summary.   Regular status reporting is the key to fair and objective appraisals. An agreement between the employee and the rater as to the format and content of the reports goes a long way toward easing the burden of the manager, as well as making employees feel they are being treated fairly.

Ongoing, Not One-Time

Performance consists of day-to-day communications, formal meetings, status reports, tasks completed, and other activities. These developments occur over time, not just at certain points in time or at the end of the review period. This means that a performance review really takes an entire year (or the equivalent review period) to complete. Every day some events happen, however small, which are part of an employee's performance profile.

Managers may give employees feedback regarding their work. Coworkers may assist an employee with a project. An employee may finish several tasks early, or complete a project well under budget. In effect, the performance review is a continuous process, happening every minute of every day.

In the previous section we emphasized the review period as a complete entity, with defined beginning and ending points. Here, we expand this definition a bit. It is important to realize that the way managers and employees perceive the review period may have a radical effect on the employee's appraisal.

Documenting events.   The most important part of documenting an event is that it be done as soon as possible, preferably while the event is occurring. There are several reasons for this.

Accuracy.   People have imperfect memories, and some events and facts seem to fade away or decay over time. Documentation is a more permanent medium that allows the employee and the manager to discuss and correct any discrepancies.

Personal growth.   People are not the best observers of their own behavior. They tend to be subjective, coloring their observations with their feelings about what is happening. Their opinions may later change based upon reflection, maturity, or opposing views from others. By documenting an event as it is occurring, the employee can then analyze the document objectively, imagining that it describes another person. Such self-analysis is important for future growth.

Management feedback. Documenting an event soon after it occurs and incorporating the documentation in the form of a status report allows the employee's manager to respond with feedback. The manager and the employee can then discuss the event, the employee's behavior, possible alternatives, and performance improvements while the event is fresh in everyone's mind.

The amount, type, and form of documentation you collect depends upon the performance review methodology being used. (These methodologies are explained in more detail in Chap. 5.)

Checklists. Events reported in the status report should be framed, using words from the appraisal checklist. In this way, the manager can convert the status report comments and descriptions directly into the appraisal format.

Critical incidents. This methodology requires that the manager and the employee document incidents during the review period, and fits in well with the principles mentioned above. The only difference may be that some events are not determined to be *critical* by either employee or manager. In these cases, the documentation can still be used in the performance appraisal process, although it may not have a direct bearing on the final result. At the very least, such documentation gives the employee experience in written communications.

Critical-incident documentation should reflect the procedures stated in the performance appraisal system. In general, this includes the circumstances that preceded the incident, the setting in which it occurred, precisely what the employee did that was effective or ineffective, the consequences of the incident, and the extent to which the consequences were in the control of the employee.

Essay reviews. One of the major problems associated with essay reviews is that they require a manager to be somewhat skilled in written communications. By documenting events that happen, by the end of the review period the manager will have accumulated a set of written descriptions that can be edited into a final document.

Management by Objectives (MBO). Here, the status report should concentrate on the employee's objectives as stated at the beginning of the review period. In this way, the manager and the employee can determine whether the incident directly affects or changes the objective in terms of its achievability, applicability, priority, or measurability. Any changes to objectives should be documented in this fashion, as this may alter the way the employee must behave to achieve their objectives.

Ranking systems. Those ranking systems that compare employees in the same job classification with each other require that managers justify their rankings. Event status reports for this type of system should be expressed in terms of what other specific employees would have done, how they would have behaved, and any similar incidents involving others in the past.

This may be extremely difficult for the employees to do, as they are not aware of many past incidents. This responsibility, therefore, falls on the shoulders of the manager. The manager must review the status report in detail with the employee, give immediate and objective feedback, and provide the employee with alternatives that will improve the employee's behavior and performance.

Rating scales. Rating scale performance appraisal systems usually require the rater to choose a numerical score for an employee in each of several different categories. These numerical ratings are usually accompanied with a word or phrase that describes the rating, such as "poor," "acceptable," or "exceeds expectations." These words or phrases should be used in status reports so that the manager and the employee can relate happenings directly to the rating scales. This will simplify the appraisal process and provide a fair and objective measurement of the employee's behavior.

Avoid report cards. From the manager's point of view, the regular status report is an opportunity to review an employee's performance for the most recent status period. The manager should examine the status report with an eye to the future performance appraisal meeting, noting incidents and achievements. The manager then should provide feedback to the employee. This feedback should be organized so that the employee understands how each item will be realized on his or her performance appraisal at the end of the review period.

Managers should avoid a report card format to the feedback—this is not its purpose. Rather, the feedback to the employees should be organized so that they understand how their recent behaviors and results will influence their appraisal.

Remember the review period. With a regular status reporting system, it will be a relatively simple matter to segregate events into separate review periods. This is important, as sometimes managers and employees allow events in one period to affect the appraisal in another. Such events can overshadow those that are more relevant, and make objective appraisals very difficult.

Summary. Regular status reporting is the key to effective measurement of employee behavior. It provides documentation of events and furnishes data regarding measurements of an employee's performance. A complementary principle is that the manager must give employees frequent feedback regarding their performance. Without such feedback, employees have little motivation for improvement.

Appraisal Forms and Their Uses

One form, many uses

One of the worst mistakes a company can make when designing a performance appraisal system, apart from having none at all, is to end up with a single appraisal form. Such a form cannot serve multiple purposes. There are many objectives for performance appraisals; the objectives determine what will be measured, how it will be measured, and how frequently it will be measured.

Following is a list of common objectives for performance appraisals, along with a description of the measurements required.

Preemployment screening. While not very common, using a performance appraisal process to screen new employees is feasible. Since potential new employees will be expected to perform adequately in their jobs, some companies use their current appraisal forms to rate likely candidates.

Using this system, the company needs the appraisal process to give them a single end result: either hire, hire on probation, or do not hire. Regrettably, most appraisal systems are not able to issue such an overall rating. Those that rate employees on a numerical scale in various categories do not lend themselves to combining scores fairly.

New employee probation. Newly hired employees usually go through a probationary period. During this period they are expected to meet certain standards and accomplish stated goals. Some appraisal systems, notably management by objectives, are aptly suited for this. Managers need the system to produce a list of objectives for the probationary period. This requires the appraisal system to develop goals specific to a particular employee in a particular job. Generic, trait-based systems are unable to do this.

Performance improvement. Systems for performance improvement generally describe several categories of employee behavior, with specific examples of acceptable and unacceptable behaviors. The appraisal then provides the employee with specific behavioral objectives that they must meet.

This kind of system must give specific standards with only two grades: acceptable and unacceptable. Scales such as low to high, or poor, average, excellent, and superior are of little use, as these words mean different things to different people.

Personnel planning. Companies planning for the future must determine which (if any) employees have the potential for promotion to higher-level positions. To do this, managers must rate their employees' *potential,* rather than their behaviors or accomplishments. Most appraisal systems fail to measure or judge employee potential adequately.

Career planning. Many appraisal systems are used to divine an employee's career goals and make sure that these are in harmony with those of the company. This requires the system to have data regarding personnel needs, company strategic objectives, divisional objectives, employee accomplishment, and work standards. Generic and trait-based appraisal systems cannot handle this. (More information about career planning is covered in Chap. 2.)

Compensation. This is the major reason for the existence of performance appraisal systems. To determine how much to pay an employee, the system must return a single, numerical measurement. This measurement will be factored into a compensation system to determine the employee's pay. The measurement must be accurate, and managers must be able to compare measurements across people.

As with preemployment screening, few systems are able to generate a single overall performance measure that fairly assesses an employee's total performance. Further, some employees have goals that differ from those of others, making it difficult to compare appraisal ratings across employees.

Multiple forms

If no one appraisal system or form can generate all of these results, then what is the solution? One possibility is for a company to use several appraisal forms, one for each performance objective. Some possible forms, matched with their objectives, are described below.

Preemployment screening. Appraisal forms for screening potential employees should list job categories and minimum standards for each category. The appraisal, or interviewing, process concentrates on determining whether the candidate meets the minimum criteria in each category. To determine this, many companies select specialists in the technical categories and execute *technical interviews.*

Each interview results in a score or rating that is entered on the appraisal form. At the end of the interviewing process the decision is simple:

- If the candidate scores well above the minimum standard in each category, they are hired.
- If the candidate scores near the minimum standards in several categories but above the standards in others, they are hired on probation.
- If the candidate scores below the minimum in any one category, they are not hired.

Using this system, the company must develop a special set of appraisal categories and standards. These may be markedly different from those of current employees as they will not take into account on-the-job training, career planning, or performance improvement.

New employee probation. This appraisal subsystem must help the manager and employee develop goals specific to the new employee in his or her new job. As this job will be different for each new employee, the appraisal form must be flexible and somewhat general. Luckily, management-by-objectives performance appraisal systems handle this well.

Performance improvement. Systems for performance improvement must describe several categories of employee behavior, with specific examples of acceptable and unacceptable behaviors. No attempt is made to score or rate these behaviors—they are either acceptable or they are not. Usually behaviors are grouped into classes relating to specific job functions or categories. In this way, an employee and a manager can organize and plan ways for the employee to improve.

No overall rating or performance measure is needed. The focus is entirely on employee behavior modification. Behaviorally anchored rating scales (BARS) are the best performance appraisal type for this purpose.

Personnel planning. Judging which employees are eligible for promotion is too often a subjective decision. Forms and procedures to help the manager in this area should concentrate on defining the minimum standards and performance criteria for high-level jobs. This should be followed by a complete and objective job analysis of these high-level jobs. The objective is to develop a complete, behavior-based appraisal system for these positions.

With this new appraisal system now in place, managers can judge potential by appraising their employees as if they already held those higher positions. Some discussion of the process and the results with the employee is necessary, as career planning must be factored into the equation.

Career planning.   Career planning is often neglected, both by companies and by employees. The general feeling is that employees are responsible for their careers, and that management is responsible for informing them about opportunities within the company. Coordinating this information requires that the employee and manager work together. The employee must gather information about his or her career goals. The manager must understand what their company has to offer, including strategic objectives and personnel needs.

No current performance appraisal system handles career planning effectively. This is a matter for professional career strategy systems, which are beyond the scope of this book. (For more information about career planning, see Chap. 2.)

Compensation.   Fair compensation demands an objective method of determining overall performance. Most appraisal systems are unable to generate a single, objective, preferably numeric, overall performance rating. As with preemployment screening, few systems are able to generate a single overall performance measure that fairly assesses an employee's total performance.

Another consideration involves comparing ratings across employees. Once employees are rated, management usually tends to reward those with higher ratings with more compensation. This, however, leads to problems when comparing two employees with dissimilar jobs who received the same rating. Who should get a raise, and how much? The one with the tougher job? What does *tougher* mean?

Forced-ranking systems attempt to resolve this problem by forcing managers to rank the total employee base from lowest performer to highest. Once this almost impossible task is finished, management can reward high achievers with high percentage raises and low achievers with lesser raises. The problems with this method are:

- It is extremely difficult to compare and rank employees with different jobs.

- Managers will be unable to determine if the highest-ranking employees are performing *barely* higher or *much* higher than the next lowest ones.

- Once a raise is awarded to an employee, it stays as a part of his or her salary for the next appraisal period.

This last point is an important one. Being rewarded a year later for high performance is not soon enough—it also is not sufficient to motivate high performance for the next appraisal period. Rewards should follow the behavior meriting them as soon as possible after the behavior. This is basic knowledge about human motivation.

Ratings and Raters

Common rater errors

Raters are only human; they make human mistakes. Depending upon the particular review form being used, raters may make one or more errors. These errors tend to occur in the following categories.

Central tendency. This is the tendency of a rater to rate an employee as average, near average, or close to the midpoint of the numerical scale. This is probably the most common rater error, and possibly the most serious. It allows the rater an easy way to evade responsibility in giving the employee a fair and valid evaluation. Another version of this bias is to rate an employee low in one category if he or she has scored high in another, thus leading to a combined score of "average."

To avoid these types of errors, raters should approach each rating category as if it were independent of the others. It may help to place each rating on a separate page where it will not influence the rater's decision on succeeding categories. Another technique is to rate all employees on a regular basis in a single category, thus assuring consistency across employees in that category. In general, raters that remember that this portion of the performance appraisal is one of simple measurement should have few problems.

The compensation effect. Somewhat akin to the central tendency problem mentioned above, this problem refers to the inclination of a rater to rate an employee low in one category if they have already scored high in another category. Conversely, it includes rating an employee high in one category if they have already scored low in another. The overall effect is to end up with an average, or near average, score.

In general, this rater has already judged the employee's performance and is fooling with the scores to get the total to "come out" right. This is a serious problem, but can be easily addressed during the regular status meetings. Both the manager and the employee should concentrate on the measurements documented in the employee's status report. These data are the *facts* that will make up the final appraisal; therefore, they should be agreed upon in writing. This then leads to rating the employee in each category during the status meeting. At these times the employee can verify the accuracy of the ratings.

The first impression. Here, raters score an employee based on their first impression, ignoring behaviors or results occurring later in the appraisal period. This happens most often when an employee transfers to a new manager or project.

It is said that one never gets a second chance to make a first impression. Employees should realize that everyone uses first impressions as guides in determining how to interact with others, and act accordingly.

This type of error can be minimized if the employee and manager conform to the letter of the performance appraisal and status reporting process. Feedback from the manager is very important here, so that the employee discerns as soon as possible how he or she is performing. Should either the employee or the manager determine that the employee has gotten off to a bad start (or something similar), both should meet and discuss the matter. This will help to relieve an otherwise strained relationship, and prevent later appraisal problems.

General bias. This is the tendency to rate all employees as lower or higher than average. "We only hire above-average employees," is a familiar saying. In this kind of corporate culture, managers tend to rate employees as if they were being compared to other professionals in similar industries, or those having the same job title in other company divisions. This leads to a compression of the rating scale, as ratings range from excellent to superior, rather than from unacceptable to superior.

Another reason for such rating compression is the inclination of performance appraisal document designers to assign words to the rating scales. For example, a scale of 1 to 5 may be labeled as unacceptable, poor, acceptable, excellent, and superior on the appraisal form. The words *unacceptable* and *poor* have negative connotations (for good reason). Some managers are emotionally unable (or unwilling) to rate their employees as unacceptable or poor.

The compression of ratings is an obstacle to good performance appraisal, as it becomes extremely difficult to compare employees to each other. This leads to inequities in pay scales, problems with promotion decisions, and difficulties discerning which employees require training.

To minimize the possibility of this kind of bias, raters and ratees alike should make a formal effort to understand the rating scales and what each of the rating scores means in real terms. If necessary, relabel the rankings with descriptions of performance, rather than one-word descriptors. Instead of "poor," the form might read, "Occasionally misses deadlines." These descriptions should conform to the rating category.

The halo effect. This refers to the tendency to rate an employee high in one category if they have already scored highly in one or more of the other categories. The high score then tends to have a ripple effect, affecting the rater's judgment in other sections of the appraisal.

This effect frequently occurs in raters that do not understand the appraisal process. They assume that the appraisal categories overlap to some extent, and that an employee whom they judge to be excellent overall must, of necessity, score high in most categories. The problem with this feeling is that of *judgment*. Managers tend to make emotional judgments about their subordinates, and they sometimes carry these feelings over into the measurement portion of the appraisal. This is both unfair and inappropriate.

Another problem is the feeling that appraisal categories overlap to some extent. In reality, while an employee's behaviors may affect ratings in several categories, each category is usually designed to be independent. It is only in this way that measurements can have meaning.

To avoid the halo effect, raters must separate in their minds the acts of measurement and judgment. This is a basic rule of objective performance appraisal. They must then follow through by discussing the issues with the employee during the regular status meetings.

The horn effect.   The opposite of the halo effect, this is the tendency to rate an employee low in a category if they have scored low in one or more other categories. Comments above on the halo effect are appropriate here.

Most recent behavior.   This is the inclination to rate an employee based on his or her most recent behavior, rather than the entire appraisal period. Almost the reverse of the first impression, in this case the manager treats the most recent behaviors as the most important. This has the effect of weighting recent events more than those at the beginning of the review period.

Complete and accurate documentation alleviates this problem. As the end of the review period nears, the manager has a file of regular status reports and notes from status meetings. These will form the basis of the performance appraisal document, making it difficult for the manager to emphasize one portion of the review period over another.

Spillover effects.   Here, the rater lets past performance appraisal results bias the rating for the current review period.

Most companies include directions in their performance appraisal procedures that require the manager to review an employee's past appraisal. While this is useful in terms of understanding how far an employee has come, the previous appraisal supplies little or no data for current appraisal *measurements*. Ratings for the present review period should reflect employee behaviors from that period, not historical behaviors.

Recommendations for Raters

In this section we summarize our advice to raters from the previous section, especially in terms of the most common rater errors. We close by recommending specific training and education in addition to some tuning of appraisal forms and procedures.

Avoiding common rater errors

Errors of central tendency and compensation. This is the tendency of a rater to rate an employee as average. This is probably the most common rater error, and possibly the most serious. It allows raters to evade their responsibility to give the employee a fair and valid evaluation. A variant of this tendency is giving an employee a low score in one category to compensate for receiving a high score in another.

First, raters should draw a clear distinction between measurement and judgment (mentioned earlier). The rater's job is to judge each set of measurements *independently*. Measurements in other categories should have no bearing on judgments made for the current category. (If this seems illogical to raters, consider this: if measurements in one category seem to logically affect ratings in another, this fact must be reflected explicitly in the performance appraisal process. This means that the appraisal forms and procedure are flawed. Such a flaw should have been detected during job analysis. Thus, we conclude either that the appraisal procedure is invalid, or that the procedure correctly separates independent categories.)

To avoid possible problems, some companies use separate raters for each job category. This allows each rater to attain a certain level of expertise in rating employees in a particular category, and prevents cross-category averaging. Another technique would be for a rater to rate an entire set of employees in a single category, thus assuring consistency across employees in that category. This method requires that large numbers of employees be rated at approximately the same time, which may not be convenient or possible.

The first impression. Here, raters score an employee based on their first impression, ignoring behaviors or results occurring later in the appraisal period. This happens most often when an employee transfers to a new manager or project.

While it is important for employees to remember that first impressions are important, it is the responsibility of the manager to make objective measurements and judgments about their behavior. This type of error can be minimized if the employee and manager conform to the letter of the performance appraisal and status-reporting process.

The most important element here will be the record of employee behavior during the review period. This record (status reports and so forth) should be examined and evaluated regularly. The manager should give the employees feedback on their progress, so that the employees may then determine what type of first impression they have made. As this may have the tendency to bias the manager, both parties must document their views during this interval. Such documentation should serve to ease any tension and streamline the future appraisal meeting.

General bias. This is the tendency to rate all employees as lower or higher than average. "We only hire above-average employees" is a common motto. In this kind of corporate culture, managers tend to rate employees as if they were being compared to other professionals in similar industries, or those having the same job title in other company divisions. Employee ratings in such companies tend to range from *excellent* to *superior,* leading to a compression of the rating scale.

This compression is an obstacle to good performance appraisal, It is difficult to compare employees with one another, as everyone has almost the same rating. This leads to inequities in pay scales, problems with promotional decisions, and difficulties prescribing training. Since the purpose of performance appraisal is to assist management in making business decisions, raters should be properly informed about what the ratings actually mean. In other words, management is responsible for defining each rating level in terms of objective criteria.

Management should relabel all rankings such as *excellent* with descriptions of actual behaviors rather than one-word descriptors or numbers. Instead of *poor,* the appraisal form might read, "Sometimes misses deadlines." In this way, raters may judge employees against behaviorally defined criteria rather than a poorly defined numerical scale.

The halo and horn effect. This is the tendency to rate employees high (or low) in one category if they have already scored high (or low) in one or more other categories. These scores then tend to have a ripple effect, affecting the rater's judgment in other sections of the appraisal.

This effect frequently occurs in raters who do not understand the appraisal process. They assume that the appraisal categories overlap to some extent, and that an employee they judge to be excellent overall must, of necessity, score high in most categories. This is a clear blurring of measurement with judgment, and undermines the appraisal process.

Raters should understand that appraisal categories must, of necessity, be independent. If categories were found to overlap during the job analysis process, then the final appraisal instrument would reflect this. Since categories must be independent for proper measurement, they must be used in this way.

Most recent behavior.   This is the inclination to rate an employee based on his or her most recent behavior, rather than the entire appraisal period. This has the effect of weighting recent events more heavily than those at the beginning of the review period.

The difficulty here is that managers naturally concentrate on an employee's most recent behaviors. As employees learn their jobs and perform tasks more quickly and effectively, their performance improves. It is this current level of performance that many managers focus on in determining task assignments, eligibility for training, and suitability for promotion. Unfortunately, these managers equate the performance appraisal with a status report, a where-I-am-now summary of employee achievement. This is not the purpose of performance appraisal. (For more information on this topic, review the previous section on The Review Period.)

To alleviate this problem requires several things. First, managers (raters) need to be informed about the purpose and procedures of performance appraisal. This may take the form of a class on appraisal coupled with required reading of relevant company policies. Second, thorough documentation during the review period is necessary. Regular, complete documentation of employee behavior and status meetings will provide the manager with the perspective of the review *over a period of time.*

Last, managers must realize that rating an employee based on an entire review period will not make it more difficult to determine task assignments, eligibility for training, or suitability for promotion (mentioned above). On the contrary, a correct and complete performance appraisal will provide an accurate account of the employee's progress during the period. This rate of progress is at least as important as the employee's current status or level of achievement, as it provides an indicator of future performance and potential.

Spillover effects.   Here, the rater lets past performance appraisal results bias his or her rating for the current review period.

Most companies include directions in their performance appraisal procedures that require the manager to review an employee's previous performance appraisal. This policy may sometimes be helpful during the judgment process, but should be avoided while reviewing and analyzing measurements. There is the danger that the rater will be influenced by the past appraisal, and that this will color his or her judgment.

Perhaps the best advice is to avoid studying the prior appraisal until after the measurement and judgment processes are completed. This lets the manager complete an objective appraisal while still giving him or her an opportunity to compare reviews from two periods. Such a comparison may seem worthwhile at that time; however, since we recommend that the entire review period be managed against the prior appraisal, this may be of limited value.

Overcoming rater errors

It may have become apparent from previous comments that most of these rater errors can be avoided by proper documentation and regular meetings between rater and employee. Indeed, most problems in life seem to be those related to a lack of communication between people. Specifically, we recommend the following:

Training. Raters must receive proper training in their company's performance appraisal forms and procedures. This should include an explanation of all terms used on the forms, such as "poor" and "excellent." It should also involve the (potential) rater in practice sessions with trainers acting as employees. In this way, problems such as those described in the previous section can be anticipated and addressed.

Another suggestion would be to give potential raters examples of good (and bad) performance appraisals. This case study approach would permit raters to learn by example, rather than by trial and error.

In addition to training the rater, some kind of performance appraisal training should be made available to employees as well. This would consist of an overview of the company's commitment to objective appraisals, the ways the company uses appraisal information, and a description of the appraisal process. Employees should receive a copy of all relevant appraisal forms for their examination. Employees who take issue with portions of the form or process should have the opportunity to discuss their concerns with a representative from the personnel department. In some cases, this may lead to changes in the review process or forms.

Documentation. We have already mentioned the regular status report as forming the basis for appraisal measurements. This process can be assisted somewhat by asking employees to arrange their status reports in a fashion similar to that of the appraisal forms. This will make the manager's job easier, as the status report becomes more of a minireview document. Further, this format gets both the employee and the manager thinking in terms of performance appraisal, thus avoiding some miscommunications.

Communication.   Both rater and employee must communicate with each other in order for proper appraisal to take place. This rather simple statement overlooks the fact that many people are poor communicators. In general, most communication problems can be traced to one thing: an inability or unwillingness to *listen.*

Effective listening skills are beyond the scope of this book. Those interested can consult any one of the many books available on the subject. Such skills are relatively easy to acquire. Indeed, this may be one of the employee's first goals.

4

Business Uses
of Performance Appraisals

Making Employment Decisions

Making the decision to hire or fire someone is probably the most important thing a manager does. Although many companies have personnel departments that get involved in recruiting, new employee interviewing, disciplinary hearings, and terminations, it is what the manager does that has the greatest impact on the final decision. In this section we examine how performance appraisal systems assist managers in making these decisions.

Hire, fire, or transfer

Deciding to hire a new employee will probably cost the company several tens of thousands of dollars. This approximate figure includes some of the following:

- The new employee's salary, probably for several months. (It may take that long to find out if the employee will work out.)
- Any on-the-job training received.
- A proportion of the employee's benefits, including medical, dental, life insurance, and so forth.
- Administrative overhead, including office space, telephone support, and secretarial services.

Should the new employee be unable to perform his or her duties, there is another cost: the *opportunity cost*. This is the benefit forever lost because the company made a bad employment decision. Had they hired an employee who succeeded, several months of work would have been saved.

What procedures do companies follow to make sure that they hire the right employees? Performance appraisal is sometimes used in several capacities when making this decision. Standard appraisal forms and procedures, with some important modifications, can be used in the stages of hiring described below.

Preemployment screening. Some companies have found it practical to use a portion of their performance appraisal system to screen potential new-hires. Since these candidates will be expected to perform the job duties of existing employees, some companies use their current appraisal forms. This is not necessarily valid, as the candidates do not have the advantage of on-the-job experience with the company. Appraisal scores, rankings, or ratings cannot be compared with those of current employees, although the company may wish to establish an entirely new set of standards for this group.

When enhancing an appraisal system to screen potential employees, the first step is to list job categories and set minimum standards for each category. (This is part of job analysis, explained in Chap. 2.) Statistics about the current employee base can be used to estimate proper standards.

The company may now use the modified performance appraisal process for prescreening. Here is how it works. Candidates are interviewed in a structured fashion according to the appraisal form. Each category is used to facilitate a portion of the employment interview. Interviewers concentrate on determining whether the candidate meets the minimum criteria in each category. To determine this, many companies select specialists in the technical categories who execute *technical interviews*. These interviews are typically in-depth question and answer sessions that attempt to assess the exact level of the candidate's knowledge and skills in the subject category.

Each interview results in a score or rating that is entered on the appraisal form. At the end of the interviewing process, the decision-making process is a simple one. The following criteria are used to determine if the potential new-hire would be an acceptable employee:

- If the candidate scores below the minimum standard set in any one category, that candidate is unacceptable.

- If the candidate scores above the minimum standard set in each category, the candidate is acceptable.

New employee probation. New employees usually go through some kind of probationary period. During this period they are expected to meet certain standards and accomplish specific goals. Typical goals include the following:

- Getting acquainted with other employees
- Learning about the operations of their new department
- Learning about the functions of other departments with which they will interact
- Reading the systems development standards manual for the shop
- Attending training classes for any required high-level languages or software tools that they will be using
- Learning procedure for handling production program abends
- Studying documentation standards
- Learning about the first applications they will assist in designing, coding, and testing

Companies must ensure that they monitor the new employee's progress during the probation period, using a formal procedure. There are several reasons for this.

Feedback.   New employees require immediate feedback regarding their performance. They are usually a bit apprehensive about their new position, and are eager to make a good first impression. Management must understand this and give them direct feedback regarding their performance. This can be accomplished in several ways.

- *Weekly status meetings.*   These meetings can be informal, as long as the manager and employee cover the employee's behaviors during the preceding week. This session will take the form of a miniature performance review session.
- *On-the-job feedback.*   If possible, the manager should walk around and visit new employees on a daily basis. This allows one-on-one contact, which is sometimes considered the best way to learn. It also makes the new employees feel as if management cares about their performance.
- *Extended employee orientation.*   Using this method, the company organizes several new employee orientation sessions that span several weeks. During the probationary period, new-hires attend the sessions, which are run by specialists from the personnel department. New employees get the chance to learn about their new jobs in manageable pieces, while retaining the services of personnel to advise and counsel them on problems and company expectations.

Uncertainty.   Many new-hires are unsure of what is expected of them. Some are unaware of their precise job title, tasks, or responsibilities. Management should anticipate this situation and prepare complete documentation regarding job titles, responsibilities, tasks assigned, and goals for each employee.

Goal-setting. As part of new employee orientation, companies should teach new-hires about company performance appraisal forms and procedures. This is especially important for new employees, as their immediate goals are apt to be quite different from those of current employees. Basically, the new employee's main goal is to *survive.* This involves leaning policies and procedures, specific task assignments, and work responsibilities. These things usually form their preliminary goals.

At the end of the probationary period, the employee will sit down with his or her supervisor and jointly determine goals for the coming review period. Up to this point the employee has been under continual review. From this point on, should the employee be retained, he or she is expected to function at the same level expected of others in similar positions. Some appraisal systems, notably management by objectives (MBO), are suitable for adaptation for this purpose.

It is interesting to note that most companies that have an MBO program rarely use it for new employee orientation. As it is remarkably suitable for such a program, such a lack of understanding on the part of many companies is somewhat confusing.

Return on investment. In data processing, a manager may not find out about the true worth of a new employee until several months have passed. This is because most analytical and programming tasks take weeks or months to complete. As most DP managers measure project progress by tasks completed, it may not be until a new employee has failed to complete several tasks that his or her poor performance is noticed.

A data processing division expends quite a lot of money in recruiting, hiring, and training DP professionals.* With the costs of making an incorrect hiring decision so high, data processing divisions are strongly urged to monitor new employee progress closely.

Hiring errors. Sometimes mistakes are made, and the wrong person is hired. This can happen for several reasons. Sometimes management is desperate, and begins hiring warm bodies. At other times, management incorrectly estimates that a candidate can be trained for the position. Another possibility is that the candidate was an expert at being interviewed, and was able to fool interviewers. In

---

* Some personnel departments estimate that, for an average computer programmer, recruiting costs average $7000; hiring costs average $3000; and three months of employment, including training, salary, and benefits, costs roughly $30,000. Total: $40,000!

any event, the company must begin by first accepting that the problem exists. Once this has been determined, the company must gather the relevant documentation regarding the recruiting, interviewing, and hiring process. At this point, the manager should include documentation from the new-hire's recent appraisal meetings.

At this point, the company must make a decision: relative to the costs expended and the potential of the new employee, what is the best solution? This process should involve the employee, as well as specialists from the personnel department. All parties must agree that a problem exists, and that a joint resolution offers the best solution.

It is not the aim of this section to help management find ways to terminate employees—such runs counter to the book's purpose. Rather, we wish to emphasize that the performance appraisal process is important to *everyone*—not just to the employee and the manager.

The appraisal system used to manage employees during the probationary period must help the manager and employee develop goals specific to the new employee in his or her new job. As such, the system will probably be a subset of the complete appraisal system, concentrating on performance improvement. Subsystems that focus on career development, training needs, and compensation need not be addressed at this time.

As the new job will be different for each new employee, the appraisal form used must be flexible and somewhat general. It must cater to several different job descriptions and be able to be adapted to specific job responsibilities. Companies that have used such systems with success usually opt for a version of the management by objectives (MBO) system, or the behaviorally anchored rating scale (BARS) system.

Employee transfer. At this point, it is time for the employee to move either laterally or upward, perhaps even into a management position. How do performance appraisal systems assist managers in making these decisions? Before we discuss this, it is advisable to look at the things that the various appraisal systems measure: *results, objectives,* and *behaviors.* It will be a combination of these three crucial measures that determines whether an employee should be transferred.

Results-oriented appraisals. These types of appraisal procedures include *essay reviews,* some *checklists,* and *rankings.* The procedures concentrate on results, sometimes to the exclusion of everything else. They are typically used by companies that emphasize the results that employees produce; some examples would include retail firms, the military services, sales organizations, and manufacturing.

The outcome of such an appraisal process is usually an analysis of the results produced by the employee (measurement) accompanied by an appraisal of the worth of those results (judgment). Little is included as to *how* the employee achieved those results, or what they should have done differently to affect their appraisal.

While some companies feel that this is sufficient information to make personnel transfer decisions, in data processing it is not enough. Jobs in DP shops are broken into tasks, each of which requires certain knowledge and skills. Further, these tasks can usually be accomplished in several ways—some of the ways being acceptable, some not. In other words, *how* the employee codes the program or writes specifications is almost as important as *what* they accomplish.

To use a results-oriented appraisal system to make personnel transfer or promotional decisions in data processing, the manager must supplement the process with additional data. This data should include a schedule of tasks, responsibilities, and goals of the employee (objectives), their record of accomplishment (results), and what they did to achieve those goals (behaviors). Many companies accomplish this by supplementing their appraisal system with the following:

- An objective-setting system, including regular meetings with the manager
- A critical-incident reporting system, so that employee and manager can monitor and enhance employee behavior

The end result of such a hybrid is a comprehensive system for appraisal and transfer/promotion. Note that this ties in with the discussion in Chap. 4 regarding the various uses of appraisal systems for multiple purposes. Again, no one system is usable in all situations.

Objective-oriented appraisals. These types of appraisals include the management by objectives (MBO) appraisals. They concentrate on objective setting, and measure performance based upon objective accomplishment. Like the results-oriented approaches, MBO systems fasten on achievement or attainment of goals, rather than on how the employee attained them or what they did to attain them.

Using the MBO style review system, the manager and the employee meet at the beginning of the review period to set goals for the employee. These goals are to be achievable, measurable, realistic, and so forth. After the meeting(s) both participants have agreed on how the employee will be measured at the end of the period, and how judgment will take place. Little time is spent on how the employee is expected to accomplish the goals—this is either explicitly stated as a part of the goal, or implicitly assumed.

Examples of goals where the *how* is explicitly stated are the following:

- "Attain a 25 percent reduction in production program abends by creating complete test benches for each subsystem. Each test bench will contain test data that thoroughly tests each logic path in each program."

- "Decrease by 33 percent the amount of time it takes to produce program specifications. Do this by selecting and installing a CASE tool that uses data design diagrams and process specifications as input, and produces program specifications as output."

It is the implicit assumptions that give new employees the greatest problems. Such a belief system is often a part of the company's culture, and is often unwritten. Some examples might include dress codes, credos such as "the customer is always right," and codes of ethics and conduct. Without this information, employees may be achieving their goals without following the unwritten guidelines that management presumed would be followed.

What employees and their managers need is more information about this corporate culture. Many companies address this issue by formalizing their culture into a corporate *mission statement* that specifies what the company's rules of conduct will be in the marketplace. This data then becomes a part of the company's corporate strategic plans, and contributes to the development of operational strategies. Once these strategies are in place, upper management develops *corporate goals*. These goals now guide managers and employees in the goal-setting process.

By incorporating the unwritten rules of conduct into the corporate goals, the company has laid out the legitimate boundaries for divisional, managerial, and employee goals, along with guidelines for goal accomplishment. In this way, goals determined as a result of goal-setting should have guidelines for goal accomplishment baked in.

There is still one thing missing from this process: employee behaviors. Current management theory describes the importance of behaviors in this way:

There are only three things that performance appraisal can measure: *people,* what people *do,* or the *results* of what people do. Measuring *people* (abilities, traits, and so forth) is subjective and unreliable. Measuring the *results* of what people do is too little, too late—the results have happened before you can manage the process that created them. The only remaining measurable thing is what people *do* (behaviors). This is the best way, as behaviors are both *measurable* and *manageable.* *

Employee behaviors are manageable in the sense that management can affect employees' behavior, thus effecting changes in their

---

* For a more complete discussion of such measurements, see *Performance Appraisal Design Manual,* by Ferdinand Fournies (F. Fournies & Assoc, Inc., Bridgewater, N.J., 1983). ISBN 0-017472-09-8.

results. To improve their performance, employees must know what to *do* differently. It is not enough to be told to increase the frequency of something by 20 percent—they must know the set of acceptable behaviors for accomplishing such a goal.

Behavior management, then, must be integrated into any system for employee transfer or promotion. Management must be made aware of employee behaviors so that they can estimate an employee's potential performance in a different job.

Merging a set of behavior measurements into an MBO program, along with data on results accomplishment, is a common alternative of companies that already have an MBO program in place.

Behavior-oriented appraisals. These types of appraisals include behaviorally anchored rating scales (BARS), critical incident systems, and some kinds of checklists. In general, behavior-oriented systems are considered to be the most useful overall. (For more information on which types of appraisals function best in various circumstances, see Chap. 5.)

The major items missing from these systems are *objectives* and *results.* Behaviors are considered the only manageable employee attributes, and are the major factor in performance improvement programs. Still, in terms of the company's goals, if no employee ever accomplished anything, the company would soon be bankrupt!

When considering employees for transfer or promotion, management must take into account the employee's contribution to the company. An analytical position, for example, will involve dealing with users, and will require that the employee have experience in particular business subsystems. This translates into having a track record of achieving results based on goals and objectives.

To incorporate such information into a behavior-oriented appraisal system, many companies choose a modified MBO approach that summarizes an employee's past goals and accomplishments. This gets included as a part of the regular performance appraisal, thereby documenting results and achievements. This is usually deemed sufficient to make an informed decision regarding a transfer or promotion.

Since employee transfer/promotion decisions depend upon a combination of the above three measures, no one type of appraisal system is adequate. No single type of appraisal form or procedure gives the manager complete information so that they can make an informed decision. The only viable alternative is to combine several review mechanisms into a single hybrid system.

One popular way to handle employee promotions is to merge one or more specialized checklists into an MBO appraisal procedure. Using this technique the manager and the employee jointly set goals, just as in the normal MBO process. This is followed by a separate meeting where they separate those goals related to the employee's promotion potential. (This assumes that one of the employee's or manager's goals is to transfer or promote the employee.) Along with these goals, the manager will provide the employee with a checklist that will be used to rate that employee's suitability for promotion.

The advantage of this technique over a simple MBO method is that the checklist provides to management information that is lacking in the MBO approach regarding results and behaviors, without forcing management to redesign the appraisal system.

Performance Improvement

Behaviors determine performance

Performance improvement is sometimes considered by managers one of the most important reasons for using performance appraisals. (It is not surprising that employees consider compensation the number one reason for appraisals.) While using appraisals to determine fair compensation requires that the system produce an overall rating, appraisals for performance improvement need no such thing. In fact, ratings or scoring is unneeded. All of these considerations are covered in the following sections.

Acceptable behavior. Systems for performance improvement must describe several categories of employee behavior, with specific examples of acceptable and unacceptable behaviors. No attempt is made to score or rate these behaviors—they are either acceptable, or they are not. The reasoning is that management should be aware of which behaviors are acceptable and which are not. Acceptable behaviors are to be reinforced; unacceptable ones are to be punished or dealt with through a performance improvement process.

Many performance appraisal systems that include some measure of behavior (critical incident, BARS, and essay review) divide behaviors in this way, allowing management to measure employee performance in this fashion.

Grouping behaviors into categories. Usually behaviors are grouped into classes relating to specific job functions or categories. In this way, an employee and his or her manager can organize and plan ways for the employee to improve by category. Some categories, such as written communications, can be improved with training. Others, such as leadership, may require experience.

Handling unacceptable performance. Most companies have formal procedures for dealing with performance improvement. Many of these

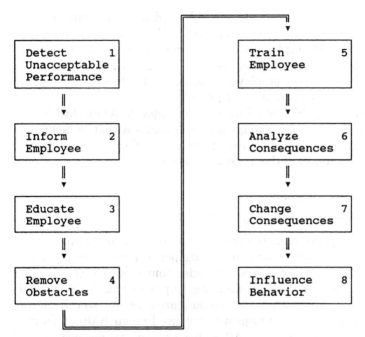

Figure 4.1   Performance problem analysis.

methods begin with an analysis of the perceived problem. Figure 4.1 shows a diagram of one company's analysis procedure. The following descriptions correspond to the numbered boxes in Fig. 4.1.

1. *Detect Unacceptable Performance.*   First, the supervisor must recognize that an employee is behaving in an unacceptable manner. This seems a simple step; however, too many managers concentrate on the results of the behavior, rather than the behavior itself.

   For example, a project leader may notice that a programmer is not completing his or her coding tasks on time. The unacceptable performance is *not* "coding tasks are late"—this is a result, not a behavior. The supervisor must investigate further to determine which behaviors are unacceptable, and which may be causing the result. Some incorrect possibilities include: insufficient knowledge of a programming language (this is an *obstacle,* not a behavior); producing inefficient, untested programs (a result); a sloppy work environment (a *symptom*—again, not a behavior).

   In this example, the supervisor must look for behaviors such as coming in to work late and/or leaving early; very slow typing speed; or working crossword puzzles during business hours.

2. *Inform Employee.*   Some managers feel that it is important to inform employees of bad behavior at the time it is observed. Others

reserve this for a regular meeting. In either case, the manager has the responsibility of informing the employee about the behavior. This is important for several reasons: performance improvement will not follow unless the employee is aware of the relationship between behaviors and performance; feedback is essential, because people are notoriously poor observers of their own behavior; and documentation of such a meeting is important in case of later transfer or termination.

3. *Educate Employee.* At this point, the manager has informed the employee about the unacceptable performance and proceeds to educate that employee about what acceptable performance is. The employee must be made aware of what is acceptable, so that he or she and the manager can develop an action plan to change the behavior. Employees must have a way of telling whether their behavior is acceptable, and may need methods of monitoring their performance.

4. *Remove Obstacles.* Sometimes behaviors are beyond the employee's control. These are called *obstacles.* A behavior such as "sitting at terminal doing nothing" may be caused by a very heavily loaded system, resulting in very slow response time. A behavior such as "not testing programs" may be because of a lack of proper test data, for which someone else is responsible. Other obstacles may cause the manager and employee to rethink the employee's objectives for the review period (for MBO-type appraisal systems).

5. *Train Employee.* In some cases it will be necessary to train the employee how to behave acceptably. A behavior such as "writes short and unreadable status reports" can be addressed by providing training for the employee in written communications. Another, such as "codes inefficient programs," may be solved by a course in intermediate programming skills.

6. *Analyze Consequences.* The manager must be careful to analyze the consequences to the employee of the acceptable and unacceptable behaviors. In general, acceptable behavior should be rewarded (if possible) and unacceptable behavior should be punished (if feasible or warranted). The manager should look for cases where positive consequences follow unacceptable behavior, or negative consequences follow acceptable behavior.

For example, consider a programming project with a programmer who is not performing well. The manager determines that the unacceptable behavior is "codes programs slowly." After following steps (1) through (5) above, the manager returns a week later to find the employee still coding programs slowly. Analysis then shows that the project leader had noticed that this programmer worked slowly, and therefore gave the more difficult coding assignments to others. In this case, positive consequences (easier programs to write) followed unacceptable behavior (slow coding)—as far as that programmer was concerned, if programmers didn't work very hard, they were given easy work!

7. *Change Consequences.* Should analysis show that the consequences of behaviors are inappropriate, the manager's responsibility is to change the consequences. In the example cited in step (6), the manager should change the consequences so that unacceptable behavior (coding slowly) is punished (extra work, transfer to lower-level job, termination, and so forth), and that acceptable behavior is rewarded (time off, challenging assignments, and so on). The manager must transform the situation to one that rewards the proper employee behaviors.

8. *Influence Behavior.* In many cases, steps (1) through (7) will be enough. If, however, unacceptable behavior persists, the manager must go through the process again. This time, the manager should verify that the acceptable behavior happens. This may require some kind of monitoring or measuring tool, a reporting mechanism, or other aid. It may be as simple as requiring employees to document the date and time of their acceptable behavior.

Should unacceptable behavior persist, the manager will be in a better position to investigate the situation, having followed this procedure.

Identifying and Rating Potential

Classical potential

Time-honored tradition treats *potential* as a set of traits such as *leadership, charisma, responsible, successful,* and the like. While such trait-based leanings are usually avoided by good performance appraisal systems, some managers use them as a basis for making decisions regarding an employee's suitability for promotion.

The problem of subjectivity

Judging which employees are eligible for promotion is too often a subjective decision. Managers are usually confronted with questions and statements such as the following:

- How near is this employee to the limit of his or her personal efficiency?
- Describe the type of work this person desires in the short and long range.
- Is this employee ready for promotion at this time?

- What position(s) could this employee be promoted to now and in the future?

- List the employees' personal and professional strengths on which they can build or achieve their future aspirations.

With guidelines such as these, it is no wonder that managers have a hard time justifying their recommendations.

Available systems

Forms and procedures to help the manager in this area should concentrate on defining the minimum standards and performance criteria for high-level jobs. This should be followed by a complete and objective job analysis of these high-level jobs. The goal here is to develop a complete, behavior-based appraisal system of these positions.

With this new appraisal system now in place, managers can judge potential by appraising their employees as if they already held those higher positions. Some discussion of the process and the results with the employee is necessary, as career planning must be factored into the equation.

Compensation Administration

Employees and managers alike consider this the major reason for the existence of performance appraisal systems. In this section we take a brief look at how such systems work.

How the system works

To determine how much to pay an employee, the system must return a single, numerical measurement. This measurement will be factored into a compensation system to determine the employee's pay. The measurement must be accurate, and managers must be able to compare measurements across people.

As with preemployment screening, few systems are able to generate a single overall performance measure that fairly assesses an employee's total performance. Further, some employees have goals that differ from those of others, making it difficult to compare appraisal ratings across employees.

Fair compensation demands an objective method of determining overall performance. Most appraisal systems are unable to generate a single, objective, preferably numeric, overall performance rating. As with preemployment screening, few systems are able to generate a single overall performance measure that fairly assesses an employee's total performance.

Another consideration involves comparing ratings across employees. Once employees are rated, management usually tends to reward those with higher ratings with more compensation. This, however, leads to problems when comparing two employees with dissimilar jobs who received the same rating. Who should get a raise, and how much? The one with the tougher job? What does *tougher* mean?

Forced-ranking systems attempt to resolve this problem by forcing managers to rank the total employee base from lowest performer to highest. Once this almost-impossible task is finished, management can reward high achievers with high-percentage raises and low achievers with lesser raises. The problems with this method are:

- It is extremely difficult to compare and rank employees with different jobs.

- Managers will be unable to determine if the highest-ranking employees are performing *barely* higher or *much* higher than the next-lowest ones.

- Once a raise is awarded to an employee, it stays as a part of his or her salary for the next appraisal period.

This last point is an important one. Being rewarded a year later for high performance is not soon enough—it also is not sufficient to motivate high performance for the next appraisal period. Rewards should follow the behavior meriting them as soon as possible after the behavior. This is basic knowledge about human motivation.

Career Planning and Development

A model for career path planning

The practice of helping a systems professional progress through the ranks of an organization is known as *career path planning*. The most valuable resource in a business enterprise is its people. And many systems people are highly motivated to progress to higher levels—or at least to different positions. A well-structured and well-publicized career path planning system can be a strong motivator of the systems staff. In addition, it can identify and help prepare people for vacancies before they arise, thus ensuring that promotions are awarded to deserving and qualified current staff rather than to outsiders. This is sometimes called *promotion from within.*

Managers who do not identify and prepare subordinates to replace themselves are seriously limiting their own opportunities for promotion. On the other hand (there is always another hand), a person identified, qualified, and eager for a promotion can become intensely frustrated if it does not come. There is the risk of that employee seeking other pastures. By all means, an organization should err on the side of staff development. An organization that does not prepare anyone for advancement and must always recruit outside may become moribund. All those with career aspirations will soon leave.

Career path planning and performance appraisal are both characteristics of an MIS shop that is at the leading edge of human resource management. What, then, are some of the components of career path planning?

- Personnel planning

- Turnover projections

- Internal sources and destinations

- Vacancy postings

- Job descriptions

- Regular career path planning meetings

Personnel planning. This should be performed at least annually and updated frequently. It is a plan, by job category and by month, of how many people of each skill level will be required to fulfill system development and maintenance commitments. The 12-month period should be planned in some detail. The next year or two should be shown roughly, by quarter instead of by month. Proceeding to the next level of detail, specific names, if known, can be penciled in to replace job category.

Turnover projections. This is an important adjunct to the personnel plan. An attempt is made to predict the number of resignations, again by job category, for the same time periods as the personnel plan. Perhaps historical data is available for a specific company, or for the industry, or the geographic region. If not, a guess might be better than nothing. Systems turnover tends to average between 15 and 20 percent annually. In a booming economy it can reach 30 percent as companies vie with each other for the available talent pool. In lean times people are less willing to move and opportunities are scarce, so turnover can shrink to 10 percent.

Turnover also varies by job category, with programmers running higher than analysts, and project managers turning over rarely. Failing any hard data, projections might look like this:

Programmers	30%
Systems Programmers	25%
Analysts	15%
Project Managers	5%

Armed with personnel requirements and anticipated turnover, the organization is now in a position to estimate *personnel needs*. These needs may be met through hiring, promotion, or use of contractors. Ideally, most hiring should be at the trainee level. A thorough entry-level training program should graduate a group of junior programmers periodically, creating upward pressure in the organization. Contracting should not be encouraged in any shop that is interested in developing internal personnel resources.

Internal sources and destinations. This entry-level training program may be used for inexperienced new-hires and also for transfers from another department. This can be an excellent source of programmer trainees. These people are known to the company and have a good track record, broad industry knowledge, but no data processing skills. DP Operations or a line-of-business department are good places to look for interested trainees. Sometimes a business specialist can be transferred in as a business analyst with no expectation that he or she will follow a technical path.

By the same logic, there can be some outflow from systems to a user area. During a systems development project, a systems analyst will learn a great deal about that part of the business and may qualify for a senior position there. This flow in and out of the systems organization is essential to the good health of the company.

Vacancy postings. These are a means to communicate available or expected position opportunities to interested staff members. An open enterprise, like an open society, is based on the free flow of information. A senior analyst who applies for a project manager vacancy can accept being told they he or she is less qualified than another candidate. But one who watches a coveted promotion from the sidelines may not overcome his or her disappointment.

Job posting, however, forces management to respond to all applicants who come forward. And posting may lead to loss of a key person from a critical project. On the other hand, awarding jobs to handpicked candidates will cost the organization more in the long run than will openly publishing vacancies.

Job descriptions. The prospect of writing job descriptions is likely to cause a red-blooded analyst's eyes to glaze over. However, in an organization contemplating a career path planning program, job descriptions are an important, if not quite essential, factor. How can staff members aspire to jobs if they cannot understand what they require?

Many shrewd managers are disdainful of job descriptions. H. Ross Perot, founder of Electronic Data Systems (EDS), believes that they often get in the way of accomplishing a mission. The story is told of the second baseman whose job description gave him responsibility for a certain piece of the territory between first base and shortstop. If a line drive went a little farther east or west, he would simply wave at it as it passed by. But business, especially big business, cannot allow people to wander all over the field chasing every ball in sight.

Job descriptions come in many varieties. Those written too specifically soon grow out of date as technology changes. But if they are sufficiently general to ensure long life, they may not say enough about what an incumbent must do currently. The proper level of detail is similar to the right amount of salt in the soup: just enough.

However, there is more to a job description than a simple narrative of the duties. For effective use in career path planning there should be:

- Salary range information
- Skill requirements
- Education and training desired
- Preferred experience
- Related positions

Job descriptions should be a matter of public record, kept where they are easily accessible by all staff members.

Regular career path planning meetings. Career path planning is an ongoing activity, but it can be focused in a regular meeting. Such meetings should be scheduled for the entire professional systems staff prior to developing the departmental budget. A key deliverable from this meeting is an annual training plan for each staff member. A copy of this plan for all employees then flows to the training administrative area, where it is consolidated and becomes the source for the annual MIS training budget.

The meeting is scheduled a week in advance so both employee and supervisor can give some thought to it. The training manager may be invited to the meeting to act as a resource. Documents brought to the meeting might include:

- The project plan for the employee
- The employee's training history
- Training course description information

The incumbents should have in mind their own goals (technical, career, and personal), and the supervisor should have an idea of possible career moves for each staff member.

During the meeting the staff members will voice their goals and the supervisor will suggest his or her own thoughts on what career moves might be appropriate for them. The organization's career ladder and job descriptions may be consulted. Both supervisor and employee will decide what kind of training experiences are necessary to pursue the stated goals. The course descriptions and the advice of the training administrator will be considered. And the time and cost guidelines must be kept in mind.

Conventional wisdom is that maintenance programmers wish to become development programmers; however, many maintenance programmers are excited by the opportunity to fight fires, to work on crises, and to see immediate results from their efforts. Development people could work for many months, even years, without gaining a sense of completion. What if Beethoven struck the keys but didn't hear the chord until Fall?

Frequently it is noted that computer operations personnel aspire to become programmer trainees. There are many success stories of this type. But in one financial organization it was a one-way street: once having studied programming, the audit rules prevented the employee from moving back to operations. There was held to be too much risk in a computer operator who had access to production files and could also write or modify programs. This requirement made the promotion a little too risky for some people.

The outcome of the career path planning discussion should be a written plan for training courses and approximate time frames for the coming year. And the more important result is the knowledge that management listens and cares about employee goals and aspirations even if they can't be acted on immediately.

Training

Now all the key components of career path planning are in place. The linkage between performance appraisal and career path planning is found in a structured training program. *Structured* is a fashionable word. Programs are structured, systems design is structured, and training ought to be structured also. The alternative is ad hoc training, with no plan in place. Training is conducted as needed—inefficiently, expensively, and with marginal results. This approach is similar to patching code, which is disdained by all unfortunate enough to have experienced it.

Providing a structured training program implies a process with certain forms and procedures in place. Adhering to the following procedures will lead to a training program that is well-planned, budgeted, administered, measured, and reported.

Course descriptions should be prepared in a standard format for all training approved by the organization. Such a description might include:

- Course name
- Duration
- Description
- Objectives
- Source
- Location
- Cost

Several training experiences might be included on a given topic. For example, there may be a two-day project management course for team members and a four-day course for team leaders. There might be a self-study and a classroom course in rapid reading. A debugging course might be available with and without a workshop. Thus, a rich variety of training would be made known to the systems management and staff. Course descriptions should be easily accessible, perhaps in a loose-leaf binder with the job descriptions.

Course evaluations should be collected and filed for the inspection of prospective students. Such evaluations are also the basis for continuing, modifying, or dropping certain courses.

Budgeting rules of thumb.   Management should decide upon guidelines for a training budget. In terms of time, many organizations set as a target an average of 5 percent of each professional staff member's time invested in training. This comes to about 2½ weeks in a 50-week year. Stated in terms of dollars, a good rule of thumb is that training expenses should approximate 2 percent of the fully burdened data processing salary budget. Then, a medium-sized shop with 100 MIS professionals might have a $5 million salary budget; the training budget could be $100,000. This might buy 500 days of training, enough for a week for each person. This is short of the 5 percent target, but group training can often be bought at a discount, self-study is less expensive, and cross-training by staff members is free.

Another consideration is the size of the MIS training group. Experience suggests one training administrator for each 100 people in the target audience. Thus in a 50-person shop it might be a half-time job. In a larger shop it is scaled up accordingly.

These are, of course, rules of thumb that will vary from company to company. Nevertheless it is useful to have some targets to shoot for.

Planning organizational training. Armed with 90 training plans (10 people couldn't get around to it), the training administrator constructs a spreadsheet, begins to see if there are clusters of requirements, and seeks vendor bids. Some training budget should be reserved for unexpected needs. The training administrator must stay in close touch with project managers to confirm that plans are still valid. Shortly before a class is to take place, the administrator will send a notice to the student and his or her supervisor.

Administering the training program. At this point, several alternatives become available. Outside instructors are sometimes available from professional training companies, and may be used as supplemental staff. Computer-based training (CBT) is another possibility. Whatever option is chosen, the training coordinator is responsible for organizing, scheduling, and monitoring the training function.

Measuring results. As stated below, it is not enough that *training* take place—*learning* must take place as well. Sadly, measuring the amount of learning a student acquires in a class is difficult. One possible method—testing—is discussed below.

Student makeup

Data processing trainers sometimes face a group of students who have a wide diversity of experience or backgrounds. Some students may even have some knowledge of the course materials, either from reading, prior training, or practical use. How can a company maximize its investment in training in this case? In other words, how do you prevent one half of the class from being bored, and the other half from being hopelessly lost?

Prevention: the best medicine. Clearly, this situation should be avoided if at all possible. One possibility is to create *self-assessment tests* for the subjects covered in the course. Such tests usually consist of multiple-choice questions that probe the student's basic and intermediate knowledge. A high score would indicate that the student may not profit from the course—a low score would signify the opposite.

Such tests are relatively easy to develop. Many standard texts on data processing include questions and exercises that can be adapted for this purpose. Information systems management can then use the pre-tests prior to class attendance to determine the actual staff training needs.

Next: pre-tests, post-tests. A logical next step would then be to greatly expand the self-assessment materials for each course into *pre-tests* and *post-tests.* These would be made available to students prior to the course, and at the end of the course to measure what the students have gained. As one instructor once remarked: "The trainer knows that training has taken place—only the students know if learning has taken place."

Not only do such tests measure initial experience levels and knowledge gained, they provide the student with a preview of the course. Questions should be organized by subject in the order the materials are presented in the course, either chronologically or in increasing order of difficulty. A comparison of the pre- and post-tests' results by the students will give them confirmation of how far they have come, and how much they have learned.

One last important comment should be made about pre-tests: the results will give the trainer a factual basis for determining the range of expertise of the students. If the tests can be implemented and scored on-line, so much the better.

If it happens: what doesn't work. Faced with a wide range of student expertise in the course materials, what is the trainer to do? There are a few logical-sounding alternatives that just don't work in practice. Let's review a few of these first. For simplicity in the following discussions we have split students into two categories: those with basic knowledge (Beginners) and those with a great deal of expertise (Experts).

Multilevel workshops. Many trainers solve the diversity problem by creating different levels of workshops, one for each level of student. The idea here is to present Beginners and Experts with challenges appropriate to their experience levels. This solution seems to be a common one, partly because it is relatively inexpensive and easy to implement.

Regrettably, this solution suffers from some basic flaws. Multiple workshops require additional overhead in terms of larger workbooks and class materials, more DASD usage for workshop data, and solutions for each workshop. In addition, the trainer must sometimes review the workshop results with the class. This, then, takes additional class time.

Last, advanced workshops require a highly skilled instructor. (Imagine telling an Expert student that you can't help him or her with the workshop.) It is sad but true that many trainers are not thoroughly enough versed in the course materials to teach it at an advanced level. This is usually not a problem for many basic data processing classes; however, the worst nightmare of many trainers is having a student who knows more than they do!

Student pairing. Some trainers solve the diversity problem by pairing Experts with Beginners. The idea seems to be that the Experts will assist and teach the Beginners, sometimes being able to answer questions that would have required the trainer. While this may sometimes work, in practice it is a bad idea.

Many Expert students, when paired with Beginners, have a tendency to "take over." They are easily frustrated with a Beginner's slow typing, and take control of the keyboard. This causes some problems. First, it hinders the Beginner's acquisition of important learning experiences (keying that reinforces a lecture, learning by making mistakes, and so forth). Second, the Expert may cover ground much too quickly for the Beginner. The Beginner then tends to learn the Expert's shortcuts, rather than the basics of the course.

Another consideration is that Expert students are not necessarily good teachers. While their motives may be good, they sometimes create more work for the trainer. Indeed, the trainer may not know exactly what Beginners are learning until it is too late!

Finally, while it is extremely helpful to have an Expert student who can assist other students in the class, one must ask whether this is the best use of the Expert's time. After all, the Expert is a student too, and deserves his or her "money's worth." Instead of being the trainer's assistant, the Expert might be better off attending a more advanced class (or even going back to work!).

If it happens: what does work.   Here are some recommended alternatives.

Computer-Based Training (CBT).   This is the perfect solution for the student diversity problem. Indeed, one of the major advantages of CBT is that students start at their current level and work at their own pace. Trainer interaction occurs during some stages of CBT. One common example is a lecture period followed by workshop materials that are in CBT format. Another example would be a classroom with CBT terminals where the instructor is available to answer students' questions.

The luxury of CBT is that it requires an expert course developer, proficient in CBT techniques. This will be someone who can address the needs of a variety of students, as the CBT courseware must allow use by Beginners and Experts alike. The courseware must be updated as new techniques and information emerge. Further, using CBT courseware requires equipment which may be expensive.

Interactive Video Instruction (IVI).   IVI is a major improvement over CBT in its use of cutting-edge technology to heighten student involvement in training. Rather than displaying just text or simple graphics on the screen, IVI combines visual images from a laser disk player with PC-generated text and allows students to control their own progress. This student control may be through a variety of input devices:

- Keyboard
- Mouse
- Light pen
- Touch-sensitive screen

The student may interrupt their course at any time. A panel is presented that asks what he or she would like to do at this point. Options might include:

- Replay this segment.
- Present a quiz on this material.
- Branch to a previous segment for review.
- Skip to the next segment.
- Show the overall course structure.
- Examine a glossary.
- Pause for a break.

The program that controls each course is loaded into the PC from a hard or floppy disk. Upon startup, the program calls for the appropriate optical disk to be mounted in the connected laser disk player. (The PC must contain a proprietary controller board.) Then the program can call for a segment of video or display text to interact with the student through any of the devices mentioned above. Text can be overlaid on visual images.

Interactive video has proven to be an attention-grabbing vehicle for training. An imaginative course designer may anticipate wrong answers and provide appropriate responses. Courseware is expensive to develop and customize, although changes to text are not difficult. Thus, stable information may be committed to visual images while volatile data (such as prices and expected release dates) can be in text.

Other limitations should be noted:

- Use of sophisticated technology for training may be daunting to some students.
- As with any visual medium, IVI works best on material that has a strong visual impact.
- There can be no free-form interaction with the trainer although some installations offer an expert to contact.

Interactive Video Instruction offers a strong alternative to classroom or computer-based training.

Two Classes.   If feasible, this is the best alternative. Beginners and Experts attend the class appropriate for their experience level. This alternative is, however, extremely resource-intensive—two classrooms, two instructors, two sets of class materials, and so forth. Still, in terms of the quality of the students' education, it gives the greatest payback.

The A-B-C Methodology.   This relatively new training methodology requires an experienced instructor and special course materials. It is described next.

The A-B-C course.   Each major course topic is divided into three sections. Section A consists of vocabulary and basic concepts. Section B includes intermediate concepts and practical applications. Section C contains advanced concepts.

Each workshop is similarly split into three levels. Level 1 includes workshop basics such as data and JCL definition, initialization of default options, program boilerplating, and so forth. Level 2 is the meat of the workshop, where most of the work is done. Typically it will include several tasks for the student: some required, some optional, and some "extra credit." Level 3 contains advanced materials such as performance and optimization considerations, software tool usage, interconnection with other workshops, or cooperation with other users in a joint project. The class progresses as follows (see Fig. 4.2).

In practice, the trainer presents sections A, B, and C of the course, in that order. Beginners attend lectures A and B; during lecture C, the beginners complete workshop level 1 and, if they have time, level 2. Meanwhile, the advanced students skip lecture A; instead, they prepare for workshop level 3. This may consist of creating test data, completing program as JCL segments, examining related tools or software packages, or even collaborating with other advanced students. After attending lectures B and C, advanced students do workshop 2 and, if they have time, workshop 3.

The above three steps are then repeated for the remaining course topics.

Minutes	Lecture Topic (Instructor)	Beginning Students	Intermediate Students	Advanced Students
:15	Vocabulary Basic concepts	Attend lecture	Attend lecture	Begin workshop 3
:35	Intermediate concepts Practical applications	Attend lecture	Attend lecture	Attend lecture
:40	Advanced concepts	Complete workshop 1	Optional workshop 1	Complete workshop 2
:45	(Workshop time)	Attempt workshop 2	Complete workshop 2	Complete workshop 3

Figure 4.2   The A-B-C methodology.

Advantages of the method. The A-B-C course methodology allows the trainer to customize the courseware to the student population. Should the students all be beginners, the trainer presents sections A and B of each topic, along with workshop levels 1 and 2. For a class of experts, the trainer presents lecture sections B and C, and assigns workshop levels 2 and 3. For a mixed class, the procedure is as outlined above.

Summary. Using A-B-C provides a company with a great deal of flexibility and leverage for its training curriculum. The training presented is customized for the audience, thus maximizing the company's return on its training investment.

Picking the method that works for your environment involves making some tough decisions. To maximize the student's learning experiences try either the A-B-C methodology or CBT. If you are strapped for resources, split the students into two classes, or try student pairing. In all these cases, get the greatest benefit you can from your training dollar by using pre-tests to determine the level of student ability.

Employee testing

Earlier, reference was made to promoting computer operations personnel to programmer trainee positions. This is an excellent source of new programmers, because operators have some knowledge of data processing, and their track record is known. Other good sources of trainee programmers might be clerical people from user departments, particularly if they have been involved in a system conversion. As before, they have knowledge of the organization and they are a known quantity. A third source is recruits from outside the company. These may be university graduates or those having completed a community college or even a trade school curriculum. Hiring requirements are dependent on company policy.

But whatever the source of candidates for programmer trainee positions, how can we tell who is qualified for this demanding position? Perhaps one person in five taken at random could achieve success as a programmer. Over the years many types of aptitude tests have been promoted as being able to predict programming ability. Among the first was IBM's Programmer Aptitude Test (PAT). As it became more widely known, it was replaced by the Revised Programmer Aptitude Test (RPAT), then by the Aptitude Test for Programming Personnel (ATPP). In addition, there have been the Wolfe test, developed by Dr. Jack Wolfe, and the Berger test. It has been suggested that musical ability is closely related to ability to master the order and logic of programming. The Seashore (named after the developer) has been studied as a possible PAT. Results of the use of these tests has been mixed, because the problems are difficult.

After all, we cannot test for programming *ability* unless the candidate has been trained—and perhaps not even then! So the IBM tests attempt to infer aptitude by evaluating reasoning ability. They present number series (1, 3, 5, 7, ?) of increasing difficulty, spatial relationship exercises (a triangle is darkened and inverted, and compared to an ellipse dealt with similarly), and logic problems (if a dog and a half can dig a hole and a half in a day and a half, how long would it take . . . ?). Such questions probably measure abstract reasoning ability, and may measure intelligence—but they do not investigate language skills or tolerance of frustration. Perhaps the best that can be said of such testing is that if a candidate does not do well he or she will probably not be a good programmer, but if he or she *does* achieve a high score we still don't know.

And another, more serious, challenge to aptitude tests emerged: their potential to discriminate on a basis other than job skills. The Equal Employment Opportunity Commission required employers using aptitude testing to prove that they were nondiscriminatory to minority groups. And, in fact, each company had to validate the test in its own environment. A blanket endorsement would not suffice.

The challenges to such validation are formidable. Briefly stated, it would be necessary to find statistically sound samples of majority groups and of minority groups, test them, and hide the results. All participants would be hired and trained. Their on-the-job performance would be tracked (which could take years), then a determination would be made as to whether the test(s) predicted the observed results. How many organizations have the resources and patience to conduct such a study? Many companies discontinued using aptitude tests instead.

5

Forms and Procedures: Advantages and Disadvantages

It is difficult to appraise the work of any professional. For example, how can a surgeon's work be reviewed, short of another capable practitioner peering into the surgical cavity?

In this chapter we review the various types of performance appraisal forms used in businesses worldwide. They fall into the following general categories:

- Checklists
- Critical incidents
- Essay reviews
- Management by objectives (MBO)
- Ranking systems
- Rating scales

Appraisal forms and procedures in each of these categories have their own special strong and weak points. We discuss these with a mind to improving their usefulness for appraising data processing personnel. The categories we will consider are the following, which were discussed in Chap. 4.

- Making employment decisions (hire, fire, transfer)
- Performance improvement
- Assigning work duties
- Identifying and rating potential

- Compensation administration
- Identifying training needs
- Career planning and development

Checklists

Simple checklists

Simple checklists (see Fig. 5.1) were probably among the earliest forms used for performance appraisal. Such checklists contained many statements or attributes that described possible employee behaviors or traits. It was the rater's job to check the appropriate items for each employee. The items on the checklist usually correspond to points on a scale from *poor* to *superior*. (So that the appraisals are objective, the ratings are usually unknown to the rater.)

As can be seen from the sample in Fig. 5.1, the simple checklist seems easy to use. Regrettably, this is one of its weak points, because many managers tend to postpone thinking about employee perfor-

Evaluation of Manager's Performance Appraisal Interview

To be filled out by the Employee.

Please rate your manager on the way they conduct performance appraisal interviews. Use the following scale:

1	Always
2	Often
3	Occasionally
4	Seldom
5	Never

1 2 3 4 5

☐☐☐☐☐ 1. Effectively used information about the subordinate in the discussion.
☐☐☐☐☐ 2. Skillfully guided the discussion through the problem areas.
☐☐☐☐☐ 3. Maintained control over the interview.
☐☐☐☐☐ 4. Appeared to be prepared for the interview.
☐☐☐☐☐ 5. Let the subordinate control the interview.
☐☐☐☐☐ 6. Adhered to a discussion about the subordinate's problems.
☐☐☐☐☐ 7. Seemed concerned about the subordinate's perspective of the problems.
☐☐☐☐☐ 8. Probed deeply into sensitive areas in order to gain sufficient knowledge.
☐☐☐☐☐ 9. Made the subordinate feel comfortable during discussions of sensitive topics.
☐☐☐☐☐ 10. Projected sincerity during the interview.
☐☐☐☐☐ 11. Maintained the appropriate climate for an appraisal interview.
☐☐☐☐☐ 12. Displayed insensitivity to the subordinate's problems.
☐☐☐☐☐ 13. Displayed an organized approach to the interview.
☐☐☐☐☐ 14. Asked the appropriate questions.
☐☐☐☐☐ 15. Failed to follow up with questions when they appeared to be necessary.
☐☐☐☐☐ 16. Asked general questions about the subordinate's problems.

. . .

Figure 5.1 Simple checklist.

mance appraisal until the last minute because of this. The net result is that the manager spends perhaps five minutes filling out the appraisal form immediately prior to the annual review meeting with the employee. The meeting then quickly degenerates into a shouting match wherein the employee and manager disagree about the manager's choices, their importance, their accuracy, and so forth.

Giving performance measurement and judgment this short shrift is unfair to the employee. Companies using the simple checklist as their appraisal system of choice should inform and train managers in its correct use. One suggestion: if the checklist must be used, have the manager use it monthly, or weekly, accumulating the completed checklists for the duration of the review period. At the end of the period, make the entire set of checklists comprise the entirety of the employee's appraisal. In this way any disagreements about forms, procedures, or ratings can be ironed out between the employee and his or her manager at an early date. Further, as the months pass by, the employee becomes more and more aware of how his or her performance will be measured. The employee may be inclined to perform better because of this.

The simple checklist is best used for jobs that are highly *determinate;* that is, jobs with predefined tasks where the employee has limited autonomy. Such jobs tend to have extremely detailed job descriptions, and employees are well aware of exactly what is expected of them. Some such jobs include officers in military services, assembly-line workers, airline pilots, accountants, and sales clerks.

The usefulness of simple checklists

Making employment decisions.   Poor. The simple checklist doesn't contain enough information about the employee's knowledge or skills. This makes it unusable for making hiring decisions. It may be acceptable as a mechanism for determining where to transfer an employee, but is usually poorly designed and too subjective to use as a basis for termination.

Performance improvement.   Good. The simple checklist specifies actual behaviors, although the employee and manager must know which behaviors are deemed *acceptable* so that the employee can improve his or her performance.

Assigning work duties.   Acceptable. The checklist concentrates on behaviors specific to a particular job. To use the results to decide which workers are assigned which tasks assumes that behaviors across the tasks are comparable.

Identifying and rating potential.   Poor. While some jobs can be described in terms of employee behaviors, others such as computer programming and systems analysis depend more on education and skills. Checklists provide management little feedback about an employee's potential.

Compensation administration.   Inadequate. The checklist provides no ratings, simply *acceptable* or *unacceptable* for behaviors. This may be enough for companies having compensation schemes that reward acceptable employees equally (i.e., the same raise). Other companies prefer some kind of sliding scale. Checklist results cannot easily be converted to a single, numerical rating.

Identifying training needs.   Acceptable. In terms of what training employees will require, most companies use the job description as the foundation. This will define the basic training needs for the job. Beyond that, the checklist can provide specific instances of unacceptable employee behavior that can be improved through training. However, in some cases this will not be enough.

Career planning and development.   Poor. The checklist provides little feedback to the employee as to his or her level of accomplishment. In addition, management requires a measure of the employee's stage of development that the checklist cannot provide.

Forced-choice checklist

There are several enhanced versions of the simple checklist. The *forced-choice* checklist (see Fig. 5.2) groups the checklist items into categories, usually three to five per category. The rater is then asked to identify the item in each category which is *most* descriptive of the employee's behavior. Sometimes the rater must, in addition, identify which item is the *least* descriptive of the employee's behavior. Upon completion, the items which were chosen as *most* descriptive are collected and scored as a group. Similar treatment is given to the *least* descriptive items.

The forced-choice system was developed during World War II for rating army officers, and is the most sophisticated of the systems described. Groups of several comments or phrases are provided, some of the statements being favorable and some unfavorable. The rater is to select from within each group the one comment that is most appropriate for the ratee and the one comment that is least appropriate. In checking one of the favorable items the supervisor will be giving credit to the ratee, but in checking another seemingly favorable item the supervisor will be giving no credit at all.

An example of one such group in the Army Officer's Proficiency Report is as follows:

a. Gives clear and concise directions

b. Is very exacting in all details

Management Appraisal Checklist

In each category of five statements, choose the <u>one most descriptive</u> and the <u>one least descriptive</u> of the manager being appraised.

Most   Least
Descriptive Descriptive

Most Descriptive	Least Descriptive	
❑	❑	Reviews work of subordinates and provides assistance as needed.
❑	❑	Follows up on all delegated assignments to ensure conformance with operating procedures.
❑	❑	Requests employee opinions and uses them when conditions permit.
❑	❑	Meets deadlines on work assignments.
❑	❑	Praises those whose workplace behavior has earned recognition.

. . .

Figure 5.2   Forced-choice checklist.

c. Fails to support fellow officers

d. Oversteps their authority

When the supervisor has completed any number of blocks of forced-choice statements, he or she has no idea of whether the officer has been favorably rated or not. The system tries to minimize the human error in rating, but the supervisor has no control in rewarding his or her ratee. The standards are preset and unknown to the supervisor. This is in contrast to the simple checklist, which is subject to bias but gives the supervisor complete control over the rating.

The usefulness of the forced-choice checklist

Making employment decisions.   The checklist provides little information to management regarding nonemployees. Management requires information such as level of education, results accomplished, and specific systems expertise from potential new-hires. Checklists furnish enough information to management on how employees will behave in other positions, and so are adequate for transfer decisions. The checklist does not give sufficient information to allow management to make objective termination decisions. While evidence of what management considers poor performance is certainly required, management must also supply documentation that the checklist is an objective measure of the job requirements. This must be supplemented by other means.

Performance improvement. Acceptable. Like the simple checklist, the forced-choice checklist provides information about employee behaviors, both good and bad. This can be used as a guide for behavior improvement, although the checklist alone provides no information about *how* to improve.

Assigning work duties. Acceptable. Such a checklist forces a manager to consider his or her employees in terms of their acceptable behaviors. This information is usually sufficient for the manager to assign employees to tasks that fit their abilities.

Identifying and rating potential. Acceptable. This type of checklist compels the manager or supervisor to select behaviors that most correctly describe the employee. This information is sometimes enough to identify how an employee will perform in another position if it is supplemented with a set of standards for each position.

Compensation administration. Poor. Again, like the simple checklist, it is difficult to create a single, numerical rating using a forced-choice checklist.

Identifying training needs. Acceptable. Assuming that the manager is aware of which behaviors are improper, the checklist helps the manager specify which employees require training in certain job-related areas.

Career planning and development. Poor. Each forced-choice checklist is directed at an individual job. While it is possible to determine whether the employee's behaviors are acceptable for a progression of jobs, no information is obtained on *how* to determine which jobs an employee should pursue.

Weighted checklist

A more advanced version of the checklist, called the *weighted checklist,* requires that items be *scored.* To create such appraisal procedures, several raters collectively rank the checklist items on a scale from (say) 1 to 9, where 1 indicates *highly ineffective* behavior and 9 indicates *highly effective* behavior. Items that raters gave comparable scores would be retained on the checklist, and would be assigned a *weight* of the average score. Items where raters had difficulty agreeing on a score would be dropped. (See Fig. 5.3.)

The result of this procedure is a checklist wherein each item has been assigned a *weight.* (For objectivity reasons, both the rater and

Employee Performance Appraisal

In each category, check those items which **best** describe the employee's behavior during the review period.

Quantity of Work

☐	Sets a work pace others try to achieve.	6.6
☐	Sometimes sleeps on the job if left alone.	0.3
☐	Lets outside interests interfere and decrease quantity of work.	1.3
☐	Recognizes limitations and abilities and prepares ahead to maintain high quality of work.	8.2
☐	Spends too much time on phone or writing personal letters during work hours.	1.1
☐	Keeps busy but may select wrong priorities.	4.8
☐	Willing to work long hours and forgo breaks to maintain high production level.	8.5
☐	Not very flexible in switching from task to task.	4.9
☐	Work is turned out on time.	5.5
☐	Uses "slack" periods to maintain quantity in other areas.	6.1
☐	Chooses priorities correctly.	6.3
☐	Wastes no time going to next task.	6.0
☐	Works rapidly.	7.1
☐	Keeps assignments organized for high production.	6.7
☐	Consistently completes all jobs, maintaining high output.	8.0
☐	Organizes all tasks for highly efficient and effective production.	7.9
☐	Usually does enough to complete jobs, seldom more.	4.1

. . .

Number of Items Checked: _____

Total of Weights: _____

Average Weighting for Category _____

Figure 5.3   A weighted checklist.

ratee should be unaware of these weights.) After the appropriate items have been checked by the rater, another staff member (a scorer) is given the responsibility of entering the appropriate weights on the form. These weights are then considered to determine the level of the employee's performance.

This method enjoys several advantages over the simple checklist. First, it provides a numerical score of behaviors that can then be used for decision making. This can be of value when deciding employee compensation. Second, the weights assigned to the various categories can be customized to particular jobs and to particular employees. Finally, the scores can be used to measure performance improvements.

The usefulness of weighted checklists

Many of the comments made for the forced-choice checklist apply here, except that the weighted checklist is deemed good for making employee compensation decisions.

Summary: Improving the checklist appraisal

Improving a company's appraisal system that is based on one of the above checklists requires using several different tactics.

First, the manager and employee should supplement the checklist with documentation that assesses the employee's current level of education and job skills. The manager should expand on this by including information on the employee's potential, both for growth in their present job and for future growth and promotion.

Second, the checklist should be expanded or enlarged to become more *granular*. By this, we mean that any behavior or quality that is measured must be measured in more detail. For example, one common trait appearing on some checklist appraisals is "works well with others," or "is a team player." This vague yes/no expression should be expanded to cover more detail: to what *degree* does the employee work well with others? In this case we recommend adding such items as "listens and understands instructions," "displays tact when interacting with others," "provides oral and/or written feedback," "assists others when able," and even "provides leadership." This increase in detail will allow the checklist results to be more easily converted to ratings, which may then be used for compensation administration.

Last, management must provide some proof that the checklist appraisal system is objective. This is necessary if the checklist is to be used for making employment decisions such as hiring and termination. This proof of objectivity may consist of documents relating to the job analysis used to create the appraisal system, or a statistical analysis of the data. The danger here is that the system may already be subjective, either in design or in use. This may open employers to claims of discrimination or unfair termination practices.

Critical Incidents

This type of review (see Fig. 5.4) is similar to the essay form mentioned later in this section. It requires managers to justify their appraisals of employees by citing *critical incidents* that occurred during the review period. These incidents are usually defined to be specific examples of employee behavior that are clearly indicative of good or bad performance.

In each instance, the manager considers the employee's typical behavior in reference to a number of important factors. As with an essay, the manager describes the employee's performance in his or her own words (prose). However, the description must be of a critical incident.

This type of review takes some time, and requires good written communications skills on the part of the manager. It also requires the man-

---

Critical Incident Form

Employee's Name _____   Employee's Job Title _____

Date of Occurrence _____   Time of Occurrence _____   Location _____

Identify Observed Behavior (if reporting hearsay information, identify source and location of actual observer.)

Date Form Completed _____   Time Form Completed _____

Signature and Title of
Person Completing Form _____

Items to be considered in identifying behavior (may be used as a checklist)

What specifically occurred?
Is there sufficient detail to support future judgement?
Have you described results of behavior?
What circumstances influenced behavior?
      Was there an emergency situation?
      Did unusual or adverse conditions exist?
Behavior Being Documented:
      Insubordination   Theft
      Attendance   Malicious Damage
      Quality of Work   Interpersonal Relations
      Quantity of Work   Acceptance of Job Enlarging Responsibilities

Second-Party Observations:

      Remote Location
      Works Independently
      Temporarily Assigned to Others

Figure 5.4   The critical incident form.

ager to keep a complete and detailed log of such incidents throughout the year.

Employees can assist their supervisors by preparing a summary of the critical incidents in advance. They do this by summarizing each incident when it happens and preparing a brief status report on the matter. Such status reports are then submitted regularly, and are summarized at the end of the review period.

After documenting a critical incident the employee should review it verbally with his or her manager. Ask for the manager's opinion about how he or she acted or reacted. Was the behavior acceptable? Were there other alternatives that should have been considered? These factors should then be documented as a part of the incident. Managers then review how the incident affected their employees' work, and whether it helped them to improve their knowledge or skills. Making a mistake may be embarrassing, but not learning from the experience can be costly.

The usefulness of critical incidents

- *Making employment decisions.*   Since this method requires historical documentation, it cannot be used to make hiring decisions. In terms of transferring or terminating employees, however, this method provides necessary and sufficient information for management to make an informed decision.

- *Performance improvement.*   Good. The critical incident technique requires the manager and the employee to review each incident in terms of what alternative behaviors were available, and which were considered acceptable. A summary of this information can be introduced directly into a performance improvement plan. In time, additional critical incidents will be used as feedback to determine the level of improvement.

- *Assigning work duties.*   Acceptable. Managers will have available to them enough information regarding incidents that describe employee behaviors, along with how much they learned from the experiences. Regrettably, this requires a lot of organizational work on the part of the manager in order to determine which employees will perform which tasks acceptably.

- *Identifying and rating potential.*   Acceptable. As with assigning work duties, the critical incident technique provides a wealth of information regarding employee behaviors; however, the manager must do a lot of work to organize the data to determine which employees may perform well in higher-level jobs.

- *Compensation administration.*   Poor.   Critical   incidents   are extremely difficult to value; hence, this method will be unable to provide the manager with either an overall single measure of performance or a relative ranking of their employees. Such information is crucial in making employee compensation decisions.

- *Identifying training needs.*   Acceptable. Each critical incident that points out unacceptable employee behavior is a possible starting point for identifying employee training requirements. Note that there is no guarantee that the sum of the critical incidents for an appraisal period will encompass all appraisal categories.

- *Career planning and development.*   Poor. Critical incidents provide little, if any, information to the manager or employee regarding career possibilities. At most, they furnish the manager with a starting point for a career planning meeting.

Summary: Improving the critical incident appraisal

While the critical incident approach to performance appraisal is considered one of the best, it has one major flaw: it requires a knowledgeable and skilled rater. To implement such a program successfully, a company must be prepared to provide comprehensive training to managers in appraisal procedures, especially in written communications.

Making this procedure acceptable for all of management's needs will involve additional work on the part of the supervisor. These items are listed below.

Keeping a detailed incident log. The supervisor must maintain a log of critical incidents. Indeed, this is the basis for the procedure. This log must contain information about each incident, including time and date, observed behaviors, observed results, and feedback. Even more, the supervisor must review such incidents regularly with the employee. This review is essential for employee growth and work improvement, as it provides the employee with feedback that allows him or her to either modify future behavior or maintain present behavior.

As this log is an integral part of the review procedure, its contents and use should be documented thoroughly in the company's policy and procedures.

Recognition of incidents. It is not enough for the manager to be trained in critical incident procedures. Perhaps just as important, managers must recognize when these incidents occur. As this usually involves observation by the manager, we conclude that managers using this technique must be continually walking around, attempting to observe employees' behaviors. Since this is not always possible, how can we ensure that most of the proper incidents are recorded? What if the manager is out of the office, attending several days of training, or simply not physically colocated with the employee?

Addressing this point requires that the employee have some training in the critical incident methodology and that the employee and his or her manager meet regularly to discuss employee status. By making employees responsible for observing and recording their own critical incidents, much of the burden on the manager is eliminated. With both manager and employee watching for incidents, it is then only a matter of them both discussing such incidents at their regular status meetings.

Valuing incidents. To make a critical incident appraisal useful for compensation administration and career planning, incidents must somehow be rated. While most such programs assign values of "acceptable" and "unacceptable" to incidents, more is required. A job analysis that results in a critical incident appraisal system usually involves collecting and analyzing many sample critical incidents. This information should be evaluated further, with the objective of determining ratings or values of the incidents. Even a general 1-to-5 scale should prove adequate.

Career planning. This is another area in which critical incident methods are sorely deficient. While such methods may produce a wealth of information about an employee's behaviors, little is learned about the employee's level of job skill, education, or promotability; however, this is usually easily remedied. The simplest method is to assemble lists of critical incidents from the job descriptions of higher-level jobs and give them to employees. Since these, by definition, constitute a description of acceptable behaviors of employees at higher levels, they therefore provide other employees with guidelines for advancement. These may then be factored in to the employee's current appraisal and covered in depth at the next status meeting.

Essay Reviews

This form of review (see Fig. 5.5) requires the manager to write prose or essay answers to certain questions. These questions are usually general ones that address topics of employee behavior. Like critical incident reviews, essay reviews are time-consuming and tiresome. A manager unskilled in written communication may have difficulty in rating employees correctly.

Managers have difficulty answering essay questions with definite statements, unless they are extremely pleased with an employee's performance. Thus, in the absence of specific guidelines, the review is highly subjective. The final rating may be a function of the manager's writing skill, not the employee's actual performance.

Managers can greatly simplify the process by requiring their employees to report their results in prose form. Employees should break down their work by project and by tasks within each project, and describe each project and its status with several sentences. The status of each task should be summarized with a short sentence. Employees shouldn't simply summarize completion of a project with the words "project complete." Instead, they should write a few sentences describing the tasks completed, and whether they were on time, early, or late. They should then finish with a summary of the total work required for the project, and note anything they learned.

Employee Performance Review

Employee's Name _____   Date of Hire _____

Job Title _____   Job Grade and Code _____

This evaluation covers the period from _____ to _____ .

1. Evaluation: (Comments on individual's performance in regard to goals previously set, measuring factors such as quality, quantity, creativity and suggestions, attendance, waste, staying on schedule, etc.)

2. Areas where improvement is needed and suggestions for attainment: (Including use of company sponsored programs; i.e., Tuition Aid, Affirmative Action Program, etc.)

3. Other remarks: (Attitude, appearance, cooperation, etc.)

4. For the time period covered by this evaluation the employee's performance has been:
    ____ Highly Satisfactory   ____ Satisfactory
    ____ Below Expected Levels   ____ Unsatisfactory

5. Employee comments (if any):

6. Goals and results to be attained and measured for new period (mutually agreed to, realistically attainable, measurable)

Supervisor's Signature _____   Reviewed By: _____

Employee's Signature _____   Date: _____

Figure 5.5 The essay review.

The usefulness of essay reviews

Making employment decisions. Essay reviews are not feasible for hiring new employees as no historical record exists for comparison. Their use to assist in employee reassignment is possible, although the employee will be subject to the communication skills of his or her manager. Essay reviews should not be used as a basis for employee terminations, as they tend to be both subjective and qualitative, rather than objective and quantitative.

Performance improvement. Acceptable, assuming that the essay information includes descriptions of all relevant employee behaviors during the review period, alternatives available, and how the employee could improve.

Assigning work duties.   Acceptable. Assuming that the review covers all of an employee's duties, this information will prove sufficient to determine which tasks the employee can perform acceptably.

Identifying and rating potential.   Acceptable. Most managers consider this form of review the best as a basis for making promotional decisions.

Compensation administration.   Poor. Most essay review systems provide no way for a manager to quantify the employee's behavior or results. This leaves the manager in the position of not being able to manage employee compensation from the review itself. In some companies this is proper, as there are other professionals who will use other methods to handle compensation. Such situations are familiar ones to assembly-line workers, teachers, and the military. Still, the essay review contains precious little information that would allow a data processing manager to make an informed salary decision.

Identifying training needs.   Acceptable. Essay reviews usually require the rater to complete a section describing the training needs of the employee, along with an action plan for follow-up. The only problem that employees have with this format of review is that of justifying what the manager has written. Sometimes it is not at all obvious why they need the training specified.

Career planning and development.   Acceptable. Again, most essay review forms contain a section for employee career development, along with an action plan. Typically, the manager and the employee will complete this section after the main part of the review has been completed.

Summary: Improving the essay appraisal

Since the essay review method is useful in so many categories of appraisal, this has caused many companies to adopt it to fulfill a variety of purposes. The major problem with using this technique is the burden placed on the manager. Not only must managers have excellent written communication skills to complete essay reviews, but they must also include sufficient detail about the entire review period for all purposes. Employment decisions will require historical data to justify them; performance improvement requires an inventory of observed behaviors and feedback; decisions as to compensation will require an overall rating; career planning decisions will require a summary of the employee's goals that are consonant with the company's. All of this takes time and demands a superior manager.

It is clear that managers will require good or excellent written communication skills. It is an unfortunate corollary that employees who are assigned to better managers get better reviews. To minimize these problems, companies can provide managers with "sample" essay answers for each rated category. This will effectively convert the essay review into a checklist or rating scale review, as each essay category will now have several possible sample answers provided, each with its own rating. This will tend to eliminate differences between managers' abilities to fill out review forms.

Management by Objectives (MBO)

With this kind of review, the manager and subordinate typically meet at the beginning of the review period and set objectives. These objectives are for the coming review period, the manager and employee set them together. At the end of the review period the manager and subordinate meet to agree on whether objectives were met, and to what degree. An example of an MBO appraisal form appears in Fig. 5.6.

Management Performance Analysis

Name: _____   Birth Date: _____   Position: _____

No. of Years in Position: _____   Reports to: _____

Analysis Prepared By: _____   Date: _____   No. Yrs. Supervised: _____

Analysis Reviewed By: _____   Date: _____

This analysis has been discussed with me _____   Date: _____
                                      (Signature of Employee)

Goal Achievements
Quantitative Goals and Results

Describe Goals	Describe Results Achieved	Describe Reasons for Differences

Qualitative Goals and Results

Describe Goals	Describe Results Achieved	Describe Reasons for Differences

Figure 5.6   An MBO appraisal form.

There are disadvantages to this method. Setting objectives can be very difficult. For example, in a sales organization, one possible primary objective is to "increase sales by 10 percent." Does this mean 10 percent more products, 10 percent greater revenue, or 10 percent higher profits?

Another disadvantage is setting the difficulty level of the objectives. Easy objectives aren't challenging: impossible or unreasonable objectives unfairly penalize employees. In both cases, appraisals may give an inaccurate picture of employee performance.

To prepare for this type of review, managers should monitor their employees' progress toward objectives carefully during the year. They must pay particular attention to circumstances beyond the employees' control that make it difficult or impossible for them to achieve their goals. Employees should document these events in regular status reports for the manager. At the end of the review period, employees summarize their progress toward their objectives. These status reports and summaries then become part of the review document.

Sometimes you must revise an objective. Unexpectedly tough competition may make it impossible for you to reach sales goals. An economic downturn may cause your company to revise its corporate goals. Employees and managers should be receptive to changing or revising employees' objectives if there is a good reason—especially if it will affect their performance appraisal.

The usefulness of management by objectives

Making employment decisions. Unless the candidate has come from a position where MBO was used, this method does not help the interviewer at all. In other cases, those of employee transfer and termination, the MBO review provides the required information for the company to justify its decision.

Performance improvement. Acceptable. As the objectives stated at the beginning of the review period are those on which the employee will be judged, the employee should always be aware of how his or her actions will affect performance. Further, should additional improvement be necessary, the MBO forms furnish the basis of an action plan, including objectives to work on and the standards against which they will be judged. Regrettably, the MBO system tells only *what* must be improved, not *how* or *why.*

Assigning work duties. Good. Typically, managers will use the pooled set of employee objectives as a measure of what talent is available to them. From this talent pool they choose employees and assign them to tasks. This works best in situations where management has set achievable, realistic goals for employees.

Identifying and rating potential.   Acceptable. Again, the set of goals set for employees provides measure of what talent is available. Managers may use this to identify employees that potentially are promotable to positions with higher, more difficult, or technically more advanced goals.

Compensation administration.   Acceptable. Although most MBO forms do not allow the rater to develop a single, overall, numerical rating, the MBO appraisal is still an acceptable medium for compensation administration. In general, managers will use a combination of goal difficulty with number and type of goals achieved to arrive at an index of the employee's performance during the review period. This measure is somewhat subjective; still, many companies use it.

Identifying training needs.   Good. In combination with setting goals for the coming period and identifying performance improvement, the MBO review provides the manager with sufficient data to recognize which employees will require training in certain areas.

Career planning and development.   Acceptable. The MBO review program is usually implemented in concert with a strategic goal-setting plan at high levels within the company. This is so the goals set by the manager and the employee are not in conflict with company goals. Against this backdrop the manager and the employee jointly address the employee's career goals. While the MBO program provides little information regarding how company goals and employee career goals can be fused, at least the information is available.

Because an MBO program can be so useful across a wide range of performance categories, many companies have adopted it as their standard. The only cautions would be the following:

Set goals from the top.   The goal-setting process must begin at the top, first with company strategic goals, then divisional goals, and so on down the line to the manager. If this is not done first, or if the process fails to produce realistic, achievable, and quantifiable goals at any point, then the program will fail.

Provide training.   Untrained managers will not keep goals comparable across employees. Some employees will be challenged, some not; some will have difficult goals, others will have easy goals; some employees will work with managers to set goals, others will not participate in the process. The key is to have management trained in employee communications, goal-setting, performance improvement plans, and career development.

Educate the work force.   Employees need training in the MBO process as much as the managers do. They must be convinced that the forms and procedures are in their best interests, and that goal-setting will assist them in performing their jobs well.

Incorporate documentation. All documentation and communications between the employee and the manager regarding goals throughout the review period should be included in the final performance appraisal document in some form. This will prevent many review-related problems, such as emphasizing recent actions over past ones, or blurring the dates of the review period. (These, and other similar considerations, are covered in a later section in this chapter.)

Summary: Improving the MBO appraisal

It seems almost heretical to suggest that an MBO program could be improved. Proponents of MBO are sometimes fanatical in their devotion to objectives, forms, goals, standards, and review procedures. Still, there is always room for improvement.

When MBO programs fail, it is usually for one of the following reasons. Most of these deal with those most elusive of concepts, *goals* and *objectives*.

Failure to set proper objectives.   This is the most common reason for MBO program failure. If objectives are too easy, everyone gets appraised as "superior." If they are too difficult, everyone becomes "unacceptable." Also, if objectives are not set from the top of the organization down, managers will have no idea which objectives are valid for their departments, let alone for employees.

To prevent this kind of failure, set objectives from the top. If a manager is placed in a position where objectives have already been set without their knowledge or consent (say, because of promotion or transfer), it is their responsibility to get explanation and clarification from top management.

Failure to anticipate circumstances or a dynamic environment.   The appearance of unforeseen competition, an economic downturn, or a merger or acquisition can result in a department or division's objectives being radically and suddenly changed. This will then cause a domino effect, as the objectives of lower-level departments, managers, and employees must now be changed.

Rather than reacting to these events, employees and managers can attempt to predict which of a set of such events may occur, and form contingency plans for those events. While this may not always be possible, it will provide perspective. This has the beneficial effect of forcing management to scrutinize current objectives and prepare alternative plans.

The program indicates what to do, but not how or why. This problem shows up in one form or another in most appraisal systems, regardless of form or technique. In general, most appraisal systems involve gathering information and making judgments about that information. Few go on to the next step: what is to be *done* regarding those judgments.

MBO programs are particularly vulnerable in this area. Much effort is put into defining and completing goals and objectives, yet little is focused on implementing changes or improvements. To address this concern, many companies have supplemented their MBO system with a separate career path planning system. This new system is then responsible for guiding employees by providing advice about job growth.

Ranking Systems

Simple ranking

Another method, which still has considerable value, is the ranking system. Supervisors rank their employees in order of the presence of traits the supervisor feels are important. Ranking overcomes a shortcoming of other approaches in which the supervisor tends to rate everyone close to the average. However, there is no way to indicate that there may be a large difference between persons 3 and 4, while persons 5 and 6 might be very close in ability. A common variation of the ranking system is known as "lifeboat order." The supervisor is told, "If you can save only one person in your group, who would you save? If your lifeboat could hold another, who would you pick?" and so forth. A sample ranking form appears in Fig. 5.7.

Another variant of ranking is known as *peer review.* Peer review was much discussed some years ago but is little used currently. In this method a group of programmers rank each other anonymously; the rankings are combined, resulting in a group ranking. The premise is that the programmers know the work of their peers better than their supervisor does. After all, how many programming supervisors review the code of their group? How many are even able to?

Several West Coast IS departments are experimenting with peer review appraisals at the top management level.

A remarkable instance of peer review appeared on public television several years ago. In a factory in communist China, a group of workers were filmed as they sat around a table discussing who among them was the most productive, thus deserving the greatest wages; who next, and who next. In this open, rather than anonymous peer rating, the workers strove to be fair to themselves and to each other, to be honest in their appraisal, and to preserve the close working harmony impor-

---

Instructions for Alternation Ranking

Attached is a list of employees. All of them may be performing satisfactorily, but some are almost certain to be doing a better job in their own assignment than are others in their assignments. You may use your own judgement as to what makes one employee better than another. Many factors may be considered: dependability, ability to do the work, willingness to work, cooperation, ability to get along with people, and any others that you think are important. On making your decision, use your own personal knowledge of the individuals and their work. Do not depend on the opinions of others.

1.   Eliminate the names of those whose work you do not know well.

2.   Eliminate the name of any person whose work in your opinion is so different from most of the others that you do not think he or she can be fairly compared with them.

3.   Decide which person you think is the best on the list. Draw a line through their name and write it in the blank space marked "1-Highest".

4.   Decide which person you think is not as good as the others remaining on the list. Draw a line through their name and write it in the blank space marked "1-Lowest". (Remember, you are not saying that they are unsatisfactory; merely that you consider the others better.)

5.   Next, select the person you think is best of those remaining on the list, draw a line through their name and write it in the blank space marked "2-Highest".

6.   Next, select the person you think is not as good as the others remaining on the list, draw a line through their name and write it in the blank space marked "2-Lowest".

7.   Continue in this manner until you have eliminated all names on the list.

Rater's Name: _____   **Date:** _____

Classification of Group Being Ranked:

1-Highest	
2-Highest	
3-Highest	
. . .	
3-Lowest	
2-Lowest	
1-Lowest	

Figure 5.7 A ranking appraisal form.

tant to their collective. Financial reward is not a group decision in a capitalistic society.

Paired comparison ranking

There are several methods for ranking employees by comparing them two at a time. One of these involves creating cards for each employee, dealing them in pairs, and choosing the best in each pair for a later dealing. Another requires the rater to place cards in three stacks, the stacks denoting above-average, average, and below-average employees. The rater then must rearrange the cards in the stacks until they are distributed with 30 percent of the cards in stacks 1 and 3.

Forced-distribution ranking

This requires the rater to allocate a percentage of the employees being appraised to certain categories, such as superior, excellent, fully effective, acceptable, poor, and unacceptable. The distribution of employees to be placed in each category usually approximates a normal distribution. This may vary according to the type of employee or business.

The usefulness of rankings

Making employment decisions. Ranking systems are almost useless for making hiring decisions, unless the raters have available a sufficiently large pool of candidates. If this is the case, then the candidates can be ranked and the top n hired (where n is the number of new-hires required). Hopefully, the top candidates will meet the company's minimum standards for the available jobs, because the ranking procedure provides no information about this.

In terms of transferring or reassignment, ranking provides a way to compare employees doing the same job. If company policy provides for regular job rotation, as in many Japanese companies, the ranking method may be used; however, it still provides no information about whether employees meet minimal standards. This also makes this technique a poor one for justifying employee terminations. After all, the lowest-ranking employee may have an excellent performance record.

Performance improvement. Poor. Ranking methods provide comparisons, but may not require the manager to justify his or her rankings. In cases where documentation of the ranking process is required, the manager's explanations should include such reasons. This information, though meager, may be enough to construct an action plan for employee performance improvement.

Assigning work duties. Poor. Again, the lack of information regarding employee knowledge and skills makes this method almost useless. The sole exception will be for jobs that require no special training, or where all employees already have such training. In these cases, rankings provide a type of *seniority* or *pecking order,* allowing the manager to assign the highest-ranked employees to the most challenging (or easiest) jobs.

Identifying and rating potential. Poor. For jobs which require little training, it may be possible to justify promoting the highest-ranking employees. Still, the technique provides no data regarding the absolute competencies of employees. The highest-ranking employee may be the best of a set of marginal employees. In another case, the lowest-ranking employee may be the worst of a set of superstars.

Compensation administration.   Acceptable. Regardless of individual competencies, some companies have a policy of *pay for performance.* By this they mean that the highest performers get the best raises. In the case of ranking methods, the highest-ranked employees are generally the best performers. To take into account that such a ranking system is relative, rather than absolute, the company looks at overall profits. If profits are high, then this is deemed evidence of good overall employee performance, and raises are high. If profits are low, this is evidence of poor overall performance, and raises are correspondingly lower.

The disadvantages of this method are: excellent performers can be overshadowed by other excellent performers in the same division; poor performers can remain hidden within other poor performers; and high-ranking employees in one division are not directly comparable to those in another division.

Identifying training needs.   Poor. In general, it might be said that lower-ranking employees need the most training. This need is difficult to justify, however, for reasons mentioned above.

Career planning and development.   Poor. Ranking techniques provide no information about goals or goal achievement.

Summary: Improving the ranking appraisal

Ranking-appraisal documents must be supplemented with additional information for them to be of much use. Typically, companies augment their ranking system with a complementary rating system. This rating system is used to rate individual employees according to their abilities. (For more information on rating scales, see the following section.)

Rating Scales

This is the most common form of performance review. The employees' behaviors or results are grouped into several categories. Managers then rate employees with a numerical score in each category. This format of review is easy to fill out.

Typical of the traits that are rated are:

- Job knowledge
- Quality of work
- Quantity of work
- Growth potential
- Attitude

A scale accompanying each trait or quality gives a full range, or number of degrees, with appropriate phrases which act as a guide in the rating. For example, if attitude is thought to be an important factor in rating, one end of the scale would be accompanied by such phrases as "uncooperative," "cannot get along with others," and so on. The other end of the scale has phrases such as "extremely cooperative," "does more than his or her share of the work," "has excellent relations with other employees," and so on. The trait rating scale allows raters to apply uniform standards but does have several problems. These are mentioned in Chap. 4. A sample rating scale review form appears in Fig. 5.8.

Managers' ratings of their subordinates, however, may easily become subjective or biased. Managers sometimes let ratings on one scale affect other ratings. Also, numerical scales mean different things to different people. For example, suppose a manager is rating an employee in a category titled "Written Communications." The rating is a 5 on a scale of 0 to 5. What does this mean? Did the employee surpass all expectations? Did they perform better than all others in your department? than others in your industry? Did they do the minimum expected, but nothing more?

Types of rating errors

Regrettably, there are many different types of errors that a manager can make when attempting to rate an employee on some type of numerical scale. These are discussed in Chap. 3.

Managers and subordinates can prepare for this type of review by discussing the procedure with each other at the beginning of the review period. Discuss and agree on what each of the categories covers and what the numerical rating scales mean. Give examples of how the rater would rate certain results or behaviors.

It is also very important that the manager and the employee agree on the standards for comparison. Will the employee be compared with others in his or her department, or with others having the same job in your company? Get agreement on this at the beginning of the review period.

The usefulness of rating scales

Making employment decisions.   Rating scales are very useful for making such decisions. Hiring new employees is best accomplished by measuring their current skills and knowledge—this is easily done with a rating system, coupled with a good technical interviewing program. Employee transfers can be managed using ratings, as the rating scores usually indicate strengths and weaknesses. Finally, performance appraisals in this system provide excellent documentation about poor employee performance, and management's attempts

Supervisory Personnel Performance Appraisal Form (cont'd)										
SECTION B	1	2	3	4	5	6	7	8	9	10
1. Leadership. To what extent does he hold the respect and confidence of associates?	Secures limited cooperation of subordinates. Does not have full control.		Has fair degree of respect and confidence of subordinates. Methods get results.		Success in getting respect and confidence of subordinates and others. Gets results without undue friction.		Leads people very capably. Results consistently good. Inspires confidence.		Outstanding, superior, inspiring, and forceful.	Exceptional.
	COMMENTS:									
	1	2	3	4	5	6	7	8	9	10
2. Manpower Utilization. Consider success in delegation of authority and proper placement.	Seldom delegates authority. Sometimes delegates authority to wrong people.		Does not always recognize and take advantage of opportunities of subordinates.		Successful in making assignments and delegating authority under normal conditions.		Successful under normal and unusual conditions. Superior ability.		Shows outstanding powers of delegation.	Exceptional.
	COMMENTS:									

. . . (portions of this form have been removed for brevity)
SECTION C

1. In area where employee scored less than "5", indicate what measures are being taken to improve his or her performance.
    1. Quality of Work   _____
    2. Quantity of Work   _____
    3. Industry   _____
    4. Dependability   _____
    5. Aptitude   _____
    6. Cooperation   _____
    7. Personality   _____

2. Do you consider this employee capable of future advancement? If yes, give reasons.

3. What is employee doing to prepare for advancement?

4. Have you formulated plans for helping this employee improve his or her performance? If so, please indicate.

Completed By: _____   Date: _____

Interviewed By: _____   Date: _____

Remarks. Indicate results of interview with employee.

Employee Signature: _____   Date: _____

Figure 5.8   A rating scale review form.

to improve it. As such, rating scale appraisals are useful in justifying employee termination.

Performance improvement.   Good. Each scale category is usually a measurement of the employee's behaviors in that category. Scales are usually ranked from low to high, and accompanied by textual descriptions and examples of poor and good performance. This provides the employees with a direct measurement of how their behavior is perceived, and details examples of acceptable behaviors in that category. Performance improvement plans can concentrate on these acceptable behaviors as a model for the employee's future.

Assigning work duties.   Good. Rating scales measure achievement. This permits the manager to assign tasks to employees efficiently.

Identifying and rating potential.   Acceptable. While most rating scales provide management data about employee behavior, they are not so good at identifying potential. Indeed, none of the appraisal methods mentioned in this book handles this well. However, since most managers find that the rating scale gives them a numerical measure of employee achievement, they use achievement as a *predictor* of future success. In other words, employees that have achieved a lot are deemed to have the greatest potential.

Compensation administration.   Good. Above all other methods, rating scales are able to produce a single, numerical, overall rating of an employee's performance. Some systems take a simple average of the ratings in all categories, while others use weighting factors. As long as the employee and manager agree on this method *at the beginning of the review period,* the rating scale forms an excellent basis for justifying compensation decisions.

Identifying training needs.   Good. Just as in the case of performance improvement, rating scales give the manager a numerical measure of an employee's competencies in various categories. These levels can then be used to develop training plans.

Career planning and development.   Acceptable. Although the rating scale method can produce what seem to be precise assessments of employee performance, there is barely enough information present regarding the company's goals and objectives. Such data is buried in the appraisal document itself—the assumption is that company goals were used to *derive* the appraisal process, and that the final result will meet those goals.

Because of this assumption, employees and their managers must assume that career planning will occur under the umbrella of the appraisal system, and that career planning meetings will use the review document as the preliminary agenda. It may be difficult to resolve employee goals with the unstated goals in the appraisal documents, but it is possible.

The rating scale is probably the best performance-appraisal methodology available for the various performance categories. Its advantages are summarized as follows:

- It is objective.
- It provides numerical measures of behaviors.
- It is behavior-based, not trait-based.

Summary: Improving the rating scale appraisal

A good rating scale appraisal system can be developed only through a complete and accurate job analysis. If the job analysis is poorly done or hurried, the resulting rating system quickly degenerates into a guessing game where managers presume that they know more about their employees than anyone else does. They will appraise employees by first guessing what the result should be, then figuring out what ratings are necessary to create that result. This can be avoided by doing the job analysis carefully.

Once created and implemented, a rating scale system must be monitored and updated when necessary. This requires an ongoing job analysis, usually done by a human resources person. Feedback from managers on ratings, categories, and descriptions is then used to update the appraisal instruments.

Optimizing Performance Appraisal

6

Using Performance Review Forms and Procedures Correctly

When Appraisal Systems Fail

Across the diverse spectrum of different corporations that have implemented performance appraisal programs in the past 50 years, only a few have succeeded in meeting all of the objectives set of them. Why should this be? In this section we discuss the most common reasons for system failure. These include:

- Lack of objectives
- No definition of development
- Forms not related to system objectives
- Poorly defined or improperly implemented procedures
- No definition of performance
- Poor appraisal interviews

As we shall see, each of these problems can occur by itself or in combination with others. In this section we summarize the major points listed above.

Lack of objectives

Performance appraisal programs with no objectives fail early in their lives. There are several interest groups associated with appraisals, one for each department or activity responsible for employee policies and procedures. This usually includes the employee's supervisor, upper management, personnel, and training. Each of these groups wishes to collect data pertinent to the employee so that they can make business decisions. A program without objectives means that it exists "to have an appraisal program," rather than to fulfill some business function. With no objectives, or with conflicting objectives, the program ends up bearing no functional relationship to the tasks at hand.

During appraisal program design, the task force involved must make a decision as to which portions of the appraisal forms and procedures are to be allotted to the various interest groups. Pressure from each group's desire to mold their portion of the same management tool distorts the tool.

A portion of the Civil Service Commission publication entitled *The Federal Manager's Responsibilities Under the Merit System* states, "Prompt, fair, and thorough appraisal of staff performance, with attention to promotion actions when warranted, can do much to create harmony and dedication within the work force."

This sounds all well and good; however, *harmony* and *dedication* are not necessarily the objectives of a performance appraisal program. Further, there is an implicit assumption in the statement that harmony and dedication will lead to increased productivity. This is not necessarily true in all cases.

Another part of the statement implies that promotional actions affect the way people will perform. Unfortunately, promotion or the potential of promotion has very little effect on the performance of the majority of the work force because of the way it usually occurs. It involves a small percentage of the work force. If you analyze the number of promotions in your organization in the last 12 months, you might discover that the number of people promoted did not constitute more than 10 percent of your total work force. If you analyzed it year to year, you would find that some of the names on the list appear more than once because of successive promotions of the same person. There are ways to make promotions involve more people and have more impact on performance, which will be explained later; but the way it is done now makes it a passive process with little effect on performance.

Regrettably, when a committee with conflicting interests gathers together to design a single performance-appraisal form, a useless tool is created.* Some of these interests, and the information they require, follow.

- *Performance improvement.* This requires that the supervisor engage in coaching the employee on a day-by-day basis, so as to detect and correct specific performance problems.

---

* As Allan Sherman once said, "The people on committees, they sit there all day / And they each put in a color, but it comes out gray."

- *Career development.* Preparing employees for the future is a long-term process. It is not directly related to current performance, but rather to the employees' ambitions and long-range objectives. Career development may involve vocational counseling.

- *Identifying potential.* This is purely a measurement process—identifying those employees who, at this moment, are promotable.

- *Salary administration.* This requires *summary* information from the appraisal process, usually with a way to directly derive a raise.

- *Objective monitoring.* Here, objectives are set and monitored over a period of time. Measurement is usually not required—it is sufficient to note whether objectives were accomplished or not.

Each of the objectives of the appraisal process requires a different measurement. Some demand immediate measurements, others are long-range in nature. Some require direct measures of the employee's behaviors or attainments, others are more subtle. What is measured, when it is measured, what is done after the measurement, and how frequently you do it, is quite different for each of these objectives.

It is not possible to design a single performance-appraisal form to accomplish more than one of the many objectives for performance appraisal.

Re-creating appraisal system objectives. If your company uses a single appraisal form for multiple purposes, consider modifying it to include information that you will need. Although changing the formal forms may take a long time, you can begin now to include relevant information about an employee in your current system. Appending additional information to an appraisal is an accepted way to do this.

Although it is difficult to change forms, we have included in Fig. 6.1 some basic guidelines for converting various types of forms to other business uses.

No definition of development

The second major reason for performance appraisal failure is related to what appear to be inaccurate and false assumptions as to what "employee development" is, and who is responsible for it.

One of the first documented appraisal programs was introduced by Samuel W. Rayburn, treasurer of the Lord and Taylor Company, back in 1914. Its concept was based on a plan created by Rayburn to develop himself when he was a young man. In that plan his development efforts were directed toward identifying his weaknesses so he could improve on them.

	Management by Objectives	Essay	Checklist	Rating Scale	Critical Incident	Rankings
Objective Monitoring	Acceptable as-is.	Acceptable, but supplement with goal-setting process.	Unacceptable. Supplement with goal-setting, regular meetings.	Acceptable, but supplement with goal-setting process.	Acceptable, but supplement with goal-setting process.	Unacceptable. Supplement with goal-setting, documentation.
Making Employment Decisions	Acceptable, except for hiring.	Unacceptable. Need objectives, measures of accomplishment.	Unacceptable. Need objectives, measures of accomplishment.	Acceptable as-is.	Acceptable, but supplement with higher job incidents, goals.	Unacceptable. Replace with behavioral measures, goals.
Performance Improvement	Acceptable as-is.	Concentrate on documenting behaviors.	Need appraisal items that show acceptable behaviors.	Acceptable as-is.	Acceptable as-is.	Unacceptable. Supplement with list of goals, behaviors observed.
Identifying and Rating Potential	Acceptable as-is.	Supplement with criteria for advancement, note behaviors.	Unacceptable. Attach checklist for high level job, appraise.	Acceptable as-is.	Need to add info. on relevant incidents and other job items.	Unacceptable. Supplement with qualitative measures.
Compensation Administration	Acceptable as-is.	Unacceptable. Add prose on goals and objectives, note behaviors.	Unacceptable. Supplement with goals, behaviors.	Acceptable as-is.	Need to match incidents to acceptable behaviors.	Unacceptable. Supplement with goals, observe behaviors.

Figure 6.1 Adapting performance appraisal forms to common business uses.

The Lord and Taylor plan was based on the assumption that if people knew what was wrong with them, they would work to improve themselves. This concept implies that if we accurately identify weaknesses in an employee, and if we in all honesty communicate our measurements to that employee, that he or she will be pleased to hear it and will work hard in correcting it. Today's *management development* concept is based on the same theory. Here is how it is usually stated.

> The primary responsibility for the development of an individual is in the hands of that individual to develop themselves. The best action a corporation can take is to create the right kind of environment for self-development and accurately communicate to that individual their weakness in areas wherein improvement is needed. That individual then works diligently to live up to the level of perfection we think it should be.*

This concept of self-development conflicts with standard management practices regarding the way we develop other resources. We don't place responsibility on any other resource we manage to develop itself. Buildings, computers, investments, and so on, do not develop themselves—they require human management for their development. Why should developing people be any different?

Consider a company that acquires several microcomputers to be used by programmers for developing software. In addition to purchasing the machinery, the company also acquires supplementary hardware such as power strips, surge suppressors, uninterruptible power supplies, and the like. Also, the company acquires some software, such as hardware diagnostic programs, "screen savers" (programs that extend the life of cathode ray tube [CRT] display screens), and utilities such as file backup and file restore.

After installing the hardware, the company will institute a preventive maintenance program. On a regular basis technicians will test the hardware for proper functionality, save copies of important files on backup media, and ensure that the machinery is working properly. On occasion, the hardware will be enhanced to increase its functionality. Some examples might include additional memory, higher-capacity hard disks, additional disk drives, expansion boards, and new peripheral connections such as a laser printer or a connection to a local area network.

This method of resource development seems to be done in reverse for human resources. Companies provide an environment for their employees to work in, but expect each individual to optimize his or her

---

* Fournies, Ferdinand F., *Performance Appraisal Design Manual*, F. Fournies & Assoc., 1983.

own effectiveness. For some reason managers have difficulty visualizing people as a resource in business.

If employees are held responsible for developing themselves, their managers are put in the position of scorekeepers. This is unacceptable. Development of their employees must be established as a management directive rather than a voluntary belief or a task delegated to their subordinates.

In *New Insights for Executive Achievement,* a collection of *Harvard Business Review* articles, author Robert Stolz in his article* refers to one company's developmental approach for managers. Top-level managers reassigned low-level managers to give them problem assignments. Facing them with the challenge of the problem assignment, they say, is the best method of developing managers. Those who fail in the face of this test show their true mettle, and subsequently are limited for future promotions.

Such a situation is not applicable in data processing. Managers should be made directly responsible for employee development, as they have a unique insight into their employees' abilities, skill levels, and experience. Giving data processing professionals problem assignments does not develop their skills or expertise unless they are provided with guidance; otherwise, they either succeed or fail, gaining nothing by the experience.

Supplementing appraisal programs with employee development. As mentioned in Chap. 5, it is possible to augment a performance appraisal program with an employee development program. This usually takes the form of a career path planning session or guide. We believe that this is not enough—that employees need and deserve something much more than this.

First, management must accept a portion of the responsibility for employee development, and a good performance appraisal program will allow them to do this. In general, appraisal forms will contain information about employee behaviors and critical incidents. At a minimum, there will be descriptions of employee behaviors, either in essays, checklist entries, ratings, or scores. This knowledge can then be transferred to the employee development system, where it can be used in conjunction with either job descriptions, critical incidents, or training programs to produce an *employee development profile.*

The next step is to alter the current appraisal system so that it includes sufficient information. This may sound impossible, especially in a highly bureaucratic organization, but it is fairly direct. Have all

---

* Robert K. Stolz, "Executive Development—New Perspective," *Harvard Business Review,* 44 (1966): 133.

managers appraising employees append an additional form to the appraisal package indicating the *action plan* to be taken. (Many appraisal systems have this already.) Include in this plan the employee development profile, and indicate how the action plan will affect the profile so as to lead to employee growth. Naturally, the employee must be involved in this process.

The final step is to see that employee action plans and development profile information are reflected in the goals, objectives, and so forth of the appraisal for the next period. For MBO programs and others where goals are set at the beginning of the appraisal period, this is straightforward. For other types of programs, the action plan and profile may become working documents that the employee and manager reference during their regular status meetings.

Forms not related to system objectives

The third major reason for performance appraisal failure has to do with the appraisal forms themselves. In most cases this relates to the differences between the objectives of the appraisal program and the way the forms are used.

Employee development.   For example, many organizations declare that one of the primary objectives of their performance appraisal programs is employee development. Regrettably, one study* found that the average space devoted to employee development amounted to only 8.5 percent of the entire appraisal form. The study went on to note that not only was available space on the form lacking, but there was also very little direction and guidance to appraisers for making specific developmental comments.

Keeping it simple.   Another popular objective of the appraisal design program is to keep it simple. Although the outward motive of this objective is to simplify procedures, the unstated goal is felt to be much more important—that is, that managers resist the work involved in appraising employees, and simplification of the forms is the only answer that will appease them. This objective sometimes results in checklist appraisals that have no bearing on performance, but are easy for a manager to fill out.

This problem is a common one. There are several objectives for performance appraisal systems. Although they were covered in detail in Chap. 4, we mention them briefly here.

---

* Ferdinand F. Fournies, *Management Performance Appraisal—A National Study* (Bridgewater, N.J.; F. Fournies & Associates, Inc., 1973).

- *Making employment decisions.* This includes decisions relating to hiring, firing, promotion, and transfer.

- *Performance improvement.* This topic involves assessing employee behaviors and developing a plan for improving weaknesses and inappropriate behaviors.

- *Assigning work duties.* Here we include all data relating to employee skill sets, knowledge, experience, and expertise, for the purpose of assigning duties efficiently.

- *Identifying and rating potential.* This includes gathering information associated with an employee's current abilities and future potential.

- *Compensation administration.* Here we include salary administration, merit pay, bonuses, commissions, and other forms of monetary pay.

- *Identifying training needs.* This topic involves setting company goals and determining how to bring the staff up to the required levels of training.

- *Career planning and development.* For the employee, these are personal goals regarding his or her career. For the company, this involves comparing and merging company and employee goals so that both benefit from an employee's experience.

Generic appraisals. Another occasional result of the keep-it-simple mentality is the generic appraisal. This is an appraisal form that is designed to be general in nature so that it can be used for a wide variety of diverse and different jobs. Regrettably, the net result is a form that is unusable. This includes one-word identifiers or short phrases to describe employees, such as *dependable, committed,* and *leadership material.* It also includes rating scales with poorly defined terms such as *poor, average,* and *excellent.*

Adapting appraisal forms to business objectives. In general, it is difficult to change business forms and company procedures, especially ones dealing with performance appraisal. Some businesses have developed their own special forms and procedures, and are loath to change them. (This is usually because someone in personnel or upper management has taken "ownership" of the process, or feels that changing it would reflect negatively on themselves.) Some companies have "adapted" programs from other companies, and installed these programs with little or no planning. This may be a sure prescription for failure, for most programs are highly dependent on industry, staff makeup, general level of competency, and various legal considerations. While some forms and procedures work best for some business purposes, the best overall programs seem to be those based on rating scales or management by objectives.

With Fig. 6.1 as your guide (shown previously), we recommend beginning by appending the appropriate information that you require to your current appraisal forms package. This additional information will help serve the business purpose for which you intend it; in addition, it will provide a basis for changing present procedures when the time is ripe.

Poorly defined or improperly implemented procedures

While some companies spend much time and effort on developing elaborate appraisal policies and forms, they sometimes skimp during implementation. Too many firms consider that "fill in the forms" is a sufficient guideline for managers and supervisors. Other companies expand upon this somewhat, giving step-by-step procedures for doing appraisals. However, in the end it boils down to the same thing: What, specifically, do managers *do* to appraise employees? Further, do all managers do the same things, in the proper order, at the appropriate times?

The problem.   The first problem a company might encounter is a lack of consistency in appraisal results across managers; however, detecting this anomaly is difficult. It requires that upper management have a way to compare employee appraisals across managers while screening out irrelevant factors.

The next problem is a legal one. If managers are evaluating employees inconsistently, or if different managers perform appraisals differently, the company may be open to charges of discrimination. In an article* on appraisal systems in the courts, Holley and Feild note several factors that influenced the courts' decisions in favor of the employee or group charging that an appraisal system was discriminatory. Some of those factors were:

Establishing a prima facie case of discrimination.   The authors note several common methods: ". . . presenting statistics to show that black or female employees are being promoted (on the basis of performance appraisals) at a lower percentage than are white males, or that older employees are receiving lower ratings on annual performance reviews." They go on to note that "If the employer fails to show that its performance appraisal system was

---

* *Will Your Performance Appraisal System Hold up in Court?,* by William H. Holley and Hubert S. Feild, *Personnel,* American Management Association, 1982.

designed and administered on the basis of the Uniform Guidelines established under the authority of Title VII of the Civil Rights Act of 1964, the court may render the employer liable for back pay, court costs, specific management training programs for and/or promotion of more female and minority employees as part of the settlement of the case."*

Whether evaluators were given specific written instructions. Courts require that managers responsible for appraising subordinates be given specific written instructions. A lack of written guidelines can throw a performance appraisal system into question.

The method used to develop the appraisal system. The Uniform Guidelines mentioned above require that job analysis be used in developing appraisal systems. The article states that one judge remarked "[T]he analyst did not verify the description by making an on-site inspection of the employee who actually performed the job . . . the former procedure was flawed insofar as it created the possibility of inconsistent descriptions, over- or under-inflation of job duties or requirements, and was associated with the lack of employee awareness of the evaluation procedure . . . The criteria actually employed by the Defendants were not developed by professional consultants, but rather adapted from a commercially available method of job analysis from which Defendants borrowed what they believed to be pertinent to their needs."†

The type of appraisal system. Trait-oriented evaluation systems are deemed by the courts to contain too much potential for partiality or subjectivity. The courts have stated that they look specifically for objective criteria or behavior-oriented evaluations. Quotes from judicial opinions bear this out: "[This court must] determine whether the evaluation method places an undue reliance on general character traits, such that complete subjectivity remains likely." "The operation of an opinion-based appraisal system . . . provides an ideal environment for disparate treatment . . . ." "[T]he evaluations were based on the best judgment and opinion of the evaluators, but were not based on any definite identifiable criteria based on quality or quantity of work or specific performance that were supported by some kind of record."‡

---

* *Ibid.,* p. 60.

† *Ibid.,* p. 62.

‡ *Ibid.,* all quotes from p. 63.

The solution. These problems point out several possible defects that may be present in a company's performance appraisal procedures. To address these, we recommend the following.

Implement systems that are easily standardized. Appraisal systems should contain specific, written instructions for managers. Managers should all receive standard training in these procedures. Upper management should be able to gauge whether, in fact, managers are appraising employees consistently.

Implement systems that are behavior-based. In addition to the courts finding such systems better than those that are trait-oriented, behavior-oriented systems usually evolve out of a proper job analysis. In short, base your appraisal system on a thorough job analysis.

Involve employees in the process. Beyond their input to the job analysis, employees must receive feedback about their performance in order to do something about it. If they are not given this chance, the entire system comes into question.

No definition of performance

As discussed in Chap. 3, designing a performance appraisal system involves deciding at an early stage what is to be measured. There are only three things that one can measure regarding people. These are:

- The descriptive qualities of people (traits)
- The things people do to produce results (behaviors)
- The outcomes or results of what people do

Sadly, the result of most performance appraisal design programs is a set of forms that mix and match these measurements without rhyme or reason. Simply putting a scale on a form and using it to measure an employee does nothing to affect the employee—and since the measurement itself does not affect performance, it is not sufficient *in and of itself* to appraise performance. And this still leaves out the question of the very definition of performance.

What is performance? This question is sometimes answered with "I can't define it, but I know it when I see it!" Such answers point out the very problem that appraisal programs are designed to solve: measurement and judgment of performance. Without a definition for performance, both good and bad, appraisal program design efforts must fail.

As described in Chap. 3, the only measurable thing about employees that is also manageable is their behavior. Personality traits do not correlate with on-the-job performance, and cannot be measured. Once a result has happened, one cannot manage it. Behaviors, however, can be observed and measured, with feedback and reward systems providing for their management. It is only logical then to define employee performance in terms of behaviors, both acceptable and unacceptable.

The problem with management performance. While the performance of computer programmers, analysts, systems programmers, and database administrators can be defined rather objectively, management performance remains a tough knot. The tendency is to concentrate on management theory and philosophy to derive performance measures. Some of these include the following:

- Span of control
- Leadership models
- The managerial grid
- Satisfiers, dissatisfiers, motivators, and hygiene factors
- Theory X, Theory Y, Theory Z

When attempting to get a handle on managerial performance, the tendency is to try to measure things that cannot be measured, and to measure the wrong things at the wrong time. One example of this confusion is that the majority of the respondents in one study* indicated a low interest in measuring personality, yet 70 percent of them included personality factors in their appraisal forms. Another example is the combination of "planning and organizing," either as a single element of performance or using the word "organizing" to describe a level of a totally different activity called "planning."

Moving toward behavior-oriented appraisals. Most progressive companies have switched to a behavior-oriented appraisal system. If your company has not, we recommend you begin to include behavior-based information in your appraisals. Not only are behaviors manageable, they tend to be more objective and minimize rater bias and errors.

Poor appraisal interviews

This last problem causes many performance appraisal program failures, and has to do with the way that appraisal interviews are structured and conducted. In general, either managers do not seem to understand the interview process, or companies have implemented a flawed program.

---

* Ferdinand F. Fournies, *Management Performance Appraisal—A National Study,* Bridgewater, N.J.: F. Fournies & Associates, Inc., 1973.

In the best cases, the appraisal interview is a summary of the employees' behaviors for the review period, as documented in their regular status reports. The interview then proceeds with the manager and the employee affirming the facts as stated, followed by objective-setting for the next period.

Unfortunately, things do not always go the best way. Companies that have not instituted a regular reporting process as part of the appraisal program are stuck with a meeting between the manager and the employee at the end of the review period. During this meeting tempers flare, emotions run high, there is lots of frustration, and much time is wasted. It is a wonder that employees remain with a company that rewards them in this way.

A training issue.   Failure during the interview is a training issue, both for employees and for managers. For most companies, managers are given very little training in how to conduct an appraisal interview. In most cases, the majority of this training involves reading the appraisal manual and forms. In only a very few cases is the manager given specific training in interviewing techniques.

Another related issue is that of employee training. Very few companies train employees in appraisal techniques, or provide them with information about their appraisal program. In many cases, employees are even prohibited from seeing appraisal forms! This kind of backward thinking only serves to isolate employees, making them feel that they are not trusted with knowing how the company views their performance.

The primary problem.   The most common problem with appraisal interviews is that too many different things are being discussed at the same meeting. At a minimum, a manager must discuss the following:

- Performance improvement
- Career development
- Setting objectives

Depending upon the company, managers may also be discussing compensation, future promotional potential, and personnel planning. This makes a total of six separate discussions. Some of these discussions will take a long time to complete, and there are possible conflicting objectives; for example, how can one set future objectives for the next review period if the employee's current performance needs substantial improvement?

Consider the following topics of discussions between a manager and his or her employee:

- Promotional opportunities available within the company and the employee's suitability for them
- Upcoming training that is important for the employee's career aspirations
- A review of the MBO objectives set at the beginning of the review period, whether they were met, and any extenuating circumstances

It is rare that both manager and employee would wish to combine all of these points into a single meeting. Each topic requires a different mind-set and a different set of data regarding performance and current skills. Further, results of each of these discussions may tend to influence the results of the others.

We will discuss improving appraisal interviews in a later section in this chapter.

Summary

In summary, the major reasons for appraisal system failure center around its design. Some of these are:

- Different and conflicting objectives for appraisal forms often make those forms useless and tedious to complete.
- Programs designed without required regular documentation will create problems during the interview process.
- Untrained managers will be unable to communicate program objectives to employees.

In the next section we discuss our specific recommendations for managers and employees.

Prescriptions for Success

The authors declare themselves

If it hasn't become obvious by now, we will state categorically that the only worthwhile performance appraisal programs are those based on a thorough, complete, careful, and accurate job analysis. We also will state that the most effective appraisal programs are either those based on behaviorally anchored rating scales or those based on a company-wide management by objectives (MBO) program. Though neither of these methodologies is perfect, they are both at least acceptable for the following:

- Providing information to management to make business decisions involving:

Monitoring employee objective accomplishment

Making employment decisions (hire, promote, terminate)

Supervising employee performance improvement

Assigning employee work duties effectively

Rating employee potential

Administering a compensation program

Identifying training needs

- Providing information to the employee to make decision regarding:

Career path planning

Training and education

What you should do now

1. If your company has no current formal performance appraisal process, we recommend, as required reading for managers and human resource personnel, *Performance Appraisal—Design Manual,* by F. Fournies. Published by F. Fournies & Associates, Inc., Bridgewater, N.J., 1983.

2. If your company already has a complete performance appraisal system in place and you feel that it could use some help, the above book will be most helpful.

3. If your company's performance appraisal system was based on a thorough job analysis and yet you feel that it lacks something, the advice earlier in this chapter should be of some assistance. Appraisal is not something that many people become experts in, so you can expect some rough edges in your system. Our advice at this point is to read the relevant chapters in our book and then begin to implement those tactics that you feel address the system's weak points. We have found that in most cases this will involve some additional documentation on the part of the employee and manager, as well as a commitment to regularly scheduled employee status meetings. If you don't do *anything* else, at least implement these two things.

To summarize

The employee and manager should document important things (critical incidents, behaviors, objectives reached, and so forth) continually.

The employee and manager should meet regularly (we recommend meeting weekly) and follow this agenda:

- Review the week's documentation for accuracy, completeness, timeliness, relevancy to previous appraisal objectives, and relevancy to job tasks. This provides the audit trail for the review period, and will constitute the bulk of the documents input to the meeting at the end of the appraisal period.

- Each party should provide feedback to the other on their feelings regarding these items. Such feedback may prompt one or the other to modify their observations or assessments. This provides both with an opportunity to respond to praise (or constructive criticism) and document that fact.

- Each item should be "mini-appraised"; that is, the manager should provide the employee with feedback as to how the incident or behavior would be judged if the appraisal meeting were held that day. This furnishes the employees with a running account of their progress, as well as almost immediate feedback on the appropriateness of their behavior.

- The manager should raise any issues regarding changing objectives, new appraisal policies, and the like. This will reduce the likelihood of misunderstandings later.

The appraisal meeting at the end of the review period then becomes a summarization of the previous status meetings. There are no surprises, and the employee is probably already aware of how his or her behavior over the review period will be judged. In fact, since most of these items have already been "mini-appraised" during the regular status meetings, the employees could probably derive their final appraisal results without assistance from their manager!

Appraisal Interviews:
Adapting to Changing Times

In the last section of this chapter we will cover (briefly) something that entire books have been written about: the appraisal interview. As we advocate the procedure outlined in the previous section for performance appraisal meetings, the final interview itself poses few problems. Indeed, we feel that there are no special problems or points of interest posed by this meeting. After all, it will be a simple review of things already covered (and documented) in previous meetings.

Still, few companies have refined their appraisal processes to this stage. This means that their appraisal interviews are still being handled in one or more of the following totally unacceptable ways:

- Interviews are scheduled once per year, and this is the only time during that year that the employees receive any feedback on their performance.

- While interviews should be *extremely* easy to schedule a year in advance, in practice they are usually weeks (or months) late. The typical excuse: the manager is "not ready."

- Immediately prior to the interview the manager begins to gather relevant information about events during the review period. Regrettably, only some of the critical incidents have been documented, and these documents the employee has never seen.

- Often the manager performing the interview has recently had the employee transfer to his or her department. The manager has little or no knowledge of these employees, their history, their goals or objectives, their career plans, or their job history.

- During the interview the employee submits to cross-examination of things that happened several months ago, some of which may not have happened in the review period.

- During the interview the manager summarizes by rating the employee either on some (seemingly) subjective criteria, or on other criteria of which the employee was unaware prior to this meeting.

- At the end of the meeting the employee feels that he or she was treated unfairly, the manager is no closer to being able to make a good decision regarding compensation, potential, or work duties, and the company has lost another opportunity to make a sound business decision.

Let us put this another way. How many managers have the authority to make a decision regarding the outright purchase of a $50,000 computer? If you were such a manager, how much time would you spend investigating alternatives, including processor speed, storage capacity, software compatibility, future expansion, required maintenance, and usability? Would you spend only half an hour?

It is this half hour that many managers spend investigating each of their most important resources: their people. Consider a senior analyst whose salary and benefits will total $50,000 per year. Would you feel comfortable making the decision to hire such a person after spending only half an hour investigating that person (and alternatives)? Consider also that this potential employee will cost your company at least $50,000 *per year.*

We have found that managers confronted with this exercise claim that they would spend an average of six hours investigating the purchase of the $50,000 computer. When asked why, they usually respond, "I have to justify my decision to upper management. If I make a poor decision, my head may roll!" Yet these managers are willing to allocate less than *one hour* on a resource that will cost their company $50,000 per year!

In summary

The appraisal interview is important solely because it is usually the only time that information about an employee's performance is formally acted upon by the company. Managers must fulfill their responsibilities by giving this meeting some of their quality time. This is not to say that employees have no responsibilities; on the contrary, employees must hold up their end of the bargain by acting on feedback provided by the appraisal system. Such feedback is most effective when it is given regularly.

You may wish to reference other books that cover appraisal interviews and interviewing in gruesome detail. (At worst, these books will provide you with examples of how bad it can be.) In the end, however, we must return to our central thesis: that managers and employees, communicating and exchanging regular feedback, will approach the appraisal meeting as a simple summary of things already documented, reviewed, and assessed.

7

Solving Common Appraisal Problems

In this chapter we approach appraisal system problems from the perspective of the people involved: the manager and the employee, or the supervisor and the subordinate. While previous chapters have covered forms, procedures, and various methods of evaluation, here we concentrate on issues and obstacles that should be familiar to all concerned.

Each major section of this chapter describes a problem or situation where the employee performance appraisal plays a major part. Following each problem description is a set of practical alternatives, together with recommendations as to how different evaluation forms and procedures should be used (or modified).

- Problem #1: The New Manager
- Problem #2: The "Transferred" Employee
- Problem #3: Salary Administration
- Problem #4: Interviewing Prospective Employees
- Problem #5: Reconciling Personal and Company Goals
- Problem #6: Handling Unsatisfactory Performance
- Problem #7: Handling Exceptional Performance

Problem #1: The New Manager

Summary

In this scenario we examine the case of the manager recently promoted, transferred, or hired. This common situation poses challenges both to managers and to their employees. Typical problems revolve around the following issues.

The manager may not know the employees.   While some newly promoted managers may have worked with their employees as peers in the past, many new managers face subordinates who are unknown to them. This unfamiliarity may lead to minor initial difficulties in dealings with employees ("personality problems"), or may blossom into productivity or attendance problems. It is important for the new manager to make a good first impression—it is equally important for the employees to do so as well.

The manager may not have received training in the current performance appraisal system.   This issue is one of proper management training, although it may also indicate poor planning on the part of those responsible for assigning the manager to the new position. Complete and thorough training in performance appraisal forms and procedures is a must for managers.

The previous manager may not have done his or her job.   This is, regrettably, the most common issue. Leading the list of offenses in this area are lack of documentation (critical incidents, status reports, objective-setting meetings), lack of a sense of responsibility (overdue appraisal meetings, unfinished evaluations), and failing to follow up on actions (responding to employee concerns, reviewing status reports, resolving disagreements).

Difficulties produced by a predecessor cause the new manager *two* problems. First, the original problems and conditions must be changed, fixed, or satisfied. Second, the employee's mistrust and doubts regarding management must be addressed. It is this second problem that generates the most work for the new manager.

Some alternatives and recommendations

First and foremost, the manager must obtain the necessary training and documentation regarding the company's performance appraisal system. Without this, the following discussion will be of no value. Managers who do not take the time and effort to fully research the extent of their appraisal process and forms risk their employees' careers (and their own). At best, the manager will evaluate employees inconsistently, perhaps subjectively. At worst, the manager may cause employees to transfer, quit, or file suit against the company for wrongful discharge or discrimination. Let's assume, then, that the manager has adequate training in current forms and procedures. What next?

The first step is for the manager to meet with his or her employees and discuss the situation. An agenda for this meeting might include the following points:

- The manager's background and qualifications
- A review of the company's performance appraisal policies and procedures
- Addressing employees' questions
- Scheduling meetings with each employee in the near future

The manager should concentrate on developing a good relationship with his or her new employees right from the beginning. It is said that one never gets a second chance at making a first impression.

After the general meeting the new manager should next schedule meetings with each of the individual employees. The subject matter of each meeting should revolve around the company's procedures for goal-setting, and should include the following:

- A statement by the manager of the company's goals, including long-range plans, marketing, divisional, and departmental goals
- A statement by the employee of his or her goals, including personal, professional, short-range and long-range
- A comparison of the two sets of goals (note that this should have already been completed and documented as a part of the employee's previous performance appraisal "objective-setting" meeting with his or her former manager)
- A discussion regarding how these two sets of goals match—whether there are any common threads, whether they are consistent, divergent, and so forth
- A discussion of the employee's status and recent progress toward his or her goals

Each meeting will be different. Some employees may be dissatisfied, as they view the process as tedious, nonsensical, or pointless. Others may be apathetic, seeing the appraisal process as no more than an exercise in filling out forms. These feelings can sometimes be eased by urging employees to contribute to the process, thus influencing their destiny.

The results of these two sets of meetings (general and employee-specific) should be fully documented by the manager. Should the files of any of their employees seem to be incomplete (or empty), these meetings may constitute the only proof that management has attempted to fulfill its responsibilities. While lack of correct documentation is not prima facie evidence of discrimination or incompetence, it will certainly make an objective performance appraisal all the more difficult.

Recommendations for specific procedures

In this section we present suggestions that are specific to the most common appraisal programs. In each case, we attempt to reconcile the types of forms used and their corresponding procedures with the situation (the new manager).

Checklists. Checklist appraisal systems are generally inadequate for organizing and documenting goal setting. This is usually because most checklists present summary information in a balance sheet format, telling where the employees are *now,* but not where they have come, where they are going, and how they are going to get there.

Checklist performance appraisal systems are usually supplemented with a separate program of employee career development and divisional or departmental project planning. The manager, then, must reconcile information from this other program to that in the checklist evaluation. Sometimes the manager is tempted to do things backward—first determine the employee's status, judge his or her performance, then input this information into career planning. The net result is an employee stuck in a one-track career, aimlessly reacting to available projects and career opportunities.

A better way of handling this situation is to do it in the right order. First, managers and employees should concern themselves with employee career planning. The results of these sessions or meetings will be employee and company goals and their commonalities. This information is then used as a basis for planning the next appraisal period, employee short-term goals, availability of training, additional responsibilities or assignments, and so forth. Finally, at the end of the appraisal period, all of this data can be consolidated into an appraisal format.

The foregoing may sound like a broken record. The gist of it has been repeated in one form or another in each chapter. At the risk of repeating it again in yet another form, the authors state the following: *measurement and documentation must occur before judgment and action.*

Critical incidents. Critical incident appraisal systems have an advantage over checklist methods in that they provide documentation of historical data as a part of the appraisal process. While this data is necessary for proper employee evaluation, it must be supplemented with some kind of goal-setting process.

In the situation of the new manager, a review of the employees' files is critical (pardon the pun). After this review, the manager should meet with the employees as recommended in the beginning of this section. In addition to the subjects mentioned, one additional item must be covered in these meetings: the current manager's understanding of each employee's situation.

While some managers are experts at documenting critical incidents, many managers (and many employees) are unable to express their thoughts in writing. In spite of classes with titles like Written Communications Skills, Writing Better Memos, and Communicate for Results!, many people never rise above a certain minimal level of competence in this area.

The most common problem with critical incident reviews (and other essay forms of review) is the ambiguous, hazy, unclear, vague, or otherwise nebulous description of the incidents themselves. To give you a feeling for what we mean here, consider the following sentence in a memo one manager wrote to another regarding recommending an employee for transfer: "You may consider yourself lucky if you get this person to work for you."

Taken one way, this sentence implies that the manager receiving the transferred employee is lucky to have gotten such a gifted worker. Taken another way, the manager may be lucky to get the employee to work *at all*.

Our point: new managers should review *their interpretation* of each critical incident with their employees. Differences of opinion should be documented.

Essay reviews. As with critical incident methods, essay reviews are adequate but require a supplementary goal-setting process. Our comments about critical incident performance evaluations apply here.

Management by objectives. Most MBO programs are tailor-made for handling this scenario. Assuming the program has been set up properly and that all participants are following procedures (two big assumptions), new managers should have no problems coping with their new situation. Lack of documentation or incompetence of the prior manager is usually best addressed by adhering to the letter of the MBO process and following procedures. These include the usual steps of goal determination, goal-setting meetings, and so forth, which are an integral part of MBO programs.

Ranking systems. Ranking appraisal systems, like checklist systems, are entirely inadequate for this situation. Knowing an employee's rank among his or her peers gives a manager no useful historical information, and (again) must be supplemented with some goal-setting or career development process. Our comments under "Checklists" above are appropriate here.

Rating scales.   Rating scale systems, especially older ones (dating from the 1960s), tend to do an adequate job of measuring an employee's current "status." While this is useful in the planning process, it still must be supplemented with a formal goal-setting program. Managers may also wish to direct such goal-setting at the appraisal form itself. For example, an employee rated "3" in some category may wish to set a goal of achieving a "4" or "5" in that category on the next appraisal. Naturally, the manager's help is required in determining exactly what must be done to achieve such a rating.

Problem #2: The "Transferred" Employee

Summary

In this scenario it is the employee who is new, not the manager. While somewhat similar to the previous problem, there are usually special circumstances regarding the employee that require special attention. These include the following.

No paperwork or documentation for the employee.   For a newly hired employee, this may be the normal case. For a veteran employee, it is an inexcusable situation. At a minimum, lists of critical incidents, goals, objectives, status reports, and the previous performance appraisal should be available.

The employee's appraisal is due soon.   Strangely, this happens much more often than one would expect. After all, if employees are appraised yearly, and if appraisal due dates are spread evenly throughout the year, then the odds of being assigned an employee whose appraisal is now due should be 1:12, or about 8 percent. Our contact with managers suggests that this ratio is, in reality, closer to 1:4, or even 1:2. In other words, employee transfers seem to be much more likely just prior to an appraisal. Since transfer decisions are supposed to be made as a *result* of an appraisal, this observed result flies in the face of common sense.

No apparent reason for the transfer.   There is always a reason for transferring an employee, whether stated or not. A good appraisal system matches and compares employee and company goals, and generates plans of action that then may translate into employee transfer.

A manager in this situation should inquire as to the real reason for the transfer. For the reader's convenience, we provide an abbreviated translation table of reasons (Fig. 7.1).

Regrettably, many of these reasons indicate that the company's appraisal system is being given lip service by management (at least in the strict sense of correct, objective performance appraisal as defined in this book). Such insincerity or hypocrisy also indicates that there is some other, perhaps informal, mechanism for evaluating employees. In cases like these, managers' and employees' efforts toward objective performance appraisal may be bypassed. Unfortunately, there is then not much the manager or employee can do.

Some alternatives and recommendations

Managers in this situation (The New Employee) should first endeavor to discover any special circumstances involved in the new employee's transfer. This investigation should include the following:

- Determining the employee's next appraisal due date
- Determining the reason for the employee's transfer
- A review of documentation regarding employee and company goals
- A review of the information (or lack thereof) in the employee's file

Stated Reason for Transfer	Translation
The employee was needed on another project	The company's goals are important, the employee's are not
It is for the employee's own good	No analysis of the employee's goals has been made
The employee needs more experience; the new department will provide it	Management failed to provide an environment in which the employee could develop
The previous manager and the employee had a "personality conflict"	Management either: (a) failed to train the previous manager correctly, or (b) failed to help the employee deal with a problem
The employee needs a manager that can do an appraisal immediately	Management is more concerned with appraisal form than with substance

Figure 7.1   Stated (and actual) reasons for employee transfer.

After this investigation the manager will be in a much better position to determine a course of action. In general, the following steps will apply.

- If any documentation is missing or incomplete, the manager should take responsibility for completing it. This may require notifying upper management.

- The manager should schedule one or more meetings with the employee to discuss the situation. These meetings may take the form of informal discussions at first—later ones should be formal and well-documented.

- The manager and employee then settle upon an action plan for the short term. These plans may include "mini-reviews," extended status meetings, interviews and discussions with prior managers or the employee's peers, and documentation of employee behaviors and accomplishments.

- Only after these steps have been accomplished can the manager continue with the normal routine, including any upcoming employee performance appraisal.

Recommendations for specific procedures

Our recommendations in this situation are similar to those in the previous problem (The New Manager). We include here only that advice which is different from or expands upon that already given.

First, let's discuss the case where the previous appraisal is missing or incomplete. While it might seem to be a fairly simple procedure, re-creating a checklist appraisal for a prior period is normally not realistic. This would require a complete set of documentation for the prior review period. (If this is available, why was the appraisal not completed?) The only condition where this is a reasonable course of action is if the document itself is missing but the prior appraisal was completed.

In cases where the prior appraisal is available, completing an upcoming appraisal will involve assembling documentation (status reports, mini-reviews, and so forth) for the current review period. If these are not available, the manager must take the responsibility of creating them. Some of this responsibility can be delegated to the employee—some might even be assigned to upper management.

In cases where it appears that there has been a breakdown (real or suspected) in the performance appraisal process, the manager must proceed carefully. These cases include a missing or improperly done prior appraisal, ignoring an employee's personal goals (see the chart earlier in this section), incompetence of the previous manager, or an incomplete or subjective appraisal system.

At this point, one has several options.

Ignore the breakdown, proceed with appraisal.   Managers do this at their peril. While it may seem that one is doing the employee a favor by continuing with the formal process and finishing the current appraisal on time, this may embroil the manager in further controversy later. Possible consequences involve legal actions such as claims of discrimination, wrongful discharge, or negligence. In these cases, the company's best defense is an objective performance appraisal system.

Refuse to continue with appraisal.   On the other hand, this reaction may be extreme. It is the manager's responsibility to help employees get work done, and this reaction doesn't do that. Such an act may be taken as insubordination by upper management (which it is).

Bring the problem to the attention of upper management.   It is the manager's responsibility to inform upper management of the breakdown in the appraisal process. Having done so, we recommend that the manager predicate his or her next actions upon the response from upper management.

1. The manager should insist that upper management provide some formal response to the problem. Without such a response, the new manager is placed in an awkward position. The employee will feel (rightly) that management condones the current situation. New managers will feel that upper management has ignored their objections and given them a task that they feel they cannot perform.

2. If company management's response is weak, or boils down to "that's the way it's done here," our recommendation is to refuse to work under these circumstances. We see the manager's position as comparable to that of an accountant who discovers unethical or invalid accounting practices, or a lawyer who suspects his or her firm of unscrupulous behavior. Any manager who disregards such practices, or permits them to continue by ignoring them, makes him or herself just as guilty.

    Refusing to evaluate an employee using a subjective or invalid appraisal system may place a manager's job in jeopardy(!). We recommend discussing the situation with someone in the personnel department, the company ombudsman, one's immediate superior, or someone else who can be expected to respond formally.

3. If company management responds positively, either with a promise to rectify the system or by addressing specific symptoms (the

previous manager, the status of personnel files, and so on), the manager may now discuss the situation with the employee. This discussion should center around the future, not the past: "Where do we go from here?"

We now finish this section with some comments specific to particular appraisal systems.

Checklists. A missing or incomplete checklist appraisal will be almost impossible to complete. (Actually, we would view this situation as positive—the authors have little use for checklist reviews.) Here, we recommend doing a "mini-review" as soon as possible. As checklist systems always require supplemental documentation, begin assembling it as soon as possible.

Critical incidents. A missing or incomplete critical incident appraisal can usually be constructed from the documentation of the incidents. If this documentation is missing or incomplete, the manager may be able to reconstruct it with the employee's help. Regrettably, this will take time.

Essay reviews. A missing essay appraisal may be a blessing in disguise. It is rare that one encounters an essay review that is well-written, objective, and fulfills goal-setting and measurement criteria. In this case, a simple compilation of remaining documentation for the period (if any) can be used as the "previous appraisal." If this documentation is not available, or is incomplete, the manager should attempt to re-create it with the employee's help.

Management by objectives (MBO). Most successful MBO systems require a well-organized support system to keep track of paperwork, employee goals, company goals, objective-setting criteria, and so forth. It is uncommon for these systems to fail on a global level. (When they do, everyone is aware of it.) Any problem noted by the manager, then, will probably be due to the company's use of appraisal information, rather than measurement or judgment errors. This is usually corrected with management training in the appraisal process.

Ranking systems. Luckily, the employee's previous appraisal in this case has little meaning (see our comments on ranking systems in prior chapters). Since this sort of appraisal is that of a "snapshot," prior documentation may not be needed to complete it for the current period. The problem comes when managers must justify their decisions regarding employee rankings. Lack of documentation leads to subjective appraisals, which are difficult to defend in court.

Rating scales.   This all-around useful system provides the tools needed to re-create or reconstruct missing or incomplete documentation. With the employee's help, the manager can review rating scale items with an eye toward the prior review period. This may also involve meeting with the employee's prior manager.

Problem #3: Salary Administration

Summary

Regrettably, the way salaries and other compensation is apportioned in data processing seems to have little to do with performance. Salary increases seem to have little effect on productivity, and create compensation unfairness as employees are paid more and more to do less and less.

In terms of providing incentive for performance, data processing salaries fail miserably. For example, a programmer coding several important application subsystem modules over a period of several months may have to wait six months to a year for an appraisal that may or may not lead to an increase in his or her compensation. This extremely long period between the behavior and the reward (if any) makes salary as a positive reinforcer highly suspect.

In terms of compensating employees fairly for what they do, it is important to note the distinction between *job evaluation* and *performance appraisal.*

> *Job evaluation* is the process of measuring jobs to place a value on the job regardless of who is performing the job. *Performance appraisal* is a process of measuring performance to place a value on how a person is performing in a particular job. The two measurements are not a connected process and can vary independently of each other.*

Without both job evaluation and performance appraisal, fair compensation administration is simply not possible.

The overall rating.   Converting performance appraisal information into a compensation decision is another bottleneck. Despite the best efforts of those who create appraisal systems, a compensation decision requires some kind of overall employee rating.

> No matter how complicated and comprehensive you design your performance appraisal program, and regardless of the reasons why you require an overall rating, the use of the overall rating reduces the entire appraisal process to the single judgment process of fifty years ago, "this employee is good, that one is bad." The answer to that single question provides no specific or meaningful information for improving performance, designing

---

* Fournies, *Performance Appraisal—Design Manual,* 1983.

training programs, or for preparing individuals for the future. It brings your performance appraisal back to the level of grading eggs.

In actual practice, managers work the process backward. They decide how much money they want the individual to have, select the overall rating which will get that much money, and fill in the front portion of the form to substantiate the overall rating.*

This sad state of affairs is all too common in data processing. Luckily, there are several evaluation systems that make determination of an overall rating relatively simple. These are discussed in the following sections.

Some alternatives and recommendations

In general, compensation administration should be kept out of the hands of managers. They are responsible for seeing that employees have the opportunity to get work done, efficiently and productively. A manager should never be placed in the position of both measurement and judgment. As discussed in earlier chapters, this leads to making assessments of an employee's value before all of the facts are in. Such subjectivity is unneeded and unwanted.

Compensation is usually left to the personnel department or to upper management. In these cases, the employee's manager may have to act as the employee's advocate, lobbying (in effect) for a particular level of compensation. This can lead to several problems.

What about other subordinates? If a manager urges the personnel department to give a sizable increase to a particular employee, what about the other employees who report to that manager? Shouldn't they receive recognition as well? What if two employees deserve recognition, but there is only a budget for one to get a raise? What if only one of the two employees is being appraised this month?

What about other employees? If the manager succeeds in getting a substantial raise for the desired employee, won't this mean that fewer dollars are available for raises to other employees?

Does the manager have the requisite skill? "The squeaky wheel gets the grease," goes an old saying. This means that managers having good oral communications skills will be able to get raises for their employees and others will not.

A manager faced with the task of compensation administration who has no formal guidelines runs many risks. Accordingly, most companies have a formal procedure for the manager to follow. Unfortunately, as mentioned above, many managers fall into the trap of prejudging

---

* Fournies, *Performance Appraisal—Design Manual,* 1983.

the employee's performance. They then manipulate the compensation system so that it produces what they have already judged as fair.

To avoid this problem many companies separate or distribute responsibility for compensation decisions among several managers. This has the advantage of allowing a manager to be somewhat objective about judging another manager's subordinates.

Most forms of compensation systems boil down to the following:

- Determine, based on company policy, profitability, and budget, what an "average" or "normal" percentage raise will be. Use this number across all employees being appraised.

- Judge each employee as being in one of the following categories:

  1. Greatly exceeded expectations

  2. Met objectives

  3. Failed to meet one or more objectives

- Employees in Category 3 get no raise.

- Employees in Category 2 get a "normal" raise.

- Employees in Category 1 get a "greater-than-normal" raise.

Naturally, the terms "normal" and "greater than normal" are extremely subjective and open to interpretation.

We end our all-too-short discussion of proper salary administration with specific comments about particular appraisal systems.

Checklists. The checklist provides no separate or overall ratings, simply acceptable or unacceptable indications for behaviors. This may be enough for companies having compensation schemes that reward acceptable employees equally (i.e., the same raise). Other companies prefer some kind of sliding scale. Further, checklist results cannot easily be converted to a single, numerical rating.

The checklist method must be supplemented with a goal system, as described in an earlier section (The New Manager). Further, it requires additional organized information about acceptable and unacceptable employee behaviors.

Critical incidents. It is very difficult to attach a value to a critical incident. Therefore, this method will be unable to provide the manager with either an overall single measure of performance or a relative ranking of their employees. Such information is crucial in making compensation decisions. Incidents must be organized and matched to acceptable behaviors.

Essay reviews. Most essay review systems provide no way for a manager to quantify the employee's behavior or results. This leaves the manager in the position of not being able to evaluate employee compensation from the information in the review itself. In some companies this is proper, as there are other professionals who will use other methods to handle compensation. Such situations are familiar ones to assembly-line workers, teachers, and the military. Still, the essay review contains precious little information that would allow a data processing manager to make an informed salary decision.

Essay review systems are unacceptable as a basis for compensation and must be supplemented with prose on goals and objectives, as well as acceptable employee behaviors.

Management by objectives (MBO). Although most MBO forms do not allow the rater to develop a single overall rating, the MBO appraisal is still an acceptable medium for compensation administration. In general, managers will use a combination of goal difficulty with number and type of goals achieved to arrive at an index of the employee's performance during the review period. This measure is somewhat subjective; still, many companies use it.

Ranking systems. Regardless of individual competencies, some companies have a policy of *pay for performance*. By this they mean that the highest performers get the best raises. In the case of ranking methods, the highest-ranked employees are generally the best performers. To take into account that such a ranking system is relative, rather than absolute, the company looks at overall profits. If profits are high, then this is deemed evidence of good overall employee performance, and raises are high. If profits are low, this is evidence of poor overall performance, and raises are correspondingly lower.

The disadvantages of this method are: excellent performers can be overshadowed by other excellent performers in the same division; poor performers can remain hidden within other poor performers; and high-ranking employees in one division are not directly comparable to those in another division.

Ranking systems will need goal and behavior measurement information to allow for true and objective compensation administration.

Rating scales. Better than other methods, rating scales are able to produce a single, numerical, overall rating of an employee's performance. Some systems take a simple average of the ratings in all categories, while others use weighting factors. As long as the employee and manager agree on this method at the beginning of the review period, the rating scale forms an excellent basis for justifying compensation decisions.

Problem #4: Interviewing Prospective Employees

Summary

Although not a new practice, few companies use performance appraisal methods or systems for interviewing prospective employees. As most appraisal systems are built with the expressed purpose of measuring and evaluating performance, it is odd that they have not been used for potential new-hires.

Part of this mystery might be explained as an interviewer's reluctance to do the work required to complete a mini-review. Still, wouldn't this information be available from the employee in the form of his or her most recent appraisal? Strangely, most companies do not trust the information in such appraisals to be accurate (although they feel that their own appraisals are accurate and objective). Also, some companies have the interesting practice of not allowing employees to retain copies of their own appraisals! Although this information is always available to employees through the Freedom of Information Act, some companies persist in trying to conceal such "sensitive" documents from prying eyes.

Types of interviews

Before the discussion on adapting appraisal systems for use as hiring tools, we need to address the various types of interviews companies use. Each interview type requires a different approach, as dissimilar information is collected.

The technical interview.   Probably the one most familiar to those in data processing, the purpose of the technical interview is to measure the applicant's knowledge and skills in certain job-relevant technical areas. Unless given in the form of an interactive or hands-on exercise, this interview consists of a set of questions for the applicant to answer. The number of correct answers then determines the applicant's level of skill or expertise.

This mode of interview is similar to the rating scale appraisal system, although here the applicants effectively rate themselves.

The career interview.   Called by many names, the purpose of this interview is to determine if the goals of the applicant are consonant with those of the company. If a good fit is not found, the applicant will not be happy, if hired. It is this interview that is potentially the most subjective. Here is where an adapted performance appraisal procedure can do the most good.

The management interview. Because applicants feel that they must dress well, this is sometimes called the "dress for success" interview. Here, upper management talks with the potential employee and tries to identify whether that person is "management material" or "there is a good fit." Typically unstructured, management attempts to determine something that is best described as subjective. Here is another case where an adapted appraisal system could help.

Some alternatives and recommendations

As most companies have a separate recruiting, hiring, and training function, managers may have little say as to interviewing and hiring procedures. Still, the manager is usually involved at some point in interviewing prospective employees. At this point, the manager must have an organized, objective approach to conducting that interview. Should current policies or forms seem inadequate (or useless), appraisal forms can sometimes be adapted for use as interview tools.

Checklists. The simple checklist doesn't contain enough information to measure the prospective employee's knowledge or skills. This makes it unusable for making hiring decisions. Management requires information such as level of education, results accomplished, and specific systems expertise from potential new-hires. Also, if checklists are used as hiring tools, management may need to provide some proof that the checklist appraisal system is objective. This is necessary if the checklist is to be used for making employment decisions. This proof of objectivity may consist of documents relating to the job analysis used to create the appraisal system, or a statistical analysis of the data. The danger here is that the system may already be subjective, either in design or in use. This may open interviewers to claims of discrimination or unfair hiring practices.

Critical incidents. Since this method requires historical documentation, it cannot be used as-is to make hiring decisions. Such forms may be modified so that the interviewer can document incidents that the employee might describe, but these will then need corroboration. This is best done through reference checking.

Essay reviews. Essay reviews are not feasible for hiring new employees as no historical record exists for comparison. Further, the time required for completing them in almost any form is usually extreme.

Management by objectives (MBO). MBO forms are not very useful during interviewing, as goals from a previous company are not likely to be compatible with your own. Even so, a "mini-review" using such a form can give the interviewer some useful information. This is recommended for both the management interview and the career interview.

Ranking systems. Ranking systems are almost useless for making hiring decisions unless the raters have available a sufficiently large pool of candidates. If this is the case, then the candidates can be ranked from least to most qualified, and the top n then hired (where n is the number of new-hires required). Hopefully, the top candidates will meet the company's minimum standards for the available jobs, because the ranking procedure provides no information about this.

The disadvantage of this system for hiring is that rankings have a tendency to be assigned subjectively. Any company using such a system for hiring purposes should be prepared (as in the case of checklists) to substantiate the objectiveness of the system.

Rating scales. Rating scales can be very useful for making such decisions. Hiring new employees is best accomplished by measuring their current skills and knowledge—this is easily done with a rating system, coupled with a good technical interviewing program. This is recommended for the technical interview.

Problem #5: Reconciling Personal and Company Goals

Summary

This is sometimes the most difficult portion of performance appraisal. Such reconciliation sometimes takes the form of a career planning session. At other times, especially using an MBO-format appraisal system, goal setting and reconciliation are part of the formal appraisal process. In either case the goals of the employee and company, both short-term and long-term, must be tuned to accommodate each other.

When managers encounter problems involving conflicting goals, they are placed in a difficult position. As a part of management they espouse the company philosophy, creed, and so forth. As supervisors, they act as advocates for the employees. It is likely they may feel torn between two conflicting sets of requirements.

We have already devoted a chapter of this book to employee career planning. At this point, what can a manager do to ease the process?

Some alternatives and recommendations

Few appraisal systems are built to settle differences between employee and company goals. (The exception is the MBO program, addressed below.) Following are some recommendations for adapting current appraisal forms and procedures to assist managers in their efforts.

Checklists. The checklist provides little feedback to the employee as to his or her level of accomplishment. In addition, management requires a measure of the employee's stage of development that the checklist cannot provide. For example, forced-choice checklists are directed at individual jobs. While it is possible to determine whether the employee's behaviors are acceptable for a progression of jobs, no information is obtained on *how* to determine which jobs an employee should or could pursue.

The checklist system must be supplemented with several additional systems. First, employees can be made aware of the contents of checklist forms for jobs at higher levels. This will assist them in that they then will have information regarding how these jobs will be evaluated. Second, the employee's manager must ascertain the company's goals. Sometimes this information is available (though sometimes somewhat ambiguously stated) in annual reports, marketing literature, or policies and procedures documents. Third, the manager and employee must meet, discuss the company goals, and document the employee's goals. Further actions will depend on the outcome of these steps.

Critical incidents. Critical incidents provide little, if any, information to the manager or employee regarding career possibilities within the company. At most, they furnish the manager with a starting point for a career planning meeting.

To make a critical incident appraisal useful for career planning, incidents must somehow be rated. While most such programs assign values of "acceptable" and "unacceptable" to incidents, more is required. A job analysis that results in a critical incident appraisal system usually involves collecting and analyzing many sample critical incidents. This information should be evaluated further, with the objective of determining ratings or values of the incidents. Even a general 1-to-5 scale should prove adequate.

While critical incident methods may produce a wealth of information about an employee's behaviors, little is learned about their level of job skill, education, or promotability; however, this is usually easily remedied. The simplest method is to assemble lists of critical incidents from the job descriptions of higher-level jobs and give them to employees. Since these, by definition, constitute a description of acceptable behaviors of employees at higher levels, they therefore provide employees with guidelines for advancement. These may then be factored into the employee's current appraisal and covered in depth at the next status meeting.

Essay reviews. Most essay review forms contain a section for employee career development, along with an action plan. Typically, the manager and the employee will complete this section after the main part of the review has been completed. Unfortunately, nothing in the essay review materials per se is applicable to employee and company goals; hence, career planning is made all the more difficult. Supplement essay reviews with MBO-style goal-setting procedures.

Management by objectives (MBO). The MBO review program is usually implemented in concert with a strategic goal-setting plan at high levels within the company. This is so that the goals set by the manager and the employee are in harmony with company goals. Against this backdrop the manager and the employee jointly address the employee's career goals. While the MBO program provides little information regarding how company goals and employee career goals can be fused, at least the information is available.

Ranking systems. Ranking techniques provide no information about goals or goal achievement. Some kind of MBO-style goal-setting and evaluating procedures must supplement it.

Rating scales. Although the rating scale method can produce what seem to be precise assessments of employee performance, there is barely enough information present regarding the company's goals and objectives. Such data is buried in the appraisal document itself—the assumption is that company goals were used to *derive* the appraisal process, and that the final result will meet those goals.

Because of this assumption, employees and their managers must assume that career planning will occur under the umbrella of the appraisal system, and that career planning meetings will use the review document as the preliminary agenda. It may be difficult to resolve employee goals with the unstated goals in the appraisal documents, but it is possible. Again, an MBO-style goal-setting procedure will be sufficient.

Problem #6: Handling Unsatisfactory Performance

Summary

Performance, productivity, attendance, and "personality" problems all seem to be lumped together in managers' minds as unsatisfactory performance regardless of symptoms, causes, or possible cures. The typical scenario is for the manager (or someone else) to notice an employee problem, either by direct observation, measurement, or as part of a formal appraisal. The unacceptable performance or behaviors are formally documented, and the employee is given a period of time to show improvement. If improvement occurs, this is documented. If no improvement occurs, the employee faces compensation decrease, transfer, or termination.

Sometimes one gets the impression that performance appraisal systems were designed specifically to address this situation. Indeed, some employees see the appraisal as a tool used to fire unwanted employees. Part of this problem revolves around something discussed in an earlier part of this book (Chap. 3), the difference between measurement and judgment. To repeat, the appraisal system is primarily meant as a measurement tool—to gather facts, record them, organize them, and so on. Judgment occurs later, as the facts from the appraisal are analyzed and evaluated. Several different types of judgments are made about the information in an appraisal. Among these are making employment decisions, performance improvement planning, identifying and rating potential, compensation administration, and career planning. Each of these types of decisions requires a different kind and quality of information. In particular, making a termination decision or setting up a performance improvement plan requires particular measurements.

What is needed

In the case of the employee displaying unacceptable or unsatisfactory performance, several things are required. Since the beginning of the review period, the employee and manager have both observed and documented incidents and behaviors. This documentation usually takes the form of status reports or "mini" appraisals. During the review period it is the responsibility of each party to interpret such reports in the context of the appraisal process, thus providing feedback on appropriateness of the employee's behavior and the effects of performance on promotional opportunities and compensation. In some cases, this ongoing analysis may prompt the manager to develop a *work improvement plan* for the employee.

Another responsibility of the two parties during the review period is that they both note how the various incidents which occur will be viewed by the eventual appraisal process. This preappraisal review requires that the performance appraisal forms and procedures explicitly state how various incidents will be rated or valued. Not only will this prevent any unforeseen or embarrassing "surprises" during the appraisal interview, it permits the manager and the employee to tune the employee's behavior during the review period. This tuning will result in a better employee, and will make the judgment process one of agreement rather than contention.

Some alternatives and recommendations

If such tuning was not possible, or the employee's behavior continues to be unacceptable, management must document it. Some appraisal systems provide this capability to some degree; others do not.

Checklists. The simple checklist at least specifies actual behaviors, although the employee and manager must know which behaviors are deemed *acceptable* and which are not, so that the employee can improve his or her performance. Like the simple checklist, the forced-choice checklist provides information about employee behaviors, both good and bad. This can be used as a guide for behavior improvement, although the checklist alone provides no information about how to improve. Assuming that appraisal items can be interpreted into a list of acceptable behaviors, this must then be supplemented by a set of *action plans* that recommend how unacceptable behaviors should be improved.

Critical incidents. The critical incident technique requires the manager and the employee to review each incident in terms of what alternative behaviors were available, and which were considered acceptable. A summary of this information can be introduced directly into a performance improvement plan. In time, additional critical incidents will be used as feedback to determine the level of improvement.

Essay reviews. Essay reviews may be used for performance improvement if the essay information includes descriptions of *all* relevant employee behaviors during the review period. This must then be supplemented with alternative behaviors available, and what the employee could do to improve.

If this information is not available, the essay review is of no use for performance improvement.

Management by objectives (MBO). As the objectives stated at the beginning of the review period are those on which the employees will be judged, employees should always be aware of how their actions will affect their performance. Further, should additional improvement be necessary, the MBO forms furnish the basis of an action plan, including objectives to work on and the standards against which they will be judged. Regrettably, the MBO system tells only *what* must be improved, not *how* or *why*. These steps must be addressed by the manager as part of a performance improvement plan.

Ranking systems. Ranking methods provide comparisons between employees, but may not require the manager to justify his or her rankings. In cases where documentation of the ranking process is required, the manager's explanations should include such reasons. This information, though meager, may be enough to construct an action plan for employee performance improvement. This is rare, however. Typical ranking schemes show where employees rank *now,* but not how they got there, whether they are improving, or what must be done to improve. In these cases ranking systems must be supplemented with a formal performance improvement program.

Rating scales.   Each rating scale category is usually a measurement of the employee's behaviors in that category. Scales are usually ranked from low to high, accompanied by textual descriptions and examples of poor and good performance. This provides the employee with a direct measurement of how his or her behavior is perceived, and details examples of acceptable behaviors in that category. Performance improvement plans can concentrate on these acceptable behaviors as a model for the employee's future, and can be based on entries in each category. Rating scale systems are by far the best for addressing employee performance improvement.

Problem #7: Handling Exceptional Performance

Summary

This problem doesn't strike many managers as being a problem at all. And yet, when it comes to appraising the superstar, most managers (and appraisal systems) fail. This is more than just a matter of the exceptional performer being outside the normal bounds of an evaluation. How does one motivate one's star performer?

Part of this problem is that procedures for identifying and rating potential are usually the last to be considered when designing an appraisal system. The result is a system built for handling compensation or termination, not for determining employee potential.

Some alternatives and recommendations

Determining employee potential for advancement, or simply for more complicated work, involves assessing things that may not be measured easily. In general, appraisal systems that measure employee behaviors or objectives achieved are poor in this respect. In fact, the easiest method of determining whether or not employees have the potential to be promoted is to appraise them as if they had already been promoted, even using the appropriate evaluation forms for that job.

Checklists. While some jobs can be described in terms of employee behaviors, others such as computer programming and systems analysis may depend more on education and skills. Checklists provide management little feedback about an employee's potential. The forced-choice checklist compels the manager or supervisor to select behaviors that most correctly describe the employee. This information, if it is supplemented with a set of standards for each position, is sometimes enough to identify how an employee will perform in another position.

Critical incidents. The critical incident technique provides a wealth of information regarding employee behaviors; however, the manager must do a lot of work to organize the data to determine which employees may perform well in higher-level jobs. Again, what is needed is a comparison of current behaviors with those of employees in higher-level jobs.

Essay reviews. Most managers consider this form of review the best as a basis for making promotional decisions. Strangely, most managers consider this form the most likely to be entirely subjective. Most managers seem to complete essay reviews with information that they have chosen as relevant for that review at that time, typically for compensation or employment decisions (hire, transfer, terminate). Seldom is this information sufficient for identifying and rating potential. It must be supplemented with documentation of employee behaviors and acceptable behaviors for higher-level jobs.

Management by objectives (MBO). MBO programs seem tailor-made for rating employee potential. The goals set for employees provide a measure of what talent is available. Managers may use this to identify employees who potentially are promotable to positions with higher, more difficult, or technically more advanced goals.

Ranking systems. For jobs which require little training, it may be possible to justify promoting the highest-ranking employees. Still, the technique provides no data regarding the absolute competencies of employees. The highest-ranking employee may be the best of a set of marginal employees. In another case, the lowest-ranking employee may be the worst of a set of superstars.

To be able to make an informed decision, the manager should supplement the ranking system with a separate evaluation of suitability for promotion. This system usually takes the form of a miniature MBO or critical incident system.

Rating scales. While most rating scales provide management data about employee behaviors, they are not so good at identifying potential. Indeed, none of the appraisal methods mentioned in this book handles this perfectly. However, since most managers find that the rating scale gives them a numerical measure of employee achievement, they use achievement as a *predictor* of future success. In other words, employees that have achieved a lot are deemed to have the greatest potential.

To ensure that this system is implemented fairly, managers should rate employees as if they were already in higher-level jobs. These ratings may then be used to determine potential for advancement.

8

Improving Appraisal Forms

In this chapter we turn to the future—what can be done to improve the current state of affairs in your company vis-à-vis appraisals and appraisal procedures. In each section we focus on practical advice rather than theory. Managers responsible for doing employee evaluations should find this chapter especially useful.

Here, we revisit some of the forms seen in Chap. 5 with an eye toward making some improvements. The areas in which the forms will be judged are shown below:

- Making employment decisions
- Performance improvement
- Assigning work duties
- Identifying and rating potential
- Compensation administration
- Identifying training needs
- Career planning and development

The forms

This chapter highlights the various appraisal and evaluation forms covered earlier in this book (Chap. 5). Our feeling is that *no single appraisal form* is sufficient in form or content for all business uses—yet almost all companies use these forms, or variations of them, to evaluate their personnel. What are managers and employees to do?

To address this situation, we recommend supplementing your in-house forms with additional information. As each type of form needs to be extended differently, we approach each type separately. For every form category, we review the advantages and disadvantages and how to make up for their weaknesses. Managers should study their own company's forms using the following approach:

Determine the type of form used. Your appraisal forms should fall into one or more of the categories described in the next section. Ascertain the form category or categories.

Examine the recommended improvements. In most cases improvements will involve collecting additional information about the employee, his or her skills, education, behavior, and goals. Understand the reasons for compiling the recommended information.

Create and implement an informal system for each type of improvement. In general, each system will be used to collect a different type of information. It is not necessary to create formal company-wide forms for this purpose; however, the forms you use should be consistent across all of your employees.

Inform management of your decision. Two caveats here. First, you are not *changing* the current appraisal process—you are merely gathering more information related to the employee and adding it to the existing system. Make sure that management understands this. Second, observe carefully management's reaction to this news. Upper management should be pleased that you are "going the extra mile" for your employees, as this should lead to more objective, fairer appraisals. If they are not pleased, beware. If upper management balks or hesitates in its approval of your extensions then something is amiss. Evaluate their reasons (if given) very carefully. This may be the first sign of one of the following problems in your organization:

- Management is aware of problems with its current appraisal system and does not want this known.
- Management is not confident in the objectivity or fairness of the current system; your supplements may point this out.
- Management feels that the success of your systems may lead to other managers being forced to use them. Such "unneeded work" will bog down these managers and not allow them to get their "real work" done.
- Management has already made decisions regarding how your employees' appraisal results will be judged. They are fearful that your supplemental information may cast your subordinates in a favorable light.

Regrettably, solving these problems is beyond the scope of this book. In the short term, it is perhaps best to maintain a low profile; however, eventually such problems will surface, perhaps with catastrophic re-

Employee Performance Appraisal

In each category, check those items which **best** describe the employee's
behavior during the review period.

Quantity of Work

☐	Sets a work pace others try to achieve.	6.6
☐	Sometimes sleeps on the job if left alone.	0.3
☐	Lets outside interests interfere and decrease quantity of work.	1.3
☐	Recognizes limitations and abilities and prepares ahead to maintain high quality of work.	8.2
☐	Spends too much time on phone or writing personal letters during work hours.	1.1
☐	Keeps busy but may select wrong priorities.	4.8
☐	Willing to work long hours and forgo breaks to maintain high production level.	8.5
☐	Not very flexible in switching from task to task.	4.9
☐	Work is turned out on time.	5.5
☐	Uses "slack" periods to maintain quantity in other areas.	6.1
☐	Chooses priorities correctly.	6.3
☐	Wastes no time going to next task.	6.0
☐	Works rapidly.	7.1
☐	Keeps assignments organized for high production.	6.7
☐	Consistently completes all jobs, maintaining high output.	8.0
☐	Organizes all tasks for highly efficient and effective production.	7.9
☐	Usually does enough to complete jobs, seldom more.	4.1

. . .

Number of Items Checked: _____

Total of Weights: _____

Average Weighting for Category _____

Figure 8.1a   A checklist appraisal.

sults. Managers should prepare for such eventualities by documenting
every action and decision. It also helps to keep one's résumé up-to-date.

Improving Checklist Appraisals

Checklist appraisals (see Fig. 8.1a) are best-suited for highly determinate jobs. Such jobs usually have formal, detailed job descriptions, and employees are compensated for completing specific tasks. While acceptable for measuring and tracking performance improvement, checklists are poor or inadequate for anything else. The following improvements are needed.

Making employment decisions

Checklists contain little or no information about employee knowledge, potential, or skills. This makes them unsatisfactory for managing new employee hiring, employee transfer, or employee termination. Strangely, the checklist format is frequently used as a guideline during employment interviews. These checklists, in concert with a final essay section, are then analyzed by various sections of the company—personnel, management, the immediate supervisor—to determine "hireability." Without some direct measure of a candidate's knowledge or skills, these procedures boil down to a subjective measure of a candidate on the part of the interviewer—something to be avoided if possible.

Employee transfer or termination is a slightly different scenario—at least the manager has some employee history to go on in the form of status reports. Still, checklists perform no useful function in making these kinds of decisions.

Performance improvement

While adequate for measuring employee performance improvement, checklists must be extended. Specific behaviors appearing in the checklist must be marked as either *acceptable, unacceptable,* or *neutral.* The checklist may now be used to monitor employee behavior by noting the occurrence of unacceptable behaviors during the review period. The employee has the additional advantage of a written list of expected behaviors.

Identifying and rating potential

As mentioned previously, checklists contain no information about employee knowledge, potential, or skills. Further, they provide the manager with little or no feedback about actual employee accomplishments during the review period. Most checklist appraisals provide a status report of an instant in time, rather than a summary of a period of time. It is this summary that the manager needs to evaluate an employee's *track record*—a record of achieving goals on a regular basis.

Compensation administration

The basic requirement for compensation administration is a single, overall rating for an employee. As the checklist appraisal consists of a set of Yes/No answers or checked boxes, there is no convenient way to convert this to a numerical rating. (While it is possible to add the checkmarks and perhaps weight them according to some scale, the validity of this method would be difficult to prove.)

Career planning and development

Career planning systems require knowledge of the company's and the employee's goals. This a major fault of checklist systems. In addition, there is little feedback available to the employee about his or her progress in this type of system. Checklist systems must be supplemented with job descriptions, company goals (both at the corporate and divisional levels), and employee aspirations.

Checklist improvements

Improving a checklist appraisal system usually involves supplementing it with additional information of a type not found in the basic checklist forms. To do this we recommend that the manager implement a system like the following.

Assess employee educational level and job skills. This information should be readily available from the employee, from a skills inventory (if utilized), or during the appraisal interview. The manager should expand on this by including information on the employee's potential, both for growth in his or her present job, and for future growth and promotion.

Expand checklist entries. The intent here is to expand or enlarge the checklist so that it contains more detail. For example, one common trait appearing on some checklist appraisals is "works well with others," or "is a team player." This vague yes/no expression should be expanded to cover more detail: to what *degree* does the employee work well with others? In this case we recommend adding such items as "listens and understands instructions," "displays tact when interacting with others," "provides oral and/or written feedback," "assists others when able," and even "provides leadership." These items can be added on a separate sheet immediately following the body of the main checklist.

This increase in detail will allow the checklist results to be more easily converted to ratings, which may then be used for compensation administration.

Include a statement of employee goals and goal achievement. Regrettably, this information may not be readily available. In general, these data are usually derived from a combination of a goal statement at the beginning of the review period and the set of employee and management status reports for the same period. If no such documentation exists, then there is no basis for objectively evaluating employee accomplishments. In this case we recommend a simple statement of employee accomplishments.

Include a statement of company goals and standards. This information *must* be available, usually in the form of mission statements, the company's annual report, or as a part of the company policy manual. (If such a statement is *not* available, then how does everyone know what job to do? If the response to this question is "I do what my boss tells me to do," the final answer then lies in what the chief executive officer or president of the company charges his or her subordinates with doing.)

One last comment: management must provide some proof that the checklist appraisal system is *objective*. This is necessary if the checklist is to be used for making employment decisions such as hiring and termination. This proof of objectivity may consist of documents relating to the job analysis used to create the appraisal system, or a statistical analysis of the data. The danger here is that the system may already be subjective, either in design or in use. This may open employers to claims of discrimination or unfair termination practices.

An improved weighted checklist appraisal form appears in Fig. 8.1*b*.

Improving Critical Incident Appraisals

The worst fault of critical incident systems (see Fig. 8.2*a*) is the considerable amount of time necessary to utilize them well. By that we mean monitoring employees' behaviors, noting critical incidents, documenting the incidents, and summarizing them at the end of the review period. Critical incident appraisals require the manager to have good-to-excellent written communication skills; otherwise, they are ineffective at best.

Making employment decisions

Critical incident systems are useless for making hiring decisions, as information about potential employees is not available. One exception to this may be the interviewee whose current company uses a critical incident system. However, in practice, appraisal systems from two different companies are not comparable. Even companies in the same business, such as retailing, manufacturing, or health care, will not have systems that share the same *basis;* that is, a thorough job analysis of current jobs.

Although not useful for hiring, critical incident systems are acceptable for making employee transfer or termination decisions. Documentation of critical incidents is both necessary and sufficient for this.

Performance improvement

Improving employee performance is feasible using critical incidents. Each incident may be used as either a good or bad example of acceptable employee behavior. Employees should view such incidents as learning experiences. Each experience provides data for improving

Employee Performance Appraisal

In each category, check those items which **best** describe the employee's behavior during the review period.

Quantity of Work

Acceptable Behaviors

☐	Sets a work pace others try to achieve.	6.6
☐	Recognizes limitations and abilities and prepares ahead to maintain high quality of work.	8.2
☐	Willing to work long hours and forgo breaks to maintain high production level.	8.5
☐	Uses "slack" periods to maintain quantity in other areas.	6.1
☐	Always understands verbal instructions.	6.3
☐	Wastes no time going to next task.	6.0
☐	Is tactful when dealing with others.	7.1
☐	Keeps assignments organized for high production.	6.7
☐	Consistently completes all jobs, maintaining high output.	8.0
☐	Always provides oral feedback.	7.9

Neutral Behaviors

☐	Work is turned out on time.	5.5
☐	Usually does enough to complete jobs, seldom more.	4.1

Unacceptable Behaviors

☐	Sometimes sleeps on the job if left alone.	0.3
☐	Lets outside interests interfere and decrease quantity of work.	1.3
☐	Spends too much time on phone or writing personal letters during work hours.	1.1
☐	Keeps busy but may select wrong priorities.	4.8
☐	Not very flexible in switching from task to task.	4.9

. . .

Average Weighting for This Category _____

[Supplement this form with company and personal goals as well as review of employee's knowledge and skills.]

Figure 8.1b   An improved weighted checklist appraisal.

behavior, and allows the manager and employee to analyze how the employee can improve.

Assigning work duties

Given a set of tasks to be performed, the manager sometimes must determine which employees perform what tasks. A critical incident appraisal system may contain enough information about employee performance to allow the manager to make this determination. Lots of work may be involved, as documentation of incidents is not usually

---

Critical Incident Form

Employee's Name _____   Employee's Job Title _____

Date of Occurrence _____   Time of Occurrence _____   Location _____

Identify Observed Behavior (if reporting hearsay information, identify source and location of actual observer.)

Date Form Completed _____   Time Form Completed _____

Signature and Title of
Person Completing Form _____

Items to be considered in identifying behavior (may be used as a checklist)

What specifically occurred?
Is there sufficient detail to support future judgement?
Have you described results of behavior?
What circumstances influenced behavior?
      Was there an emergency situation?
      Did unusual or adverse conditions exist?
Behavior Being Documented:
      Insubordination   Theft
      Attendance   Malicious Damage
      Quality of Work   Interpersonal Relations
      Quantity of Work   Acceptance of Job Enlarging Responsibilities

Second-Party Observations:

      Remote Location
      Works Independently
      Temporarily Assigned to Others

Figure 8.2a   A critical incident appraisal.

---

organized or classified by task. The manager must examine each incident, preferably at the time of its occurrence, and collect data about task performance.

Identifying and rating potential

Again, critical incidents provide an abundance of information regarding employee track records, skills learned, knowledge gained, and future plans. It is possible for the manager to reorganize this information to predict how employees will behave in the future. Unacceptable behaviors that recur may point to lack of learning; acceptable behaviors that grow more frequent may lead to an ability to accept new challenges.

Still, without some kind of formal procedure for determining which employees are ready for promotion, the critical incident system requires lots of work on the part of the manager to organize and categorize data into a more usable form.

Compensation administration

Determining employee compensation requires a single, overall measure of the employee's behavior during the review period. Most critical incident systems do not provide this. To do so requires that each incident be given some *value,* and that multiple values may then be combined into a final one.

Valuing incidents is difficult, and sometimes impossible. An acceptable behavior may mean more to a new employee than to an experienced one who is expected to behave appropriately. Different jobs may require varying behaviors that may also vary over time. Different employees may approach the same job in different ways. All of this makes putting a value on incidents perplexing, subjective, and potentially inaccurate.

Combining such values adds another level of uncertainty. Should values be averaged? Should they be weighted? If weighted, who determines what the weighting factors should be?

To make proper decisions about compensation, a manager needs additional information to that provided by critical incident forms and procedures. We recommend that the job analysis that led to the development of the critical incident system be continued and extended. Job analysis can be used to assign values to incidents, assuming that a set of *base,* or *expected,* incidents can be developed. These incidents are then analyzed and importance assigned to each on a job-by-job basis. This then forms the core of the incident valuation system.

In the absence of such information, managers and employees must develop their own rating or valuing system. Values placed on incidents may be either *relative* or *absolute,* whichever is determined to be more appropriate. (Note that relative values are always relative to some standard. Choosing a relative scale means that the employee and manager agree on the standard. Some possible standards are: all employees in a particular department; all employees having jobs with the same title or job description; or some industry standard.)

Identifying training needs

The set of critical incidents for a particular employee is usually sufficient to point out major training needs. Problems such as unacceptable behaviors can sometimes be traced to a lack of skill or education. Thus, additional education or training can be recommended.

There is one danger: the manager and employee must be certain that the incidents documented completely cover all expected job behaviors. If not, a major training area may be missed.

Career planning and development

Critical incident systems are not designed to properly handle employee career planning. They must be supplemented with employee goals and company job opportunity information.

Critical incident improvement

While the critical incident approach to performance appraisal is sometimes considered one of the best, it has one major flaw: it requires a knowledgeable and skilled rater. To implement such a program successfully, a company must be prepared to provide comprehensive training to managers in appraisal procedures, especially in written communications.

Making this procedure acceptable for all of management's needs will involve additional work on the part of the supervisor. These items are listed below.

Keeping a detailed incident log. The supervisor must maintain a log of critical incidents. Indeed, this is the basis for the procedures. This log must contain information about each incident, including time and date, observed behaviors, observed results, and feedback. Even more, the supervisor must review such incidents regularly with the employee. This review is essential for employee growth and work improvement, as it provides the employees with feedback that allows them to either modify their future behavior or maintain present behavior.

As this log is an integral part of the review procedure, its contents and use should be documented thoroughly in the company's policy and procedures.

Recognition of incidents. It is not enough for the manager to be trained in critical incident procedures. Perhaps just as important, managers must recognize when these incidents occur. As this usually involves observation by the manager, we conclude that managers using this technique must be continually walking around, attempting to observe employees' behaviors. Since this is not always possible, how can we ensure that most of the proper incidents are recorded? What if the manager takes two weeks of vacation?

Addressing this point requires that the employee have some training in the critical incident methodology and that the employee and his or her manager meet regularly to discuss employee status. By making employees responsible for observing and recording their own critical incidents, much of the burden on the manager is eliminated. With both manager and employee watching for incidents, it is then only a matter of them both discussing such incidents at their regular status meetings.

Valuing incidents.   To make a critical incident appraisal useful for compensation administration and career planning, incidents must somehow be rated. While most such programs assign values of "acceptable" and "unacceptable" to incidents, more is required. A job analysis that results in a critical incident appraisal system usually involves collecting and analyzing many sample critical incidents. This information should be evaluated further, with the objective of determining ratings or values of the incidents. Some type of numeric scale should prove adequate, perhaps a range from 0 to 10.

Career planning.   This is another area in which critical incident methods are sorely deficient. While such methods may produce a wealth of information about an employee's behaviors, little is learned about his or her level of job skill, education, or promotability; however, this is usually easily remedied. The simplest method is to assemble lists of critical incidents from the job descriptions of higher-level jobs and give them to employees. Since these, by definition, constitute a description of acceptable behaviors of employees at higher levels, they therefore provide other employees with guidelines for advancement. These may then be factored in to the employee's current appraisal and covered in-depth at the next status meeting.

Improving Essay Reviews

Like the critical incident review procedure, essay reviews (see Fig. 8.3) require the manager to have good-to-excellent written communications skills. They are also time-consuming and laborious to complete. Essay reviews suffer from all of the shortcomings of critical incident reviews, with one addition: they do not include any examination of specific incidents, goals, events, or behaviors that can be objectively measured. This exposes essay reviews to charges of subjectivity, charges that are difficult for a company to defend.

Making employment decisions

As mentioned in the section on checklists, essay reviews are commonly used as an attachment to a checklist during employment interviewing. However, the essay, by itself, may contain little or no useful data to make an employment decision unless all such essays are in a common

---

Critical Incident Form

Employee's Name _____   Employee's Job Title _____

Date of Occurrence _____   Time of Occurrence _____   Location _____

Identify Observed Behavior (if reporting hearsay information, identify source and location of actual observer.)

Date Form Completed _____   Time Form Completed _____

Signature and Title of
Person Completing Form _____

Items to be considered in identifying and rating behavior (may be used as a checklist)

What specifically occurred?   Was this behavior acceptable? _____
Is there sufficient detail to support future judgement?
Have you described results of behavior?
What circumstances influenced behavior?   What rating is assigned? _____
        Was there an emergency situation?
        Did unusual or adverse conditions exist?
Behavior Being Documented:
        Insubordination   Theft
        Attendance   Malicious Damage
        Quality of Work   Interpersonal Relations
        Quantity of Work   Acceptance of Job Enlarging Responsibilities

Second-Party Observations:

        Remote Location
        Works Independently
        Temporarily Assigned to Others

ATTACH COPY OF CRITICAL INCIDENT SUMMARY LOG

[Supplement form with summary log of incidents and ratings.]

Figure 8.2b   An improved critical incident appraisal.

format with common content, including ways of rating or evaluating statements. But this is the definition of a rating scale review!

Essay reviews are acceptable for use in employee transfer or promotion, as long as the supervisor writing them has good written communication skills. As a part of implementing an essay appraisal system, a company should train its managers in completing the forms. In addition, several examples (say, a dozen) of completed appraisals should be provided as examples of good, acceptable, and poor reviews. This will help managers in determining the effects of the content of a review.

Unfortunately, essay reviews are unacceptable as vehicles for documenting or driving employee terminations. They are considered too

---

Employee Performance Review

Employee's Name _____   Date of Hire _____

Job Title _____   Job Grade and Code _____

This evaluation covers the period from _____ to _____ .

1. Evaluation: (Comments on individual's performance in regard to goals previously set, measuring factors such as quality, quantity, creativity and suggestions, attendance, waste, staying on schedule, etc.)

2. Areas where improvement is needed and suggestions for attainment: (Including use of company sponsored programs; i.e., Tuition Aid, Affirmative Action Program, etc.)

3. Other remarks: (Attitude, appearance, cooperation, etc.)

4. For the time period covered by this evaluation the employee's performance has been:
    ____ Highly Satisfactory   ____ Satisfactory
    ____ Below Expected Levels   ____ Unsatisfactory

5. Employee comments (if any):

6. Goals and results to be attained and measured for new period (mutually agreed to, realistically attainable, measurable)

Supervisor's Signature _____   Reviewed By: _____

Employee's Signature _____   Date: _____

Figure 8.3   An essay review appraisal.

subjective and not quantitative enough. A potential employee termination may not be an employee problem—it points out that there may be possible hiring problems, management problems, and employee appraisal system problems! An essay appraisal system will not provide a company with enough information to justify a decision to terminate an employee.

Performance improvement

Despite their weaknesses, essays are acceptable ways of noting avenues for employee performance improvement. This assumes that the supervisor is aware of the range and bounds of the employee's behavior, and that this is documented regularly and summarized in the final appraisal. Full coverage of behaviors is required in the document.

In addition to simply mentioning areas of possible or potential improvement, the manager must give quantitative information as well. How much better? How much more (or less) frequently? How well must skills be learned and in what period of time? This may require the supervisor to append an additional form to the appraisal that summarizes an employee's performance improvements during the appraisal period.

Assigning work duties

Assuming that the essay review covers all of an employee's duties, the set of recent reviews of all of a manager's employees should provide sufficient information to permit him or her to assign appropriate work duties. Again, this assumes that the reviews fully cover the range and scope of acceptable employee behaviors.

Identifying and rating potential

An employee's potential may well be a subjective thing—at least that's the way many managers view it. The essay review seems to be the perfect place for identifying employee potential, as it allows the supervisor to state why he or she believes an employee deserves more responsibilities, a promotion, or some future assignment. Still, such a recommendation is usually based on specific incidents or value judgments. If such incidents exist, they should be documented as a part of the appraisal (this now becomes a critical incident appraisal!). If the supervisor is making judgments about an employee's potential, this is usually based on perceived abilities, aptitudes, or talents. These, also, should be documented in the review, along with the supervisor's evaluation (this now becomes a rating scale review!).

Compensation administration

Essay reviews are a poor vehicle for making compensation decisions. Statements on an essay review are, by definition, not quantifiable. (If they were, we would have a rating scale review or critical incident review.) However, there are some jobs where compensation is not directly determined by an appraisal, but is set in advance. These jobs include public school teaching, some trade professions, and some piece-work jobs. In these cases, essay reviews are usually used to determine *merit,* or bonus compensation. But here, too, essay reviews are not a viable or practical source of quantifiable information.

Managers making compensation decisions based on essay reviews should supplement the review process with a formal evaluation procedure. This procedure should strive to value the content of each essay review in an attempt to standardize all reviews across managers. Failing in this, we recommend appending goal-setting and achievement information as described above under *checklist* reviews.

Identifying training needs

Required employee training can be documented in an essay review, although a manager may find it difficult to justify based on the review alone. The manager should add to the review enough information about employee training levels and achievements to explain his or her recommendations.

Career planning and development

Essay reviews are an acceptable means of documenting employee career planning and development. As the employee's career and the company's future plans should be examined together, we recommend that the manager supplement the essay review with a summary of the company's future plans and goals, along with the employee's plans and goals. This should then become the basis for a goal-setting meeting between employee and manager at the beginning of the next review period.

Essay review improvement

Since the essay review method is useful in some categories of appraisal, many companies have adopted it to fulfill many purposes. The major problem with using the essay review technique is the burden placed on the manager. Not only must managers have excellent written communication skills to complete the essay reviews, but they must also include sufficient detail about the entire review period for all purposes. Employment decisions will require historical data to justify them; performance improvement requires an inventory of observed behaviors and feedback; decisions as to compensation will require an overall rating; career planning decisions will require a summary of the employee's goals that are consonant with the company's. All of this takes time, and demands a superior manager.

With these things in mind, we recommend the following:

Implement training in written communications. This training is *not* just for the manager, but for the employee as well. Not only may an employee become a manager some day, but the employee and the manager should work together in concert to complete the essay review form. This has several advantages. First, the evaluation now becomes a joint project, not an adversarial one. Second, the employee has a lot at stake. Assisting in drafting the review makes him or her a part of the process, not an outside observer. Finally, managers should welcome employees supporting them in their jobs. Any situation where a manager feels daunted by an employee contributing to his or her own appraisal points out a management weakness in the corporation.

Supplement the review process with examples.   It is an unfortunate corollary that employees who are assigned to better managers get better reviews. To minimize these problems, companies can provide managers with "sample" essay answers for each rated category. This will effectively convert the essay review into a checklist or rating scale review, as each essay category will now have several possible sample answers provided, each with its own rating. This will tend to eliminate differences between managers' abilities to fill out review forms.

As we feel the essay review is virtually useless without much supporting documentation, we do not show an improved form here.

Improving MBO Appraisals

The MBO review format (see Fig. 8.4*a*) is one of the most fashionable. Management by objectives, popularized by Peter Drucker in the 1960s, involves employees and management jointly setting and monitoring objectives during the review period. Unfortunately, this objective-setting process is difficult. It requires that several processes go well.

Setting objectives.   Setting employee objectives requires that management know its own objectives first. This only comes from the top of the company down. Only after the board of directors sets general guidelines are the company's goals known. From these goals, each division can set its own goals; from these, each department, and so on, down to the employee.

This top-down goal-setting process demands competence at each level, for if any level sets goals that are unrealistic, unattainable, or contrary to the goals from above, all goals set at levels below become defective, erroneous, or even harmful.

Revising objectives.   Another part of the process is goal-monitoring. On a regular basis at each level of the company, goals are analyzed, goal progress is measured, and decisions are made regarding expanding, revising, or deleting goals. When this happens, each level of the company below the one revising goals must analyze and perhaps revise their own goals as well. This continues downward in the chain, until it reaches the employee and his or her supervisor. At this point, goals set a short while ago may be completely unrealistic,

Management Performance Analysis

Name: _____   Birth Date: _____   Position: _____

No. of Years in Position: _____   Reports to: _____

Analysis Prepared By: _____   Date: _____   No. Yrs. Supervised: _____

Analysis Reviewed By: _____   Date: _____

This analysis has been discussed with me _____   Date: _____
                                    (Signature of Employee)

Goal Achievements
Quantitative Goals and Results

Describe Goals	Describe Results Achieved	Describe Reasons for Differences

Qualitative Goals and Results

Describe Goals	Describe Results Achieved	Describe Reasons for Differences

Figure 8.4a   A management by objectives (MBO) appraisal.

unattainable, unmeasurable, or contrary to those of higher levels or the company as a whole. Regrettably, few companies follow this process to its logical conclusion; instead, managers simply monitor employee goals against previously set department standards at the beginning of the review period. Only in cases where goals must be drastically revised will they go to the trouble of reviewing them.

Measuring objective attainment.   Even with the best of intentions, many managers do not give their full attention to developing measurable, attainable, feasible goals. As a result they have a great deal of difficulty measuring goal attainment at the end of an employee's review period. As this measurement directly affects the employee in many categories, employees should spend quality time with their supervisors during goal-setting meetings.

Despite these defects, MBO appraisals have many good qualities, and are extremely useful in many employment situations.

Making employment decisions

Like many appraisal forms, MBO review forms are not very useful for making potential employee hiring decisions. As discussed previously (see checklist appraisals), a combination of a rating scale appraisal and some real-world testing is best in this situation.

MBO appraisals are excellent vehicles for documenting and justifying employee transfer or termination, as they include goal-setting and achievement information. The only caveats are:

- As employee and company goals are interdependent, MBO appraisals should include a statement of the divisional or departmental goals from which the employee's goals were derived.

- Managers should take care to include any special circumstances that may affect goal attainment or measurement, such as economic conditions, business circumstances, or competitive information.

Performance improvement

MBO appraisals are an acceptable means of making employee performance improvement recommendations, but they have one shortcoming: although they specify *what* goals were or were not attained and why, they do not relate *why* or *how*. This seems to be left to the manager's judgment.

We recommend supplementing the MBO appraisal with information regarding why and how goals were attained (or not attained). In addition, the manager should document specific and relevant employee behaviors during the review period. This information should then be highlighted or summarized for performance improvement purposes.

Assigning work duties

Choosing which employees perform which tasks can be a difficult decision for a manager, especially if certain tasks or jobs are highly valued by employees. The MBO appraisal is a good vehicle for this, assuming that goals and work duties are interrelated (as they should be).

One interesting consequence of this is that managers who feel they must justify their decisions may find themselves in the position of divulging appraisal information that the company (and employees) consider confidential. Managers should attempt to avoid this by announcing their decisions to the entire group.

Identifying and rating potential

While the MBO appraisal can be used effectively in rating employee potential, it still only contains information about what *did* happen, not why, or how, or what might have happened under different circumstances. Managers attempt to infer this information based on "what they know" about the employee. This subjective decision by the manager cannot be justified by material in the appraisal.

Predicting an employee's future behavior, which is what *potential* really boils down to, is a difficult challenge. The most effective solution seems to be thorough job analysis, coupled with appraising an employee using the list of acceptable behaviors from other, higher, job descriptions. For example, a programmer could be appraised using the forms for a senior analyst. The results may then be indicative of how the programmer will behave if he or she is promoted to the higher position.

Compensation administration

Although it is acceptable for use in making compensation decisions, MBO appraisals suffer from the same flaw as many other styles: they do not provide a single numerical rating of the employee's performance. Although it is possible to derive a number or rating from the sum of the employee's attained objectives, this number will only be useful if all employees having the same or similar job descriptions have similar objectives. Even in this case, such objectives must change over time. This results in re-creating the complete appraisal system on a regular basis.

We recommend supplementing the MBO process with either a standard set of goals for similar jobs or a method of valuing goal attainment. Either or both of these methods should be discussed with the employee during goal setting.

Identifying training needs

Assuming that goals were set in accordance with the MBO approach, a failure to attain a goal is a direct measure of an employee's training needs. The only caution here is that it assumes goals set for an employee cover the extent of the employee's expected behaviors. Otherwise the employee may have a training need but no corresponding goal in that area for the review period.

Career planning and development

As with training needs, MBO appraisals provide sufficient information for a manager to assist an employee with his or her career development. Managers can use their history of company, divisional, and departmental goals to indicate where the company is going. This can then be supplemented with recommendations for possible training, education, transfers, or promotions.

MBO improvement

It seems almost heretical to suggest that an MBO program could be improved. Proponents of MBO are sometimes fanatical in their devotion to objectives, forms, goals, standards, and review procedures. Still, there is always room for improvement.

When MBO programs fail, it is usually for one of the following reasons. Most of these deal with those most elusive of concepts: goals and objectives.

Failure to set proper objectives. This is the most common reason for MBO program failure. If objectives are too easy, everyone gets appraised as "superior." If they are too difficult, everyone becomes "unacceptable." Also, if objectives are not set from the top of the organization down, managers will have no idea which objectives are valid for their departments, let alone for employees.

To prevent this kind of failure, set objectives from the top. If managers are placed in a position where objectives have already been set without their knowledge or consent (say, because of promotion or transfer), it is their responsibility to get explanation and clarification from top management.

Failure to anticipate circumstances or a dynamic environment. The appearance of unforeseen competition, an economic downturn, or a merger or acquisition can result in a department or division's objectives being radically and suddenly changed. This will then cause a domino effect, as the objectives of lower-level departments, managers, and employees must now be changed.

Rather than reacting to these events, employees and managers can attempt to predict which of a set of such events may occur, and form contingency plans for those events. While this may not always be possible, it will provide perspective. This has the beneficial effect of forcing management to scrutinize current objectives and prepare alternative plans.

The program indicates what to do, but not how or why. This problem shows up in one form or another in most appraisal systems, regardless of form or technique. In general, most appraisal systems involve gathering information and making judgments about that information. Few go on to the next step: what is to be done regarding those judgments.

MBO programs are particularly vulnerable in this area. Much effort is put into defining and completing goals and objectives, yet little is focused on implementing changes or improvements. To address this concern, many companies have supplemented their MBO system with a separate career path planning system. This new system

---

Management Performance Analysis

Name: _____   Birth Date: _____   Position: _____

No. of Years in Position: _____   Reports to: _____

Analysis Prepared By: _____   Date: _____   No. Yrs. Supervised: _____

Analysis Reviewed By: _____   Date: _____

This analysis has been discussed with me _____   Date: _____
(Signature of Employee)

Goal Achievements
Quantitative Goals and Results

Describe Goals	Describe Results Achieved	Describe Reasons for Differences

Qualitative Goals and Results

Describe Goals	Describe Results Achieved	Describe Reasons for Differences

Attach Goal Description Documentation describing when goals were set, by whom, when changed, etc.

Action Plan
Describe how each goals will be achieved — give specific approach, including dates and man-hours

---

[Supplement with detail training on goal-setting for managers and employees. Note
that Goal Description document describes why goals were set, changed, and so on.]

Figure 8.4b   An improved management by objectives (MBO) appraisal.

is then responsible for guiding employees by providing advice about
job growth.

An improved MBO appraisal form appears in Fig. 8.4b.

Improving Ranking Systems

For most jobs, especially in data processing, ranking appraisal systems
(see Fig. 8.5) suffer from several major flaws.

Instructions for Alternation Ranking

Attached is a list of employees. All of them may be performing satisfactorily, but some are almost certain to be doing a better job in their own assignment than are others in their assignments. You may use your own judgement as to what makes one employee better than another. Many factors may be considered: dependability, ability to do the work, willingness to work, cooperation, ability to get along with people, and any others that you think are important. On making your decision, use your own personal knowledge of the individuals and their work. Do not depend on the opinions of others.

1.   Eliminate the names of thise whose work you do not know well.

2.   Eliminate the name of any person whose work in your opinion is so different from most of the others that you do not think he or she can be fairly compared with them.

3.   Decide which person you think is the best on the list. Draw a line through their name and write it in the blank space marked "1-Highest".

4.   Decide which person you think is not as good as the others remaining on the list. Draw a line through their name and write it in the blank space marked "1-Lowest". (Remember, you are not saying that they are unsatisfactory; merely that you considers the others better.)

5.   Next, select the person you think is best of those remaining on the list, draw a line through their name and write it in the blank space marked "2-Highest".

6.   Next, select the person you think is not as good as the others remaining on the list, draw a line through their name and write it in the blank space maried "2-Lowest".

7.   Continue in this manner until you have eliminated all names on the list.

Rater's Name: _____   **Date:** _____

Classification of Group Being Ranked:

1-Highest	
2-Highest	
3-Highest	
. . .	
3-Lowest	
2-Lowest	
1-Lowest	

Figure 8.5   A ranking appraisal.

They contain no information about minimum standards. What were the standards that employees had to meet? To rank employees there must be a standard of some sort. The problem here is that without minimum standards employees in one ranking group cannot be accurately compared with those in another.

The manager's decisions are hard to justify. Why is one employee ranked higher than another? Without hard data, this is a highly subjective decision. Suppose data did exist. For example, Employee A has attained ratings of 3, 4, and 5 in three categories, while Employee B got ratings of 1, 3, and 9. Who should be ranked higher? A rated higher than B in two of the three categories. B got a higher total rating (13) than A did (12).

For a manager to justify ranking one employee higher than another requires some kind of internal, undocumented, subjective rating scale.

The appraisal contains no absolute information—only relative. By comparing employees within a group with one another, the rater gets relative rankings. This information is useless when comparing across groups. Highly ranked employees in one group may be less competent than low-ranking employees in another. An extremely competent (or incompetent) employee will not be recognized as such.

There is no goal-related information. A ranked list of employees contains no information about whether attainable goals were set, whether they were met, or to what degree employees attempted to meet goals.

While ranking appraisal systems occur in some specific instances (the military, for example) they are of little use in data processing. A DP manager confronted by such a system should go to whatever lengths necessary to change it.

Making employment decisions

Rankings are almost useless for choosing new employees from a pool of potential new-hires, since rankings contain no information about minimum standards. They are also difficult to use when justifying meaningful termination decisions, except in certain cases. For example, when it is necessary to lower staffing levels in a group of employees, a ranking system may be used to terminate the lowest performers. This should be used independently of any measures of productivity or performance; it may become necessary to let go one or more employees that are performing well. In fact, in a group of good performers it is rarely a happy event when one or more must leave. In these cases it is imperative that management document the reasons for termination, especially when performance is not an issue.

Performance improvement

Again, rankings are useless for this. A relative ranking list may consist of all excellent (or all incompetent!) employees. The rankings themselves contain no performance-related information.

Assigning work duties

For the same reasons as stated previously, rankings cannot be used meaningfully here.

Identifying and rating potential

Due to the relative nature of the rankings, employee potential usually cannot be determined.

Compensation administration

In certain cases, ranking systems are acceptable for determining compensation. These cases usually consist of a set of employees doing a job where each employee is assumed to be performing to a minimum standard. With this assumption in place, higher-ranked employees may be paid more than those ranked lower. Still, by *how much?* Again, since the rankings are relative it is difficult to come up with a meaningful formula.

Identifying training needs

While it might be assumed that lower-ranked employees require more training than those ranked higher, exactly what training do they need?

Career planning and development

Ranking systems do not include any useful data about employee career planning or company goals.

Ranking improvement

Ranking appraisal documents must be supplemented with lots of additional information for them to be of much use. Typically, companies augment their ranking system with a complementary employee rating system. This rating system is used to rate individual employees according to their abilities. In effect, this new system becomes the employee performance appraisal system. What, then, is the ranking system used for? We do not recommend its use.

Improving Rating Scales

When they first appeared in academic literature, rating scale appraisal systems (see Fig. 8.6) were hailed as the best thing since sliced bread. Since then, companies that implemented such systems have learned to live with some of the difficulties inherent in such systems. In particu-

Supervisory Personnel Performance Appraisal Form (cont'd)									
SECTION B	1	2	3	4	5	6	7	8	9	10
1. Leadership. To what extent does he hold the respect and confidence of associates?	Secures limited cooperation of subordinates. Does not have full control.		Has fair degree of respect and confidence of subordinates. Methods get results.		Success in getting respect and confidence of subordinates and others. Gets results without undue friction.		Leads people very capably. Results consistently good. Inspires confidence.		Outstanding, superior, inspiring, and forceful.	Exceptional.
COMMENTS:										
	1	2	3	4	5	6	7	8	9	10
2. Manpower Utilization. Consider success in delegation of authority and proper placement.	Seldom delegates authority. Sometimes delegates authority to wrong people.		Does not always recognize and take advantage of opportunities of subordinates.		Successful in making assignments and delegating authority under normal conditions.		Successful under normal and unusual conditions. Superior ability.		Shows outstanding powers of delegation.	Exceptional.
COMMENTS:										

. . . (portions of this form have been removed for brevity)

SECTION C

1. In area where employee scored less than "5", indicate what measures are being taken to improve his or her performance.

    1. Quality of Work   ——
    2. Quantity of Work   ——
    3. Industry   ——
    4. Dependability   ——
    5. Aptitude
    6. Cooperation   ——
    7. Personality   ——

2. Do you consider this employee capable of future advancement? If yes, give reasons.

3. What is employee doing to prepare for advancement?

4. Have you formulated plans for helping this employee improve his or her performance? If so, please indicate.

Completed By: ——————————————————————— Date: ———————————

Interviewed By:——————————————————————— Date:———————————

Remarks. Indicate results of interview with employee.

Employee Signature: ——————————————————————— Date: ———————————

Figure 8.6   A rating scale appraisal.

lar, problems with rating scale systems revolve around issues relating to the scales themselves and how raters use them.

Making employment decisions

Rating scales are very useful in making hiring decisions. Assuming that raters are able to appraise candidates and judge their worth on some scale, these data are superior to those gathered using any other method. The same can be said for employee transfer or termination decisions. Assuming that they are backed up by hard data, rating scale appraisals provide enough information to justify such decisions.

Performance improvement

As rating scales are usually behavior-based, ratings in each category point out areas for employee performance improvement. Employee goal setting can also be rating-based by setting the attainment of particular ratings in certain categories as goals.

Assigning work duties

Ratings afford the manager an objective measurement of employee accomplishment and behavior. As such they are extremely useful as a basis for assigning tasks or work duties.

Identifying and rating potential

As stated previously, predicting employee potential is a highly subjective area; however, rating scale appraisals for higher-level jobs may be used to appraise employee performance. This gives management an indication of how the employee would behave if transferred or promoted.

Compensation administration

More than any other appraisal system, rating scales can be used effectively to determine or compute a single, overall performance rating. Doing such requires weighting each category according to job description and employee competence level. Once this is accomplished, a simple calculation determines the overall rating.

Identifying training needs

As with performance improvement, training needs can be estimated based upon ratings. Poor ratings may indicate training needs in that area, although the manager must analyze the situation to determine if other factors are at work.

Career planning and development

Though ratings in specific categories may indicate an employee's strengths, more information is needed to determine the match between employee and company. To do this requires a statement of company goals. This, coupled with the employee's goals and plans, can be used during the career planning process. Note that completion of specific goals can be rated as separate items.

Rating scale improvement

The most difficult experience that companies have with rating scale appraisal systems is developing them. A good rating scale appraisal system can be developed only through a complete and accurate job analysis. If the job analysis is poorly done or hurried, the resulting rating system quickly degenerates into a guessing game where managers presume that they know more about their employees than anyone. They will appraise employees by first guessing what the result should be, then figuring out what ratings are necessary to create that result. This can be avoided by doing the job analysis carefully.

Once created and implemented, a rating scale system must be monitored and updated when necessary. This requires an ongoing job analysis, usually done by a human resources person. Feedback from managers on ratings, categories, and descriptions is then used to update the appraisal instruments.

Changes we recommend include supplementing the appraisal form with company and employee goal information (if not already included). This data will be needed for career planning and determining training needs.

9

Improving Appraisal Procedures

In this chapter we turn to another part of the future—what an be done to improve appraisal procedures. Again, in each section we focus on practical advice rather than theory.

The procedures

Every company has its own procedures, written and unwritten, for employee evaluation. These procedures range from a simple "fill out the appraisal form and do your best" to elaborate objective-setting and monitoring processes. In addition, as discussed in Chap. 4, business appraisals are used for a variety of purposes. For ease of reference, we repeat these major categories here.

- Making employment decisions (hire, fire, transfer)
- Performance improvement
- Compensation administration
- Career planning and development

As discussed in Chap. 4, each of these major reasons for evaluating employees requires both a different collection of information about the employee and a different evaluation procedure for that information. Here, we analyze the differences between the various procedures and recommend how they may be improved. As most companies seem to merge two or more procedures into one, our typical recommendation will be to formally separate the procedures. This can be accomplished most easily by using a different set of current appraisal forms (and the recommended supplements) for each procedure.

The raters

Many popular books about job interviewing are available. With statements like "hard-hitting answers to tough interview questions" and "winning responses to interview situations," prospective employees and managers are presented with a magic elixir, panacea, or crutch that will guide them through such a meeting. Strangely, few books have appeared about the appraisal interview itself. Those that have done so approach the interview as an adversarial one, where the manager and employee confront each other in stylized combat, probing for weaknesses, parrying and thrusting for the slightest advantage. Instead of objectively evaluating or rating an employee's behavior, managers are compelled to approach the appraisal interview as a bargaining session where they negotiate the results of the appraisal.

In all of these books little is said about the raters themselves: how they should be trained, what their primary role is, and how they themselves are appraised. (Oddly, appraisals of managers seldom evaluate how such managers appraise their employees. This seems to directly contradict the primary goal of managers—to help their employees get work done.)

Here we reexamine the difficulties of rating people, and recommend training and methods of improving one's rating skills. Finally, we discuss how upper management can measure the effectiveness of its appraisers.

Improving Appraisal Procedures

Appraisal categories

Although companies differ in many ways (size, industry, culture, and so on), the reasons for doing employee evaluations remain constant:

- Making employment decisions (hire, fire, transfer)
- Managing employee performance improvement
- Identifying and rating potential
- Compensation administration
- Career planning and development

Each of these categories requires a different approach to gathering information, a different organization of that information, and a different technique for evaluating and acting on it. Each of these was covered in detail in Chap. 4. Here, we briefly review each of these areas with an eye toward improving the process.

Making employment decisions. Making the decision to hire a new employee or terminate an existing one may be the most important thing a manager does. (Not only that, it may be the most painful.) Although many companies have personnel departments that get involved in recruiting, new employee interviewing, disciplinary hearings, and terminations, it is how the manager gathers data and what he or she does with it that has the greatest impact on the final decision.

Preemployment screening.   Appraisal forms sometimes may be used in preemployment screening as a device for measuring a potential employee's value in a certain job; however, such forms are seldom built specifically for this task. Usually the forms are adapted from the present evaluation system. The procedures themselves seem to vary widely among companies. Most commonly a degenerate appraisal form is used as a list of desirable job skills and checked against applicant resumes. After passing this initial screening, applicants are interviewed with the form being used as an agenda (sometimes hidden).

This procedure can be improved somewhat by incorporating the appropriate rating scale review form(s). This is most easily done by developing a rating scale appraisal system for current positions, but can also be accomplished by deriving its equivalent from present forms. The purpose of this is not to create the perfect screening system; rather, it is to ensure that the preemployment screening procedure is enhanced to the point where it is more likely to be fair and useful.

Care should be taken at this point to ensure that the resulting forms and procedures are valid and do not unfairly discriminate against groups protected by law (see "Legal Considerations," later in this chapter). This is achieved through the *validation* process, which is beyond the scope of this book. (Interested companies should direct their inquiries on this matter to a professional human resources consultant.)

Employee transfer and promotion.   Transfer and promotion decisions should be as simple as appraising the employee with the evaluation forms for the new job as the basis. Their score or rating for this evaluation could then be compared against incumbents or against other applicants for a position to determine who is best qualified.

Employee termination.   Sadly, this is probably the most likely company procedure to be fully documented. Past problems with fired or laid-off employees have prompted many companies to expend much time and effort on their termination documentation and procedures.

Management's job is to *get work done through people.* To this end most managers are responsible for assisting their employees to succeed in their jobs. Those employees that do not succeed should be given assistance in the form of regular performance appraisals, action plans, goal setting, and performance improvement plans. Each of these steps involves documenting employee results and behaviors. As these documents are usually the basis for business decisions that will affect the employee (compensation, termination, promotion), it is in the interests of manager and employee alike that both understand and agree to the documents' contents.

Should an employee fail despite all efforts, termination becomes likely. It is prior to this point that managers can improve their procedures. Any attempt at changing termination procedures is probably best avoided. Our recommendations in this area are focused on the manager's responsibilities.

Managing employee performance improvement. Alan Brache* defined several assumptions that managers and organizations make when attempting to deal with workforce productivity. These assumptions, most of them false, are described here, along with their relationship to correct performance appraisal.

The most significant productivity improvements result from actions directed at the people in the job. This is akin to attempting to improve your golf game by buying better clubs. People, like golf clubs, are only a single element in a complex system. Brache says, "The performance system in which people function contains not only the skills and attitude of the men and women in the job but also a number of components in the environment in which these people work. These environmental influences include the performance that is expected, the available resources, the physical job setting, the workflow, the rewards and punishments, and the information provided to the employees."[†]

The DP manager who attempts to influence programming performance by training, motivating, or replacing employees may be completely off the mark. We would liken this to a golfer who reacted to a persistent slice by buying new clubs every time. Programming performance standards are sometimes unclear, ambiguous, or vague; the workplace environment may interfere with effective productivity; or rewards and feedback may not immediately follow the desired behaviors. Each of these elements indicates that environmental factors may be more important contributors to performance than simple knowledge or skills training.

---

* Brache, Alan, "Seven Assumptions that Block Performance Improvement," *Management Review,* March 1983.

[†] *Ibid.,* p. 22.

Such a philosophy is consistent with behavior-oriented appraisal systems that incorporate some kind of goal-setting and monitoring procedures. These include MBO, rating scale, and some critical incident appraisal systems.

Training, reorganization, goal setting, and positive reinforcement are effective productivity improvement interventions. Each of these methods is a possible tactic for performance improvement; however, the manager must take care that the intervention selected treats a cause, not a symptom.

For example, a manager notices that programming productivity, measured in lines of code produced per day, has steadily declined in each of the first few weeks of a project. Attributing this to a lack of proper skills, the manager sends all programmers to a two-day training session where they learn effective techniques for programming. Strangely, productivity declines again the next week. The manager now institutes a goal-directed performance appraisal program, where the manager and each employee meet to mutually decide upon productivity goals. Still, productivity declines. Attributing this to poor morale, the manager initiates a "positive reinforcement" campaign wherein programmers producing above a certain amount of code every week are rewarded. Strangely, productivity declines again the next week. Now thoroughly confused, the manager calls in their lead analyst and asks for an opinion. "Simple," replies the analyst. "As programmers write more and more code, their programs are getting bigger and bigger. This translates into longer compile and linkedit times, as well as longer test sessions. As more code is produced, the amount of compile, linkedit, and test time increases, thus also increasing the system load."

As this example shows, the manager neglected to perform an analysis of the presumed productivity problem, and instead applied a standard remedy. This not only failed to relieve the problem, but actually made things worse. Managers must make sure that they tie such performance improvement tactics together with the appraisal system being used.

People understand what's expected of them on the job. Regrettably, most job descriptions are result-focused, in that they concentrate on what employees are expected to produce, rather than how they are to do it. While this may work quite well for some jobs, most data processing jobs require that tasks be performed a certain way. In many cases the method determines the effectiveness or productivity of the individual.

Many companies approach this problem by attempting to quantify job performance in the appraisal document. Others take this one step further by placing task descriptions in the appraisal document ("writes effective, easily-maintainable code"), while embedding the standard of measurement in goal-setting sessions. Such standards usually take the form of thresholds, or steps, where each step of greater production leads to a higher rating in the corresponding category.

The data processing manager cannot presume that all of his or her employees know what is expected of them. This fallacy usually results from assuming that every employee is aware at every instant of his or her performance, how it is being measured, and how it will be judged at the end of the review period. While some of the best employees may reach this pinnacle of effectiveness, most are too busy concentrating on the task at hand to worry about their upcoming appraisal meeting many months away.

Managers can avoid this problem by using the appraisal form as the agenda for regular employee meetings. As employees are reminded of the evaluation criteria at every meeting, they will begin to use it in evaluating their own performance on an ongoing basis.

The organization reward system supports productive, high-quality performance. Except in the case where the DP organization has a formal quality assurance system in place, this assumption is simply unfounded. The formal reward systems of salary, bonuses, and promotions occur too infrequently to have an impact on employee performance. As discussed in Chap. 1, such rewards do not follow immediately after the desired performance; hence, they do not reinforce the performance. Also, DP people in general are not as strongly motivated by salary as they are by working conditions, challenging work, and more responsibility. (For more on this subject, see the discussion in Chap. 1.)

Too often the *informal* reward system reinforces undesired behavior. A project leader of our acquaintance found that one programmer was not as productive as others. Since the project leader needed to get the project completed, this programmer was given easier assignments so that more complex assignments would be completed by others. Note what happened: the programmer was rewarded for slow work by being given easier assignments!

The annual performance appraisal provides the feedback that employees need to improve or sustain performance. Readers of this book should find this assumption clearly false and unwarranted. Feedback is required on a *continual* basis for employees to act on it. As a manager, do you really want to wait for almost a year before you give employees information or training that might improve their performance? Further, after the annual appraisal meeting, will you wait another year to see if action plans or performance improvement plans are carried out?

Regular meetings have already been discussed as a vehicle for monitoring employee performance (see Chap. 6).

There is no need to be concerned with those parts of the organization that are meeting or exceeding their goals. While it is tempting for a manager to concentrate on parts of the organization that seem to need the most help, this may lead to a "fire fighting" mentality. It is also possible to miss some golden opportunities. First, the manager should determine why certain departments or staffs have met or exceeded their goals. Were their goals too lenient? Were there extenuating circumstances or environmental (external) factors beyond the organization's control that contributed? Finally, is the work done by these people comparable to that in other parts of the company?

After this initial analysis, the manager should continue to monitor goals and goal-setting processes. In general, a department that exceeds its goals for a review period is given tougher goals for the next period.

Performance management.   While a complete description of this topic is beyond the scope of this book,* the key elements of Performance Management bear a striking resemblance to those of effective performance appraisal.

Performance Management is based on the theory that behaviors will occur more frequently when positive consequences are known to follow. Though reinforcement is an effective tool, formal Performance Management consists of the following five factors.

- *Pinpoint behaviors and results.*   List or otherwise document what results are expected and what behaviors are desired to achieve those results.

- *Measurement.*   We measure the results to recognize whether improvement has occurred. If so, part of the measurement process will be an indication of the improvement.

- *Feedback.*   Document and communicate to the employee the results measured and behaviors noted. Contrast these with the expected results and behaviors.

- *Goals and subgoals.*   Performance Management emphasizes immediate and obtainable subgoals that will allow the individual more opportunities for success and positive reinforcement. Through recognition of success the system creates enthusiasm and energy for achieving further successes.

---

* Interested readers are referred to *Performance Management,* by A. C. Daniels, Performance Management Publications, Tucker, Ga., 1989.

- *Positive reinforcement.* This is given for subgoals attained, both for results achieved and behaviors achieved.

Compensation administration. There are almost twice as many ways of compensating employees as there are appraisal systems. Some of these are listed here.*

- *Pay for time worked.* Usually an hourly rate, this figure does not vary based on performance or productivity. Of course, it varies based upon attendance.

- *Pay for performance.* In its purest sense this type of pay is exemplified by many "piece rate" systems. Here, employees are paid a fixed amount for every task completed. The more tasks you complete, the higher you are paid.

- *Pay for position.* Specific positions are assigned base salaries. An employee receives a raise if either the position itself is revised and upgraded (with a corresponding increase in pay) or the employee is promoted to another position with a higher pay rate. This is commonly found in salespeople's "base" salary.

- *Pay for probation survival.* Many employees new to a position are given substandard pay during a fixed probationary period. At the end of this period, assuming that their performance warrants, their pay is upgraded to some minimum amount.

- *Pay raise for merit.* Usually a gift awarded for outstanding or superior. Almost always a poor choice for a company, once given it remains part of the employee's base pay, regardless of future performance.

- *Pay for survival.* This is pay presented for seniority. Many union jobs and teaching positions have this.

- *Pay for cost of living.* A raise that is given across the board due to either a negotiated contract or philanthropy on the part of upper management.

- *Bonus for performance.* A one-time reward for outstanding or superior performance. Commonly used for sales commissions.

- *Bonus.* A one-time reward that is not tied to performance. Some companies use this as a tactic to get people to work for less base pay with the promise of the future bonus that will make up the difference.

To determine how much to pay an employee, the appraisal system must return a single, numerical measurement. Few appraisal systems

---

* Adapted from *Performance Appraisal Design Manual*, by F. Fournies & Associates, Inc., 1983.

are able to generate a single overall performance measure that fairly assesses an employee's total performance. Further, some employees have goals that differ from those of others, making it difficult to compare appraisal ratings across employees. Fair compensation demands an objective method of determining overall performance.

These factors require that the appraisal system be specifically and carefully designed. (Our recommendations on the subject for these changes can be found in Chap. 8.) Once this is done, how will compensation be administered?

An excellent method described by Fournies* is to break down the overall employee performance category as follows:

_____ Unsatisfactory Performance

_____ Satisfactory Performance

_____ Outstanding Performance

The actual method of assigning an employee to a category will be a function of the appraisal system used. The final overall performance measure will determine into which category an employee fits. At this point, compensation administration proceeds as follows:

1. Employees in the Unsatisfactory Performance category get no raise.

2. Employees in the Satisfactory Performance category get the "standard raise."

3. Employees in the Outstanding Performance category get the "standard raise" plus a merit raise.

All that is required of the compensation administrator is to determine what the standard raise and merit raise percentages should be. This may be derived from an analysis of company profits and the number of employees (and their salaries) in each category. This compensation system is easiest to implement companywide at regular intervals, although it is possible to determine the proper percentages on an ongoing basis.

Career planning and development.   Career development as an adjunct to performance appraisal has been described[†] as ". . . a process that can attain its fullest promise only within a context of full understanding

---

* *Ibid.,* p. 16-1.

[†] Kaye, Beverly L., "Performance Appraisal and Career Development: A Shotgun Marriage," *Personnel,* March–April, 1984.

and readiness among all involved. To be successful, a career development program must be undertaken as a step-by-step process that is integrated with organizational goals and other human resources development strategies." This goal of "fullest promise" is something that is rarely reached, although many companies strive for it.

Employee career development revolves around three key questions.

Where am I?   This is information about the employee's current knowledge, skills, and training. In addition, it takes into account current tasks, projects, work in progress, and other job responsibilities.

Management can assist the employee in this area by providing a complete and accurate job description of the employee's current position. This should give the employee a base from which to start. In addition, management should provide regular, behavior-oriented performance appraisals. This provides the employee a measure of individual rate of progress.

Where am I going?   Here the employee is concerned with options and alternatives. Management should provide job descriptions of other possible jobs for comparison, along with regular status meetings. The most important meetings here are those where goal setting is involved. Companies with MBO programs may have an advantage in this respect.

How can I get there?   Again, these are options and alternatives. Here employees need to know what they must *do* to attain their goals. The company should furnish employees with career path planning information that is relevant to their department or division.

There are several advantages to combining career development planning into a regular performance appraisal program. Some of these are listed here.

A realistic view of performance appraisal.   Employees may now view the evaluation process as progress reports on their career plans. In addition, appraisal information can now be examined in the context of career development.

Career planning as part of performance.   Employees may now view regular career planning itself as a goal or task to be accomplished during the review period. Their performance ratings may now depend upon how well they do such planning.

Motivation to improve performance.   With a direct tie between performance and career advancement, many employees will be motivated to improve their performance as a direct consequence of career evolution.

Legal Considerations
and Performance Appraisal

An overview of relevant legislation

Probably the single most important piece of federal legislation that affects the way we do performance appraisals is Title VII of the Civil Rights Act of 1964. This prohibits employment discrimination against individuals on the basis of race, color, religion, sex, or national origin. Over the years various court cases have sought to determine which employment practices the Act includes. In particular, the courts have ruled that discriminatory operation of performance evaluation systems is within the legitimate interest of the Act. This act, enforced by the Equal Employment Opportunity Commission (EEOC), has been interpreted to require employers to meet certain conditions. Some of these are as follows.

Employment tests. In 1966 the EEOC issued *Guidelines on Employment Testing Procedures,* a document that gave procedures for validating employment tests. If such a test was determined to have an unfair impact on minorities protected by the Act, these guidelines required the employer to justify the impact on the basis of business necessity.

Employee evaluation. In 1970 the EEOC issued *Guidelines on Employee Selection Procedures,* which broadened the scope of what was meant by "test." The definition used included the following language:

> . . . the term "test" is defined as any paper and pencil or performance measure used as *a basis for any employment decision* . . . the term "test" includes all formal, scored, quantified, or standardized techniques assessing job suitability including, in addition to the above, specific qualifying or disqualifying personal history or background requirements, specific educational or work history requirements, scored interviews, biographical information blanks, *interviewer's rating scales,* scored application forms . . . [emphasis added].

In 1978 the EEOC republished an updated edition titled *Uniform Guidelines on Employee Selection Procedures.* These new guidelines were substantially the same as those published in 1970. The essential points were as follows.

The overall selection process should be evaluated for any evidence of adverse impact on the employment of any group protected by the law. A statistical definition of adverse impact, known as the "four-fifths" rule, is provided. It states, "A selection rate for any racial, sex, or ethnic group which is less than four-fifths . . . of the rate for the group with the highest rate will generally be regarded by the federal enforcement agencies as evidence of adverse impact."*

Where evidence of adverse impact is demonstrated, the individual components of the selection process should be investigated to find out what specific step(s) or techniques are contributing to the adverse impact. This guideline applies to any selection procedure, including interviews, physical examinations, training programs, work-experience requirements, and the full range of assessment techniques.

Once a procedure has been shown to result in adverse impact, it must be either discarded, changed so that the adverse impact is eliminated, or proved to be job-related and therefore in compliance with the requirement of business necessity. The proof of job-relatedness must be in the form of acceptable evidence of validity.

Encouragement of cooperative validation studies by groups of organizations.

In performing validation studies, an investigation should be made of "suitable alternative selection procedures" that are equally valid but may have less adverse impact. When equally valid procedures are available, the one with the least impact should be adopted.

Additional legislation.   Several other federal regulations and laws apply to performance appraisals. Some of them are as follows.

- The Age Discrimination in Employment Act
- The National Labor Relations Act
- The Occupational Safety and Health Act
- The Vietnam Era Veterans' Readjustment Assistance Act
- The Vocational Rehabilitation Act
- The Whistle Blowers' Protection Act

In addition to the above, many states have passed legislation in several similar areas. It is probably not necessary for the manager to memorize each piece of legislation and the relevant court cases and opinions. However, each business must be aware of these laws and regulations when it develops or uses a performance appraisal system.

---

* *Federal Register,* August 25, 1978, p. 38297.

Performance appraisal and the Civil Rights Act

In *Rowe* v. *General Motors Corporation,* the Court of Appeals for the Fifth Circuit concluded that the failure of blacks to be promoted resulted from a defective performance appraisal system. The court listed five factors that they felt demonstrated that the system was in violation of Title VII of the Civil Rights Act:

1. The supervisor's recommendation was the indispensable, single most important factor in the promotion process.
2. Supervisors were given no written instructions pertaining to the qualifications necessary for promotion.
3. The standards that were determined to be controlling were vague and subjective.
4. Employees were not notified of promotional opportunities.
5. No safeguards designed to avert discriminatory practices existed in the procedure.

In *Brito* v. *Zia Company* the court concluded that performance evaluations were based on the "best judgments and opinions" of the evaluators, but not on any identifiable objective criteria that were supported by some kind of record.

A summary of the guidelines. To summarize: the *Uniform Guidelines on Employee Selection Procedures* and court opinions to date suggest that employers take a long, hard look at current performance appraisal systems. In particular, we encourage upper management to focus on the following recommendations.

- *Do a formal job analysis of all appraisable positions.* This will help to ensure that the resultant appraisal system is job-related.
- *Perform a validation study.* This study will analyze the job analysis information to determine if the criteria developed are sufficient, relevant, necessary, and nondiscriminatory. Statistics gathered during this process will be used in later steps.
- *Ensure that objective criteria are used.* Although the courts have generally frowned on using subjective criteria for measuring and evaluating employees, these data must sometimes be included. If so, ensure that the subjective measures are only one portion of the overall evaluation system.

- *Provide adequate training for evaluators.* Include written instructions and clear, specific descriptions of job or promotion qualification criteria.

- *If using quantitative measures, fix any weights in advance.* Weighting factors for measures are usually used to indicate that certain criteria are more important or more job-relevant than others. These weights should not be applied in retrospect, but delineated prior to the appraisal period.

- *Publicize opportunities for promotion or transfer.* Make such notices available to employees.

- *Standardize the administration and scoring of appraisals.* Any method of scoring or judging the appraisal results should be tightly controlled and standardized.

- *Formalize appraisal procedures.* As appraisal procedures should be in writing and available to evaluators and evaluatees alike, such procedures should be formally documented and available to all parties.

Summary

The performance appraisal process is considered a "test" under EEOC guidelines. It is clearly in the best interest of an organization to see that its evaluation forms and procedures meet the criteria established by the EEOC.

Improving Appraisers

Rating, judging, and evaluating

Each of these terms connotes an opinion or estimate of another person's worth. As it is nearly impossible to prevent subjectivity and human error from creeping in, it is in the best interests of all parties to develop and refine the appraisers themselves.

In Chap. 3 we reviewed common rater errors. We revisit these common errors here, along with our recommendations.

Errors of central tendency. This is the tendency of a rater to rate an employee as average. This is probably the most common rater error, and possibly the most serious. There are several ways for raters to avoid these types of errors. All of these require the rater to *view rating categories independently.* This portion of the review is one of measurement, not judgment. There are several techniques available. A manager may regularly rate *all* employees in a single category, perhaps using a different category every week. Not only does this ensure consistency of ratings across employees, there will be less of a tendency for other errors to creep in (see The Compensation Effect, The Halo Effect, and The Horn Effect following).

Another possibility is to use separate raters for each rating category. Individual raters now have the opportunity to attain a certain level of expertise in rating employees in their category.

The compensation effect.   This is the inclination of a rater to rate an employee low in one category if he or she has already scored high in another category. Such "compensating" tends to generate overall ratings of "average" or "near average." This sometimes stems from a manager's emotional feelings about an employee. If a manager deems an employee as average, then it is only logical to conclude that a high rating in one appraisal category must be balanced by one or more low ratings in others.

As with errors of central tendency, compensation effects can be greatly reduced or eliminated by viewing rating categories independently.

The first impression.   Here, raters score an employee based upon their first impression, ignoring or minimizing behaviors or results occurring later in the appraisal period.

The most important element required to eliminate these types of errors will be a record of employee behavior during the review period. This usually consists of status reports, minutes of appraisal, goal-setting and career planning meetings, and the like. It is always a good idea at the beginning of the review period for the manager and employee to meet often to agree upon the goals and subgoals for the coming period. During these early meetings the manager should give the employee feedback on his or her initial progress, so that the employee may then determine what type of first impression has been made. This then becomes a point of discussion for future meetings. The documentation should serve to ease any tension, and streamline the future appraisal meeting.

General bias.   This is the tendency of a manager or an organization to rate all employees as lower or higher than average. Such a disposition leads to a compression of the rating scale, as "normal" ratings now range from "excellent" to "superior."

Another possible reason for such bias is the inclination of performance appraisal document designers to assign words to the rating scales. For example, a scale of 1-to-5 may be labeled as unacceptable, poor, acceptable, excellent, and superior on the appraisal form. The words *unacceptable* and *poor* have negative connotations (for good reason). Some managers are emotionally unable (or unwilling) to rate their employees as unacceptable or poor.

Dealing with this kind of bias may mean upsetting an entire corporate culture. After all, any attempt to make major changes to such an appraisal system will suddenly make the majority of employees *acceptable* or *satisfactory*. Many will be upset by this "devaluation" of their appraisal system.

First, to minimize the ill effects of this type of bias, the manager and employee should meet at the beginning of the review period and formally agree (and document) their understanding of the rating scale steps. For example, for the rating of *acceptable* they might agree that this means "codes programs that seldom require maintenance," or "completes all programming and testing assignments within allotted deadlines." The final appraisal can then measure the employee's behaviors in terms of these descriptions.

The halo and horn effects.   These tend to rate an employee high (or low) in one category if they have already scored high (or low) in one or more of the other categories.

Avoiding these biases is relatively easy to do. As with compensation errors and errors of central tendency, managers must view the appraisal categories independently. The manager's feelings belong in the area of judgment, not measurement. While it may seem logical that an "excellent" employee that scores high in one category should naturally score high in several others, this is a false assumption. Since the act of judgment follows that of measurement, it should be the facts that determine the rating, not the other way around.

Most recent behavior.   This is the inclination to rate an employee based on his or her most recent behavior, rather than the entire appraisal period. This has the effect of weighting recent events more than those at the beginning of the review period.

To avoid this problem, we recommend complete and accurate documentation during the appraisal period. Since the final appraisal meeting is (or should be) a simple summary of the entire review period, it will be difficult for the manager or the employee to give more recent behaviors greater weight.

Some managers feel that the most recent behavior is naturally more important. After all, if the employee was initially unskilled and is now fully trained, shouldn't the appraisal reflect this? The answer is *yes,* the appraisal should reflect this, but in the proper way. The rate of an employee's progress is at least as important as the employee's current status or level of achievement, as it provides an indicator of future performance and potential.

But basing category ratings on most recent behavior or achievements will compress the meanings of the rating scales. Since most employees improve over time, this makes it impossible to compare employees who have performed satisfactorily for twelve months with those who were unsatisfactory for nine months and satisfactory for three. As upper management will probably wish to distinguish between these two categories of employees (at least as far as compensation is concerned), raters must make sure that this is reflected in the ratings given.

Spillover effects. Here, the rater lets past or previous performance appraisal results bias their rating for the current review period.

This is unfortunate, as it indicates a lack of awareness on the part of the manager of the difference between measurement and judgment. Although the prior appraisal may have formed the basis for current action plans or performance improvement plans, it should have no bearing on current ratings.

Ratings for the present review period should reflect employee behaviors from that period, not historical judgments. Perhaps the best advice is to avoid studying the prior appraisal altogether until after the current measurement and judgment processes are completed.

Overcoming rater errors: General advice

We feel that most of these rater errors can be avoided or eliminated by proper documentation and regular meetings between rater and employee. Indeed, most problems in life seem to be those related to a lack of communication between people. Specifically, we recommend the following.

Rater training programs. Raters must receive proper training in their company's performance appraisal forms and procedures. This should include an explanation of all terms used on the forms, such as *excellent* and *satisfactory*. It should also involve the rater in practice sessions. In this way, problems such as those described in the previous section can be anticipated and addressed.

Potential raters should be given examples of good (and bad) performance appraisals. This case study approach would permit raters to learn by example, rather than by trial and error.

In addition to training the appraiser, performance appraisal training should be made available to employees as well. This would consist of an overview of the company's commitment to objective appraisals, the ways the company uses appraisal information, and a description of the appraisal process. Employees should receive a copy of all relevant appraisal forms for their examination. Employees who take issue with portions of the form or process should have the opportunity to discuss their concerns with a representative from the personnel department. In some cases, this may lead to changes in the review process or forms.

Formal documentation procedures.   We have already mentioned the regular status report as forming the basis for appraisal measurements. Employees should organize their status reports in the same order as that of the appraisal forms. This will make the manager's job easier, as the status report becomes more of a mini-review document. Further, this format gets both the employee and the manager thinking in terms of performance appraisal, thus avoiding some miscommunication.

Regular communication.   Both rater and employee must communicate with each other in order for proper appraisal to take place. This rather simple statement overlooks the fact that many people are poor communicators. In general, most communication problems can be traced to one thing: an inability or unwillingness to *listen*. Effective listening skills are beyond the scope of this book. Those interested can consult any one of the many books available on the subject. Such skills are relatively easy to acquire. Indeed, this should be one of the employee's first goals.

Appraising the appraiser

One interesting aspect of appraisal not dealt with in detail so far is that of appraising the performance of raters themselves. This is not a new problem. First posed by early philosophers (*Quis custodes ipsos custodes?*—Who shall guard the guardians?), this problem has no simple solution, but some of those in use today are described here.

Multiple raters.   There are several companies that divide the measurement aspect of performance appraisal among several raters. Each rater is responsible for one or more rating categories across the entire employee base. An internal expert in written communications would evaluate all employees in this category, another skilled in quality assurance would evaluate work quality, and so forth.

A variation of this method is for employee appraisals to be done by two or three managers, either working separately or in concert. This tends to greatly reduce biases, including general bias errors, first impression errors, and recent behavior errors. One possible disadvantage of this method is the amount of time spent by management in the appraisal process. Still, this time is spent in the judgment phase, rather than the measurement phase.

Separation of powers.   Using this method, the employee's immediate manager performs measurement tasks, while upper management is responsible for those of judgment. This tends to reduce halo and horn effects, as upper management is less likely to have formed personal opinions or biases about every employee.

Automation.   Several small software firms have produced programs that attempt to do automated performance evaluations and follow-up (compensation administration, promotion recommendation, and the like). While these systems would seem to offer the advantage of objective ratings and customized features, they tend to oversimplify the appraisal process. Indeed, they depend on the user to input *all necessary information.* As this information usually includes fifty-two weeks of employee status reports, interpreting and entering the correct information may be somewhat tedious.

Upper management observers.   Using this method, a representative of upper management observes the appraisal process; in actuality, this observer only observes the appraisal meeting. With a properly designed appraisal system there will be little to observe at this meeting, as it is designed to summarize an entire year of employee behavior.

A better idea would be for upper management to participate as observers in weekly employee meetings. This, however, will probably be seen as taking too much of management's time.

Rater raters.   This latest trend in performance evaluation is for a professional evaluator to appraise management performance. This professional, commonly an outside consultant, first reviews all appraisals completed within a specified period. The evaluator then interviews each manager, reviewing specific appraisals. On occasion, the consultant will observe an employee meeting or appraisal interview. The evaluator may also require the manager to reperform an employee evaluation for analysis.

This is probably the most fair and impartial method of rating managers on their employee appraisals. Although it may seem expensive, the cost should be weighed against the realization that any serious problems a company may have with raters and appraisals may not surface for years after they first develop.

Chapter

10

Sample Appraisal Forms

In this chapter we round off our look at various methods of employee evaluation by exhibiting some examples of appraisal documents. These sample forms were compiled by the authors in the course of their lives and do not necessarily match those of any organizations at this time. Some are blends of two or more forms, and some have been completely redone by their sources. In each case, however, the intent of the form was to appraise the performance of data processing personnel.

These forms illustrate the wide variety and diversity of thought regarding measuring and evaluating DP employee performance. To get the most out of these examples, we invite the reader to examine and analyze each one using the criteria in this book. Specifically, can these appraisal forms be used for the following:

- Making employment decisions?
- Performance improvement?
- Assigning work duties?
- Identifying and rating potential?
- Compensation administration?
- Identifying training needs?
- Career planning and development?

In addition to these, we suggest that the reader analyze the forms from the perspective of *objectivity:* is the information requested objective or subjective? Is it fair? Is it non-gender-specific? Do items concentrate on observable and measurable behaviors, or do they ask for managers to measure things like *dependability, attitude,* and *devotion?*

Rating scale appraisals

The rating scale type of appraisal form seems to dominate data processing departments, perhaps because it assigns numbers to behaviors or skills. Fully half of the organizations surveyed by the authors used some form of rating appraisal. While they seem to be well-constructed, all still contain fatal flaws.

The ratings and how to use them. Some of these forms include explanations of the rating numbers or categories on the form itself. For example, in Fig. 10.1 the term *outstanding performance* is defined. Regrettably, it is defined in terms of other words or phrases that are subjective, such as *far exceeds, peak performance,* and *totally dependable.* Far from helping a manager to rate an employee, such descriptions obscure the measurement process, sometimes turning appraisal meetings into childish arguments about the meanings of the words *excellent, superior,* or *above average.*

Other forms leave such interpretations to the manager, being content to leave the rating scale as *low* to *high* (see Fig. 10.2), or to assign check boxes to certain levels defined in short phrases (see Fig. 10.3). Others (see Fig. 10.4) simply leave a bracketed line on the form and leave it to the appraiser to figure out!

The rating category descriptions. Some of these types of forms define the rating categories briefly, as in Figs. 10.1 and 10.5. Others print only the category title itself. Figure 10.2 contains an appraisal like this. Imagine using this appraisal to rate an employee as a *4* in the category of Creative Thinking!

Overall. All of these rating scale appraisal forms lack the following:

A time-valued basis. Is an employee who has been a *superior* performer for a year to be rated the same as one who gradually matured from *average* to *superior* in the course of the review period?

A description of the standards against which the employees are being measured. Excellent compared to what? Last year? Other employees that were judged *excellent* this year, or in previous years? The manager's idea of what *excellent* means? Compared with others of the same job description in a department? Across the company? Across DP organizations in general?

An analysis of which categories are applicable or are more (or less) important for a particular employee at certain times. Different projects may require different skill sets. COBOL programmers may need different communication skills than programmers developing client/server applications using CASE tools.

Rating Scale Appraisal Form

Employee Name _____   Emp-ID _____   Title _____

Location _____   Department _____   Review Period _____

Rating Categories

5   Outstanding Performance. Far exceeds job standards. Outstanding producer, Turns in peak performance. Extremely accurate worker, rarely makes errors. Completely understands the relationship and duties of related jobs. Totally dependable in performing, including non-routine assignments.

4   Highly Effective Performance. Considerably above standards. Consistently above average producer. Organizes all work assignments well. Work is consistently well done, negligible amount of error, handles assignments with minimum amount of direction. Consistently dependable in accomplishing job assignments. Requires minimum of supervisory follow-up.

3   Effective Performance. Meets all job standards. Output is consistent with job standards on most assignments. Work assignments are consistent with a minimum amount of error. Fulfills responsibilities and follows instructions with limited supervision. May require assistance on non-routine assignments.

2   Conditionally Acceptable. Generally meets many job standards. Requires additional supervision to complete assignments. Sometimes fails to meet job standards. Requires additional counseling, training, and experience to meet job standards in some areas of job assignments. Does not always fulfill responsibilities.

1   Inadequate Performance. Frequently below standards. Organizes assignments poorly. Work assignments seldom meet specified quantity or quality standards. Does not perform full scope of job responsibilities.

_____ 1. Planning and Organizing. Develops sound plans for operation within guidelines of policy and statistical data. Delegates work systematically so that subordinates understand assignment allocation, even in absence of supervision.

_____ 2. Innovation. Initiates change in operation based on sound planning and wise use of resources available.

_____ 3. Controlling. Has developed systematic and efficient methods for keeping track of all activities for which responsible. Has set standards and defined exceptions for operation so subordinates know under which circumstances to report for special instructions and help.

_____ 4. Communicating. Gives instructions, both oral and written, which result in prompt and accurate performance by subordinates and associates. Grasps spoken and written communication accurately, speaks and writes clearly and concisely.

_____ 5. Motivating. Generates cooperation and creative initiative from both subordinates and associates. Encourages frank discussion and so is aware of subordinates' attitudes and problems.

_____ 6. Developing Subordinates. Selects, trains, and develops subordinates so that they can function effectively with a high degree of versatility and independence and without close supervision. Identifies potential in subordinates and recommends developmental guides toward future.

Comments

Figure 10.1   Rating scale appraisal form.

Tie-ins to career development and personnel planning.   An employee rates *superior* in the category of Developing Subordinates. Is this good? Was it related to his or her job? Do the employee's career plans include supervision of others? Do the company's goals and career development plans for this employee include management?

Coordination with the normal reporting system.   Where in these forms does one indicate the derivation of the manager's ratings? An

Rating Scale Appraisal Form

Name _____   Locn/Dept _____

Position Title _____   Date _____

(1)   The employee should be reviewed on each of the factors below in relation to the present position. For each of these factors, check the box which reflects most typically the employee's performance.

(2)   Some factors are particularly significant in certain positions. Circle the three factors which are particularly important in reviewing an employee in this position.

Group	Factor Number		Low 1 2 3 4	High 5
	1	Position Knowledge	☐ ☐ ☐ ☐	☐
	2	Analytical Ability	☐ ☐ ☐ ☐	☐
Position Performance	3	Planning and Execution	☐ ☐ ☐ ☐	☐
	4	Acceptance of Responsibility	☐ ☐ ☐ ☐	☐
	5	Dependability	☐ ☐ ☐ ☐	☐
	6	Creative Thinking	☐ ☐ ☐ ☐	☐
	7	Relationship with Others	☐ ☐ ☐ ☐	☐
Personal Performance	8	Attitude	☐ ☐ ☐ ☐	☐
	9	Emotional Stability	☐ ☐ ☐ ☐	☐
	10	Health	☐ ☐ ☐ ☐	☐
Supervisory Performance	11	Delegation of Responsibility	☐ ☐ ☐ ☐	☐

Figure 10.2   Rating scale appraisal form.

employee rated *acceptable* in the category of Quality might be annoyed by this if his or her status reports for the review period contained nothing but documentation of high-quality work.

Checklist appraisals

These types of appraisal forms rarely appear in data processing organizations, unless they are a holdover from the parent enterprise. (In other words, some human resource professional felt that forms applicable to other personnel would be applicable in DP.) Checklists usually materialize in one of two forms: *simple checklists* and *weighted checklists.*

The simple checklist.   An example of a simple checklist occurs in Fig. 10.6. Here, the manager reads the description of the category, such as Knowledge of Work. Then the manager reads each of the behavior descriptions

---

Rating Scale Appraisal Form

Name _____ Date_____

Position _____ Salary Group _____

Division/Department/Location _____

Analysis of Performance. Using the scale definitions shown below, indicate your appraisal of the employee on each of the factors listed below by checking the appropriate box under each factor. Use the space provided under each factor for any explanatory comments your may wish to provide.

Accomplishments — Consider results achieved by the employee in terms of quantity, accuracy, thoroughness and timeliness, and indicate the employee's level of effectiveness in completing agreed-to tasks and/or objectives.

❏ RE   ❏ CE   ❏ MR   ❏ MM   ❏ FM   ❏ ?   ❏ NA

Organization — Consider the employee's effectiveness in ordering and completing tasks according to priority, keeping records current, providing support data when needed, and indicate the employee's level of effectiveness in planning and organizing work.

❏ RE   ❏ CE   ❏ MR   ❏ MM   ❏ FM   ❏ ?   ❏ NA

Job Knowledge — Consider the employee's skills and grasp of work and procedures and indicate the level of the employee's job knowledge and effectiveness in applying this knowledge.

❏ RE   ❏ CE   ❏ MR   ❏ MM   ❏ FM   ❏ ?   ❏ NA

Independent Action — Consider the employee's ability to work with little or no supervision and indicate the level of effectiveness in taking independent action.

❏ RE   ❏ CE   ❏ MR   ❏ MM   ❏ FM   ❏ ?   ❏ NA

Rating Scale Factors. Taking all significant factors into consideration (accomplishments, organization, job knowledge, independent action) along with any special circumstances which may have helped or hindered the employee, check one of the following:

❏ RE   Rarely equaled in exceeding job requirements   ❏ FM   Fails to meet job requirements
❏ CE   Clearly exceeds job requirements   ❏ ?   Undetermined: insufficient data
❏ MR   Meets all job requirements and all expectations   ❏ NA   Not applicable
❏ MM   Meets minimum job requirements

Figure 10.3   Rating scale appraisal form.

for that category, checking the most appropriate one. This method has several advantages, assuming the form was designed properly.

- The manager evaluates without any subjective ratings or rating-descriptive words such as *average.* As the checklist entries describe *behaviors,* these words tend not to appear.

- The manager measures behaviors, not traits—what he or she sees the employee *do* (Needs Instruction or Guidance), not what the employee *is* (Highly Dependable from Fig. 10.2).

- Checklist items are easily cross-referenced to normal reporting tools such as status reports and mini-reviews.

Rating Scale Appraisal Form

Employee Name _____   Review Date _____

Instructions: In the column to the left of each factor place the number (weighting factor) which indicates your judgement of this factor's importance to the successful performance of the incumbent's job.

> 1 Absolutely critical to success on the job
> 2 Important but not critical
> 3 Not really important to success on the job

After weighting the factors, place an A (Actual) on the continuum for each factor to indicate the developmental level actually achieved, and a D (Desired) to indicate how much development remains to be achieved with regard to that particular factor. (The assumption here is that it may not be desirous or efficient that the incumbent aspire to the optimum of each factor.)

MEASURING AND CONTROLLING

A.   The identification of performance activities or functions to be measured.

_____ |——————————————————————|——————————————————————|

B.   The planning, developing, and implementing of the means for collecting and analyzing performance information

_____ |——————————————————————|——————————————————————|

C.   The identification and establishment of performance standards, job related goals, rates of progress towards reaching these goals, and acceptable levels of deviations from goals.

_____ |——————————————————————|——————————————————————|

D.   The positive steps the individual took in utilizing collected information to correct deviations from established plans, goals, objectives, and standards.

_____ |——————————————————————|——————————————————————|

LEADERSHIP

E.   The incumbent's skill in influencing subordinates to accomplish desired goals.

_____ |——————————————————————|——————————————————————|

Figure 10.4   Rating scale appraisal form.

- Checklists lend themselves well to compensation administration. This assumes that the manager filling out the form has no idea how the items are used in determining salaries. One such method is to assign each checklist entry a weight; the weights are then summed at the end of the appraisal to determine an overall rating. However, should a manager find out what the weights are, then the objectivity of the appraisal process is in question. The manager now knows what checklist items to check to get the employee a raise (or deny one).

Rating Scale Appraisal Form

Employee Name _____   Review Period _____

1.   Initiative. The degree to which the employee acts independently in new situations; the extent to which
      the employee sees what needs to be done and does it without being told.

A.	90—100%	Superior. Little or no supervision needed. Highly resourceful and aggressive.
B.	71—89%	Good. Thinks and acts independently. Resourceful in new situations.
C.	31—70%	Acceptable. Initiative is satisfactory. Requires average supervision.
D.	11—30%	Improvement Needed. Requires frequent instruction. Needs close supervision.
E.	1-10%	Unsatisfactory. Must be told everything to do. Takes no personal initiative.
F.		Unable to Rate.

2.   Productivity. The actual work output of the employee relative to other employees. Consider what the
      employee actually produces, rather than what the employee may be capable of producing.

A.	90—100%	Superior. Definitely a top producer.
B.	71—89%	Good. Produces more than most. Above average.
C.	31—70%	Acceptable. Average output definitely meets requirements.
D.	11—30%	Improvement Needed. Low output, below average.
E.	1-10%	Unsatisfactory. Extremely low output, definitely not acceptable.
F.		Unable to Rate.

3.   Quality. Freedom from errors and mistakes; accuracy; quality of work in general.

A.	90—100%	Superior. Highest possible quality. Final product virtually perfect.
B.	71—89%	Good. Quality above average; few errors and mistakes.
C.	31—70%	Acceptable. No more mistakes than should be expected; quality definitely acceptable.
D.	11—30%	Improvement Needed. Meets only minimum standards. Improvement needed.
E.	1-10%	Unsatisfactory. Excessive errors and mistakes. Very poor quality.
F.		Unable to Rate.

4.   Effort. The degree to which the employee does the best to be a top employee, without regard to how
      effective the employee may be. Consider conscientiousness and motivation.

A.	90—100%	Superior. Intensely motivated. Exerts maximum effort.
B.	71—89%	Good. Exerts more effort than most. A hard worker.
C.	31—70%	Acceptable. Satisfactory effort. Average motivation level.
D.	11—30%	Improvement Needed. Low motivation. Could perform much better than currently.
E.	1-10%	Unsatisfactory. Exerts effort only when the employee is forced to do so.
F.		Unable to Rate.

Figure 10.5   Rating scale appraisal form.

Regrettably, in our opinion these forms are rarely designed correctly.
The checklist items still contain subjective terms such as *lacks imagination, dependable and thorough, satisfactory team worker,* and *very
capable.* This takes the review totally out of the realm of objectivity
and fairness.

The weighted checklist.   As shown in Fig. 10.7, this type of appraisal
form incorporates a weighting factor for each category. Despite its simplicity, this form suffers from the same problems as the simple check-

---

Checklist Appraisal Form

Name _____   Position Title _____
Department _____   Location _____   Date _____

Instructions: Evaluate the employee's performance in their present position by checking the most appropriate square. Use the Remarks section for significant comments.

A.   **Knowledge of Work:** Understanding of all phases of work and related matters including quality.
☐ Needs instruction or guidance
☐ Has required knowledge of own and related work
☐ Has exceptional knowledge of own and related work

B.   **Planning and Organizing:** Ability to plan ahead so as to make most effective use of personnel, materials, time and equipment.
☐ Needs frequent help
☐ Normally plans and organizes
☐ Very effective under all conditions

C.   **Analytical Ability and Judgement:** Ability to size up a problem, get and evaluate facts, and reach sound conclusions.
☐ Normally requires assistance
☐ Generally analyzes problems and uses judgement
☐ Outstanding analytical ability and judgement

D.   **Initiative:** Ability to originate or develop ideas and to get things started. Works to improve self and job.
☐ Lacks imagination
☐ Generally exhibits independent thought
☐ Exceptionally resourceful

E.   **Dependability:** Reliability in following through with thoroughness and accuracy on assignments and instructions.
☐ Requires more than normal follow-up
☐ Dependable and thorough on most assignments
☐ Exceptional in all assignments

F.   **Cooperation:** Ability to get along with fellow workers; i.e., disposition, tact, sincerity, and courtesy.
☐ Reluctant to work with others
☐ Is satisfactory team worker
☐ Works effectively with others to best interest of all

G.   **Development of Others:** Recognition and development of the abilities and capacities of others.
☐ Contributes little to their development
☐ Strives to develop the potential of others
☐ Very capable and active in developing their people

Figure 10.6   Checklist appraisal form.

list. In addition, the measurer or rater now has knowledge regarding what final rating will be assigned.

The MBO appraisal

Management by objectives took the management world by storm several decades ago. Championed by Peter Drucker, this method advocated managers and subordinates jointly setting goals for the review period and monitoring those goals periodically. However, this descrip-

Weighted Checklist Appraisal Form

Name _____ Cost Center _____ New Grade _____

Current Position _____ Grade _____ Merit _____

Former Position _____ Date Left _____ Status _____

New Position _____ Approved Grade _____ Init _____

Major Areas of Responsibility	Weight (Total=100)	Decimal Factor Applied	Performance Points (Weight x Factor)
1.			
2.			
3.			
4.			
5.			
6.			
7.			
8.			
9.			
10.			

Total Performance Points: _____

Decimal Rating Factors

2.0 Distinguished
1.5 Highly Satisfactory
1.0 Satisfactory
0.5 Marginal
0.0 Unsatisfactory

Final Rating

170-200 Distinguished
130-169 Highly Satisfactory
90-129 Satisfactory
50-89 Marginal
< 49 Unsatisfactory

Comments

Rater _____ Rating Date _____

Figure 10.7 Weighted checklist appraisal form.

tion was a drastic oversimplification, as many managers soon found out. Compounding this was the lack of understanding of what appraisal meant in such circumstances. After all, if the goal was to meet your objectives, how could one be rewarded for exceeding them? To put it another way, *meeting an objective* is a binary, yes/no operation. One either meets an objective or one does not. Even objectives couched in numeric terms may not lend themselves well to being "exceeded." Consider the following objective: *Reduce the staff by five percent.* Suppose a manager reduced his or her staff by 100 percent; should he or she be rewarded for greatly exceeding the objective?

MBO appraisal forms used in data processing tend to have lots of formatted empty space for managers to fill in; hence, they require a manager to have good written communication skills.

Figure 10.8 shows one example of such a form. The manager and the subordinate fill in the agreed-upon objectives at the left. At the end of the appraisal period the manager rates whether the objectives were achieved. Note that on this form the manager must determine *to what level* the objectives were achieved (satisfactory, outstanding, and so

MBO Appraisal Form

Name _____   Rating Period _____

Department _____

1. Achievement of Maintenance Objectives. List the maintenance objectives that have been set for this individual for the rating period. These objectives should reflect the basic responsibilities of the position or assignment that are usually reflected in the position description. Rate each objective at the end of the rating period on the basis of results achieved.	Less than Satisfactory	Satisfactory	More than Satisfactory	Outstanding

2. Achievement of Innovative Objectives. List additional objectives that should contribute to improvement and effectiveness of area operations. They could be termed "plus" or "stretch" objectives, but the important consideration is that they bring an added dimension to the effectiveness of the position or assignment. Quantify when possible. Rate each objective at the end of the rating period on the basis of results achieved.	Less than Satisfactory	Satisfactory	More than Satisfactory	Outstanding

Figure 10.8   MBO appraisal form.

on). Thus, the rating problem appears again as it did with rating scale appraisals.

Figure 10.9 is much better organized. Here each item is assigned several *indicators* that will be used to measure objective accomplishment. These are *minimum permissible, average expected,* and *maximum probable.* In this way the manager and employee can agree not only on the

MBO Appraisal Form				
Name _____ Date _____ Objectives for Period _____				

Part I — Routine Duties and Goals

List major areas of responsibility related to your routine duties and goals. Every item that can be quantified should be included in the indicators column on the right. Be sure that you have listed "trade-off" responsibilities.	Indicators			Actual Achievement During Period
	Minimum Permissible	Average Expected	Maximum Probable	
List major areas of responsibility related to routine duties and goals that do not have specific quantitative indicators				

Part II — Other Goals and Objectives

Instructions: Categorize goals and objectives (problem solving, creative and personal development). Establish priorities according to the following codes: A — Maximum contribution to position and company objectives. B — Average contribution to position and company objectives. C — Minimum contribution to position and company objectives. D — Postponable (until A through C are complete or until next MBO review meeting.)

Objectives and Goals — Improvement Expected	Standards of Performance — How Results Will be Measured	Target	Priority

Figure 10.9 MBO appraisal form.

objectives but also on the scale by which they will be measured. This is a giant step forward for this kind of appraisal form. Combined with documentation for a formal goal-setting process, this appraisal form may well be the best all-around for data processing personnel.

Conclusions

It would have been extremely satisfying to conclude this book with an example of a perfect appraisal form for DP personnel. Regrettably, no single form can satisfy all needs. Clearly, certain combinations of MBO and rating scale forms can satisfy management's needs for monitoring objectives, making employment decisions, improving performance, identifying and rating potential, and compensation administration. We doubt that many organizations will take the time and resources to completely rethink their appraisal systems. However, they might be responsive to recommendations from middle and upper management as to enhancements that would do the following:

- Make terms on appraisal forms understandable, fair, objective, and behavior-based
- Make the manager's job of employee review easier
- Add any forms and procedures necessary to competently measure and judge employee performance

In these and other ways, management is accountable to the employee base to compensate them fairly for the work they do.

Societies and Associations

The information in this appendix is included so that readers may be made aware of the various professional societies and associations that are involved in some aspect of data processing. This list is not meant to be exhaustive, but should serve as a guide to prospective members.

ACM   Association for Computing Machinery
            11 West 42nd Street, 3rd Floor
            New York, NY 10036
            (212) 869-7440

AICCP   Association of the ICCP
            2200 E. Devon Ave., Suite 268
            Des Plaines, IL 60018-4503
            (708) 299-4227

AIM   Association for Information Management
            7380 Parkway Dr.
            La Mesa, CA 91942
            (619) 465-3990

ASM   Association for Systems Management
            P.O. Box 38370
            Cleveland, OH 44138-0370
            (216) 243-6900

AWC   Association for Women in Computing
            41 Sutter Street, Suite 1006
            San Francisco, CA 94104

CIPS   Canadian Information Processing Society
            430 King Street West, Suite 205
            Toronto, ON Canada M5V 1L5
            (416) 593-4040

COMMON   An IBM User Group
              401 N. Michigan
              Chicago, IL 60611-4267
              (312) 644-6610

DAMA   Data Administration Management Association
              152 W. Northwest Highway
              Suite 103
              Palatine, IL 60067
              (708) 934-6875

DPMA   Data Processing Management Association
              505 Busse Highway
              Park Ridge, IL 60068-3191
              (708) 825-8124

FNUG   Federation of NCR User Groups
              Mail Station USG-1
              Dayton, OH 45479
              (513) 445-3131

ICCA   Independent Computer Consultants Association
              933 Gardenview Office Parkway
              St. Louis, MO 63141
              (314) 997-4633

ISCA   Information Systems Consultants Association
              P.O. Box 467190
              Atlanta, GA 30346
              (404) 458-3080

ISTE   International Society for Technology in Education
              1787 Agate St.
              Eugene, OR 97403
              (513) 686-4414

NaSPA   National Systems Programmers Association
              4811 S. 76th Street, Suite 210
              Milwaukee, WI 53220-4352
              (414) 423-2420

Data Processing Tasks and Responsibilities

In this appendix we take a look at how all of the data processing staff interact with each other to solve business problems. We approach this from the perspective of the Systems Development Life Cycle (SDLC) (see Fig. B.1). Each of the phases of the SDLC brings different talents to bear on the functions and tasks being performed.

Developing user requirements. In this phase, management personnel meet with user representatives to discuss and develop user requirements. In some organizations the users will submit requests to the information systems (IS) department for automated applications they wish developed. It is then the responsibility of IS to respond to these requests. Such responses usually involve performing a *feasibility study* and a *cost/benefit analysis*.

A task force performs a feasibility study to determine if it is *possible* to develop the required system. The study takes into account hardware requirements, program and file design, and user service needs such as on-line access to data or high performance. If the task force determines that development is feasible, they then begin the cost/benefit analysis. This analysis lists the costs of systems development in terms of additional hardware, third-party software, new software development, staff requirements, and quality assurance procedures. It then describes the benefits of the system, including such things as money saved, orders processed more quickly, higher inventory turnover, reduced overtime, and sometimes even higher profits. These costs and benefits are then compared and submitted to management to make the decision whether or not to proceed with systems development.

Traditional   **Modern**

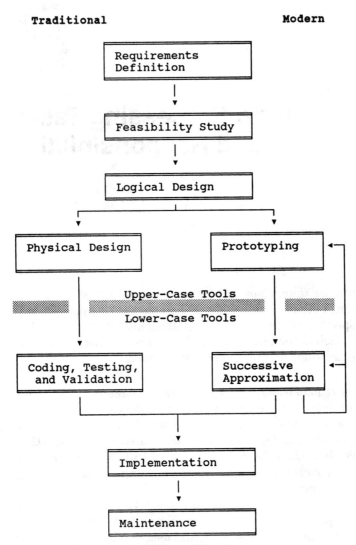

Figure B.1   The systems development life cycle.

Should management decide to proceed with development, a task force is formed to create a *user requirements* document. This document will become the contract between the IS department and the users. It defines precisely the description of the system to be developed and delivered to the users. The following are some typical requirement items.

A statement of the business problem.   For example, "Permit telephone order takers to enter customer orders into an on-line screen or screens. Verify that order items are on-hand in inventory; if not, backorder such items. Calculate shipping and state sales taxes (if any); provide customers with order total; for credit card orders, perform credit check."

A statement of constraints.   Some typical constraints might be:

- All tax calculations must conform to any relevant federal and state laws.

- The system must run in an environment that includes the present Accounts Payable, Accounts Receivable, and Inventory Systems, and all associated files.

- All on-line screens must provide a response to the user within three seconds 95 percent of the time.

A timetable or set of deadlines.   This is sometimes the fuzziest part of the requirements document. It is not enough to say, for example, "The system must be completed by March 1." The word *completed* is not well-defined. Most IS departments have standard timetables for system development that include such things as subsystem programming completion dates, testing deadlines, a date for user acceptance testing, and user training.

With the requirements document complete, the information systems department now begins systems development.

Analysis and design.   Sometimes called *logical design* and *physical design,* these two processes sometimes go hand-in-hand. *Analysis* deals with the translation of user requirements into data items, entities, relationships, dataflows, and processes. (We will not define these items here, as complete descriptions are not necessary to understand analysis.) This translation is done by an *applications analyst.* (Note: another type of analyst, the *systems analyst,* is primarily concerned with analyzing *operating systems,* not user applications. We will meet the systems analyst in a later phase of the SDLC.)

The applications analyst interprets the user requirements and converts them into some kind of graphic diagrams that will be suitable for the next step. These diagrams depict collections of data and how they will be processed by the system. This is all done at a logical level. What is *not* described, therefore, are specific programs, files, databases, or even the computer the system will use. These are determined in the next step.

After the applications analyst has completed the diagrams and logical systems description, he or she passes along this information to the *application designer.* The designer is charged with taking the logical design and determining the correct hardware and software environment for the new system. This may involve many decisions.

Data storage.   The designer must decide where application data will be stored. Some options include flat files, databases, and distribution across a network. The designer must take into account where any interfacing systems currently exist, as some of this data may need to be made available to the new system.

Hardware platform.   While most organizations will assume that new systems will be developed to run on currently available hardware, some shops have reached the limit of their computer's capacity. Adding new systems or data will only slow down already lethargic applications. In this case, the designer must take into account possible upgrades to current hardware, addition of new hardware, addition of distributed processing capabilities across a network, and placement of microcomputers at the user site.

Database environment.   When the choice has been made to store data on a database, there may be several alternative data base management systems (DBMS) available. Most database organizations can be classified into one of the following types: *hierarchical, network, multilist,* and *relational.* Each of these choices has its own advantages and disadvantages in terms of performance, ease of use, ability to define data structures quickly, convenient security mechanisms, and backup and recovery procedures.

Programming language.   Although most shops have settled on a single standard programming language, sometimes the choice is not so clear-cut. Most high-level languages such as COBOL and PL/I are not known for their execution speed. If speed is a system requirement, then some programs or often-used modules may be coded in (say) assembler.

   Another alternative in this area is using a computer-assisted software engineering (CASE) tool. New tools now coming out are able to read as input the diagrams made during the analysis step. These tools then produce an output program code, ready for execution. These *code generators* are relatively new in data processing and have not yet established themselves with a track record.

Choice and selection of programs.   Many of the processes defined in the analysis step involve complex data manipulation. These more complex processes may then be split up into several simpler processes, with each process then defined as a program. Simpler processes, on the other hand, may be combined into a single program.

With these decisions made, the designer is ready to proceed to the next step. The designers and analysts meet with the user representatives and conduct a *design walkthru.* This process is designed to uncover any serious errors in the analysis or design documents. This is probably the most cost-effective way to fix errors. Errors found during programming, for example, may be much more costly, as they may lead to required design changes and possible additional required programs or data.

Each program must now be completely *specified*. This operation means taking the process descriptions and transforming them into *program specifications* that a programmer can understand. These specifications may take the form of *flow charts* that delineate the flow of control of the program, or *dataflow diagrams* that depict dataflow through a maze of processes that alter the data. Another popular diagramming method is the *structure chart* that portrays program control flow in a hierarchical manner.

Along with the program specifications, the designer must include data descriptions. In general, data items are grouped into bundles called *entities*. These will then be transformed by the designer into *files* or *database* entries. The totality of data items and entities for a system is grouped into a *data dictionary, or repository*.

One last document for complete and correct program specifications is the *program test plan*. This plan tells the programmer what tests will be performed to verify that the program is working correctly. This provides the programmer with more information on what the program is expected to do, as well as how the data will be processed.

Programming. With the programs defined and the specifications completed, program coding can now begin. (Actually, the phases of design, programming, and testing need not be completed exactly in that order. If the IS department waits for the analysts and designers to finish completely before beginning programming, many programmers may have to sit idle as more and more specifications are completed. Instead, there is usually some overlap.) As designers finish program specifications they usually have the option of approving them for immediate programming. One must take care, however. Sometimes Program B requires data produced from Program A; in this case, Program A should be written first.

For large application systems (those having scores of programs), IS management will collect all of the tasks that must be performed up to this point and enter them into a *project management* tool. Management then uses this tool to determine the best sequence of program design and coding. Such a tool usually has added benefits: most will calculate total staff resources required, and will inform you as to whether the project is on schedule or not.

Testing and debugging. As the programmer finishes coding a program, testing may begin. (Note: there are some tools that will allow the programmer to interactively test a program before coding is complete.

These are not considered here.) Some shops have designated *testers* who create test data and test programs. These testers are skilled in testing programs, and gain a certain level of expertise in the system being tested. They coordinate with programmers to make any changes to programs that are required due to failing one or more tests.

In many environments it is the responsibility of programmers to test their own programs. Using the test plan provided with the program specification, the programmer performs each test, some singly, others in groups. The results are then documented so that the program can be approved to enter the next phase.

Quality assurance.   This phase is not a normal part of the systems development life cycle. It is included here for completeness.

At this point, the programmer has completed *unit testing* of the program. There is additional testing to be done before the program can be accepted as finished. Before this step, however, the programmer usually meets with the application analyst and designer for a *program walkthru* meeting. The purpose of this meeting is to determine how well the program conforms to requirements, including coding standards (if any). Any errors found become the programmer's responsibility to fix, although sometimes these meetings end up pointing out file or database design errors.

Additional testing.   Apart from the final *user acceptance test,* the program must be *integration tested* with any programs with which it interfaces (i.e., shares files). It must also be *regression tested.* Regression testing provides a methodology for constructing a complete program test scenario. When programs are modified later on, the regression test is rerun, and the results compared to the first run. In this way, one can determine what effect a program change has on program processing.

Implementation and maintenance.   With testing complete, programs are now moved to the production environment, or one close to it. Actual moving of programs to the new environment is usually done by the *systems analyst,* who moves program source code, executable modules, operations information (Job Control Language, and so forth), and some data to the production environment. Execution of programs now becomes the responsibility of computer operations.

Systems support and computer operations.   Once programs are transferred from the test environment to production, they are ready for execution. *On-line* programs will be available immediately, as they involve communication between the user and the program using a *terminal.* *Batch* programs, on the other hand, are scheduled for execution either upon the request of the user or on a regular basis. An *operations analyst* uses the program descriptions and documentation to construct a *job execution* plan. This plan may take many forms depending upon the hardware and software environments, and tells the *computer operator* what order the programs should be run in, as well as what procedures to follow in the event of an abnormal termination. Batch programs that execute on IBM mainframes using the MVS operating system will require Job Control Language (JCL) statements that specify to the system what files the program will require for input and output.

Most batch jobs that run on a regular basis are run automatically by a *job scheduling system*. These systems assist computer operations by relieving the computer operator from running programs manually. Manual program execution may sometimes take several minutes as the operator collects information about the job, verifies that it is being run in the correct order, and types in computer console commands to start the program. With a scheduling system this process is done just once, as the operations staff specifies when the programs are to be run, in what order, and beginning at what time of day.

Meanwhile, other things are happening. The operating system that comes with the hardware is responsible for servicing program requests such as accessing files. The *systems programmer* is charged with maintaining the operating system and diagnosing systems problems. Most systems also include a variety of *utility* programs that perform various commonly used functions such as file sorting and report printing. The systems analyst may be involved in evaluating several such utilities, some available from third-party vendors.

Management. Almost forgotten in the life cycle was management. What were they doing during this process?

Estimating. Management is responsible for estimating work efforts for the analysis and design phases. At the beginning of the analysis phase, the *project manager* will develop a *project plan* that specifies what DP staff will be assigned to the various tasks to follow in the life cycle. To do this, the project manager must be aware of various estimating *metrics;* that is, measurements of resource requirements for standard tasks. Some of these metrics include the following:

- How long it takes to code certain types of programs, graded by size of program and complexity
- How long it takes to create test data and test certain types of programs
- What hardware resources (central processor speed, memory usage, data storage) are required for certain processes.

Project management. As the analysis phase begins, the project manager must allocate resources (staff members, mostly analysts and some designers at this stage). This involves assigning tasks to each staff member across the life of the project, from analysis to implementation. Once the schedule is complete and the project gets under way, the project manager *tracks* the project by monitoring the number of hours each person spends on the assigned tasks. If a task is taking too long, the manager must make a decision–assign someone else to the task, assign additional resources, rearrange the project plan, or perhaps allow the task to go over budget. Sometimes these situations lead to problems and make the entire project late.

Change control. This is the process of managing changes to programs, both in the test environment and in production. If already-completed programs must be changed, a *change control specialist* monitors the moving of the program source code from the production source library to a test library. After any changes have been made, the specialist inspects the changes, examines the program test results, and (usually) approves the change. The specialist then *migrates* the program back to the production library.

All of these procedures help to prevent two types of errors. First, programmers may make invalid changes to programs, either intentionally or unintentionally. Change control procedures minimize this risk. Second, it would be unfortunate if two programmers were each making changes to the same program simultaneously without the other knowing. Without proper management, this could lead to chaos.

Another aspect of change control is that of data security. Many sensitive systems, such as payroll and personnel systems, contain data that is sensitive, either from a corporate or a private point of view. Change control provides a mechanism for limiting access to programs and data to those making required changes.

Personnel management. Last, but not least, is personnel management. Here we include normal personnel functions such as paying employees, providing work space and administrative assistance, and performance appraisal. Unfortunately, performance appraisal seems to be the last on the list, as management and staff concentrate on getting the system analyzed, designed, coded, tested, and installed.

If managers and employees concentrated on performance appraisal *first,* the goals and standards set would form a basis for personnel planning and project task assignments that everyone would comply with and thereafter coexist in harmony.

C

Function Point Analysis

Software Metrics

Increasing emphasis is being focused on software *metrics*—that is, objectively measuring key aspects of software development. The two measurements most important to management are software *quality* and *quantity*.

Quality measurements in software borrow from two concepts long used in defining quality of hardware: *mean time between failures* (MTBF) and *mean time to repair* (MTTR). Mean time between failures for hardware refers to the time that can be expected to elapse, on average, between hardware failures. It is often applied to disk drives, power supplies, and other critical hardware components. MTBF can be used to help determine the frequency of scheduled preventive maintenance or the need to provide backup components.

Mean time to repair refers to the time needed to bring a hardware component back into service once failure has occurred—again, on average. Service companies may write a contract guaranteeing that MTTR will not exceed a certain figure. Equipment subject to failure can be designed for ease of repair. Some ways to achieve this are to build hardware interfaces with predetermined *test points,* and organize hardware into *modules,* each with limited function. The service technician can often use test points to isolate the failed module, then quickly remove and replace it.

Hardware Measurements
as Applied to Software

These measures of hardware quality have important applicability to software. For many years the quality of software development was difficult to measure. There were few standards of what constituted "good" software. Even in those few installations that had published standards for software development such as

- Naming conventions
- Rules for indentation of source code
- Depth of nested loops
- Use of program switches

seldom was code measured against these standards. Usually the excuse was that too little time was available to evaluate quality, but a more likely reason was that few supervisors were qualified to review programs.

Consider the practice of medical surgery: How shall we judge the performance of a surgeon? The default is to keep an eye on the postoperative patient. But a patient may do well *despite* rather than *because of* the surgery. The best—perhaps the only—way to judge a surgeon is for a peer to peer into the surgical cavity.

The difficulty of measuring program quality used to be comparable, but is no longer. Software Engineering has evolved tools that can automatically (without human intervention) apply predetermined standards to program evaluation.

In fact, one enlightened installation has adopted a policy of annually evaluating the programs in its production portfolio. The measuring tool applies a point value (on a scale of 100 = perfect) to the programs, then calculates an average across the portfolio. The goal is to gradually increase the rating over a period of years. New programs are expected to rate higher than old ones. And, when an existing program is opened for major maintenance, changes in structure are made to improve its rating. Thus the portfolio rating improves, rather than degrades, as it ages.

How can the concept of hardware test points be applied to software? In testing electronic equipment, circuit diagrams will provide expected voltages at key interface points. Use of a voltmeter will confirm the appropriate signal strength at that point. In modern software development it is recognized that key test data and expected results for each program should be preserved in a library. The concept of *regression testing* provides that, whenever a change is made to a program, it must be subjected to new tests for the change at hand, as well as all prior test data. The new test cases become part of the test script in the development library. Thus a process analogous to hardware test points can be performed on software as well.

Hardware modularity applies even more directly to software. In the distant past, programs were monolithic—all functions were combined into one structure. This led to the pejorative term *spaghetti code,* meaning that branches and loops were so convoluted that the logic was exceedingly difficult to follow. Thus it was difficult to maintain such programs. Even the person who wrote the program had a hard time following the logic. The advantage was efficiency of execution. But as CPU cycles became *less* expensive and human-hours became *more* so, economic factors led to the advent of structured programming.

Along with its sibling *structured design,* structured programming isolates program functions into specific modules.

Now when maintenance or enhancement is required, only the specific module or modules involved need to be opened. When a program failure does occur, it is easier to identify the responsible module. Program maintenance is less difficult and less expensive; mean time to repair is reduced.

Use of structured design and programming, and their more recent permutation, *object-oriented programming,* may lengthen the development cycle but the total cost over the life of the application will be reduced. And through these software engineering techniques, life expectancy of the system should increase.

Thus have the hardware quality measurement concepts of test points and modular design improved the MTBF and MTTR metrics of applications software.

So far the discussion has focused on measuring software quality. How can metrics be applied to software quantity?

Quantity of software has long been an elusive concept. Perhaps we can count programs. An application may consist of 100 "programs." But some run daily, some monthly, a few are executed only once a year, others run only on request. Should they count as heavily as a daily job? And some are sorts or backups, or are provided and maintained by a vendor. Should we count those in our application portfolio? One program may be ancient and monolithic, written in assembler language for an obsolete machine and currently being emulated on another. Should it count as one program in our list of responsibilities, or is it the equivalent of a dozen modular, well-documented COBOL programs?

Or, if counting programs seems misleading, let us count lines of code. We may find that our production library consists of 500,000 lines of code. Then a case could be built that a certain number of programmers is required to maintain it. But what is a line of code? Does a COBOL program's DATA DIVISION count? How about a CALL, that in itself is a single line, but may bring in 100 lines from the object module library? If programmers realize they are being measured on lines of code generated, they can easily write programs with lots of lines.

Further, programming languages are at great variance in coding efficiency. COBOL is often criticized for its verbosity, while a language such as APL is remarkably succinct. In APL, a matrix can be inverted with a single instruction. Aficionados of APL pride themselves on short programs and compete to see who can write the shortest routing to accomplish a task. Such a program may occupy a single line! (Of course, few commercial programs are written in APL.) But "lines of code" clearly has shortcomings as a measure of program quantity and of programmer productivity.

Some additional metrics that have been used to this point by various organizations are listed in Fig. C.1.

Function point analysis

This new technique is gaining considerable acceptance as a means of quantifying software development effort. Through function point analysis (also referred to as *feature point analysis*) the anticipated workload in a new or enhanced project can be estimated. In brief, the number of points where function is delivered by the proposed application is counted. The level of effort required to code each point is gauged, and the result relates to the staff-hours required for programming.

Before looking at details of the process, some limitations should be recounted. Function point analysis cannot be undertaken until the system has been clearly specified—at the earliest, after completion of detailed systems design.

Productivity guidelines are dependent on several factors: whether applications or systems software, whether a commercial or military system, whether journeyman or trainee programmers will be assigned, and the rigor of standards for design and quality assurance in use at

---

- Pages of documentation
- Number of variables
- Number of decision points
- Number of external interfaces
- Number of modules
- MIPS per person

- Depth of testing and number of tests
- Count of changes made per unit of time
- Count of discovered defects

- Percentage of reusability
- Staff years of experience
- Staff turnover rate

- Elapsed time to design, code, and test
- Person-hours to design, code, and test
- Dollar cost to develop
- Ratio of nonproject time to project time
- Ratio of planned to actual development time

Figure C.1 Quality and productivity metrics.

the installation. Even recognizing these limitations, function point analysis offers the best opportunity for applying metrics to the otherwise undisciplined process of building software. It should be noted that there are some 200 corporate members of IFPUG, the International Function Point Users Group, who are attempting to refine the following methodology.

Function Point Methodology

Significant features

The methodology recognizes five significant features of computer applications: Inputs, Outputs, Inquiries, Data Files, and Interfaces. Further, it recognizes that these features can be rated in terms of complexity as low, average, or high. A matrix summarizing these characteristics would look like Fig. C.2.

Definitions of these significant features are as follows:

INPUT	Screens or forms through which human users of an application add new data or update existing data
OUTPUTS	Screens or reports which the application produces for human usage
INQUIRIES	Screens which allow users to interrogate an application and ask for assistance or information, such as HELP screens
DATA FILE	A logical collection of records which the application modifies or updates. A file can be a flat file such as a tape file, one "leg" of a hierarchical database such as IMS, one table within a relational database, or one path through a CODASYL network database
INTERFACE	Files shared by other applications, such as incoming or outgoing tape files, shared databases, and parameter lists

SIGNIFICANT FEATURE	COMPLEXITY MULTIPLIER		
	LOW	AVERAGE	HIGH
INPUT	3	4	6
OUTPUT	4	5	7
INQUIRY	3	4	6
DATA FILE	7	10	15
INTERFACE	5	7	10

Figure C.2 Matrix of complexity multipliers.

In using this table, each significant feature in the proposed application would be evaluated to determine if it is of low, average, or high complexity. The IFPUG Handbook provides guidelines to aid in the determination. If, for example, there are five inputs, two of low complexity (multiple = 3), one is of average complexity (multiple = 4), and the remaining two are highly complex (multiple = 6), all the system's inputs provide 22 points. These are subject to further adjustment for influence factors.

How shall we evaluate the complexity of an input screen? The guidelines are shown in Fig. C.3.

So if our input screen requires that 12 fields be completed and four different records must be referenced to construct the data, this input is of high complexity and is worth six points. Each significant feature should be considered separately in making this judgment.

Example: Function point calculation

Assume an average project with 6 inputs, 8 outputs, 12 inquiries, 1 data file, and 1 interface. Further, to simplify the example, assume that in each case the function point is of average complexity (thus its weight will fall into the middle of the multiplier range). The calculation would appear as in Fig. C.4.

Influence factors

Next, the function point process recognizes that certain factors, if present in the development process, exert a global influence on the project duration. Fourteen such factors have been identified, and are listed in Fig. C.5.

To account for the impact of these factors, determine which are present, and in each case assess the extent of its influence on a scale of 0 to 5. For example, if the installation is making a concerted effort to build a library of reusable modules for this as well as other applications, consider the "code reusability" factor. Modules need to be designed to be parameter-driven and exceptionally well-documented in order to be

Record Types	Data fields on screen:		
Referenced for this	1 to 4	5 to 15	=> 15
Screen 0 or 1	Low	Low	Avg.
2	Low	Avg.	High
more than 3	Avg.	High	High

Figure C.3 Guidelines for evaluating screen complexity.

FEATURE	WEIGHT	RESULT
6 Inputs	4	24
8 Outputs	5	40
12 Inquiries	4	48
1 Data File	10	10
1 Interface	7	7
Unadjusted total 129		

Figure C.4   Sample function point calculation.

- Data communications
- Distributed data or processing
- Performance objectives
- Tight configuration
- High transaction rate
- On-line inquiry/data entry
- End-user efficiency
- On-line update
- Complex processing
- Code reusability
- Implementation/installation ease
- Operational ease
- Multiple site installation
- Facilitate change

Figure C.5   Factors influencing function point calculations.

reusable. The impact of this factor may be judged to be 4. Accordingly, estimates are made for all 14 factors.

The applications' total points will be multiplied by a constant derived from these influential factors. But first it must be put into standard form. That is, if no factors were present, we multiply by zero and our project would disappear. To provide a floor for the calculation, we mark it off as a decimal, then add a constant of 0.65. Now, if no factors are present, we multiply by this minimum value, 0.65, thus reducing our scope but not off the map. In other words, follow these steps:

1. Assess each influential factor on a scale of zero to five (zero if not present at all; five if strongly present).

2. Add the factors and convert the sum to a decimal by multiplying by 0.01.

3. Add a constant of 0.65 in order to provide a minimum complexity multiplier.

4. Multiply the unadjusted function point total by this complexity multiplier to derive the final Adjusted Function Point Total.

Returning to our earlier example, which had an unadjusted total of 129 points, we must derive a multiplier. Following the previous steps,

1. For ease of illustration, assume our project has low weights of 2 for all 14 influential factors.

2. Multiplication results in (14 × 2) 28 influence points. Converting to standard form (28 × .01) gives .28.

3. Add the constant (.28 + .65) results in 0.93.

4. Adjust our example's total (129 × 0.93) to obtain 120.

We have scoped out our project at 120 adjusted function points.

What does this metric mean in terms of programmer productivity? To answer, we approach the issue of how long it takes to write the code for an average system's function point.

To this end, data has been collected by IBM and others for actual projects, and a considerable body of productivity figures is available. Without delving into the variables of size of project, programmer experience, and others, the number suggested for an average COBOL programmer on a commercial application is *105 source statements per function point.*

If this process can be accepted, next we must search for a figure assessing typical programmer productivity—say, source statements per day.

A figure often seen in the literature is 10 statements per day. If this number seems low, bear in mind that it includes studying the specs, any flowcharting, coding, desk checking, testing, and documentation. Also, be aware that a workday is 6 hours long, at the outside, in terms of productive project effort. For military command-and-control applications, the productivity estimate could be much lower than 10 statements per day, perhaps as little as half that level.

Given 10 statements per day, and 120 function points at 105 COBOL statements each, results in:

$$120 \times 105 / 10 = 1260 \text{ person-days.}$$

At 250 working days per year, we have estimated our project at the level of a 5-person-year effort.

Index

ABOUT THE AUTHORS

LOCKWOOD LYON is vice president of RDE Systems, Inc., a mainframe and microcomputer software training company. He has more than 20 years of experience as an IMS/VS database analyst, a DB2 systems specialist, and consultant for several Fortune 500 companies in North America. He was a project leader and manager for a major consulting firm, specializing in IMS/VS, DB2, and EDI applications, and is the author of several references and dozens of articles on database management systems, data processing certification, performance appraisal, and entry-level training.

FRED A. GLUCKSON is a senior consultant with Compuware Corporation, an international software developer. He has more than 20 years of experience as a data processing practitioner, consultant, and manager, and has published numerous articles in the field.